how to write
Magical Words
A Writer's Companion

Edited by
Edmund R. Schubert

BellaRosaBooks

BellaRosaBooks

HOW TO WRITE MAGICAL WORDS: A Writer's Companion
ISBN 978-1-933523-80-4

First Edition: January 2011

Library of Congress Control Number: 2010941759

Printed in the United States of America on acid-free paper.

Cover photograph by David B. Coe

BellaRosaBooks and logo are trademarks of Bella Rosa Books.

10   9   8   7   6   5   4   3   2   1

Table of Contents

Butt In Chair

On Writing Fantasy

A Writer's Life

"This is the best idea for a writing book that I've ever seen. It's like sitting in a room full of professional writers, and after each one delivers a riff on one aspect of writing, the others weigh in to buttress, amplify, refine, or add to what was said. It's an extended conversation with writers who know what they're talking about— and what matters in writing fiction that really communicates with readers."

— Orson Scott Card

Introduction

It goes without saying that the book you hold in your hands is the product of a tremendous amount of work. If you spend even a few minutes reading from among the one hundred essays contained in these pages, you'll quickly realize that writing books is hard work. This book, we hope, will make it a bit easier for you to write the novel percolating inside *you*.

But this volume, *How To Write Magical Words: A Writer's Companion*, is also the product of forces that were . . . well, magical. It was born of kismet, inspired by years of camaraderie and a shared passion for the written word, and forged in the combined energies of a group of committed, talented people who we are proud to call our friends and colleagues.

MagicalWords.net, the web site devoted to the craft and business of writing, and the place where all the material in this book originated, went online in January 2008. It began as the brainchild of the original three contributors: Faith Hunter, Misty Massey, and David B. Coe. People talk about networking all the time, but sometimes networking isn't a plan. Sometimes it just happens. Sometimes you attend a conference, take one look at a person, or in this case a couple of people, and tsunamis start. Professional tsunamis, friendship tsunamis—it's not always easy to tell where one ends and the other begins. But when they happen, writers have choices—they can swim away, they can be overwhelmed and swallowed whole. Or they can ride the wave. When Faith, Misty, and David first met it was like that—instant, indefinable energy, powerful and intense.

We began by bringing the wonderful C.E. Murphy into the mix, and, after Catie left us, first we added A.J. Hartley and Stuart Jaffe, and then Edmund Schubert. But no matter the personnel, the energy has remained and Magical Words has thrived—thanks in large part to our growing readership and the willingness of those who visit the site to join in our online discussions.

Since our first post, Magical Words' regular writers and guests have contributed over six hundred essays dealing with everything from business contracts to worldbuilding. The roster of writers and guests has changed and expanded to include not only bestselling authors, but also agents, editors, and other professionals in the publishing industry. The appearance of the page has evolved and grown more sophisticated. Traffic at the site has increased at a rate of over thirty percent a year. But always, Magical Words has remained a labor of love for all of us.

And that original tidal wave of energy has continued to build. In the spring of 2010, during a convention in North Carolina, all of us—Faith and her husband Rod, Misty and her husband Todd (our wonderful web guru), David, A.J., Stuart, and Edmund, and of course our beloved minion, Beatriz—gathered in Faith and Rod's RV. Though we came together to speak of the future of Magical Words, none of us knew what to expect. But maybe that's when magic is most likely to strike.

What began as a night of laughter and fun, turned into something else entirely. It's odd to think of an RV as a setting for the brainstorming session to end all brainstorming sessions. But it was. The space positively crackled with creative energy. And out of that night came the idea for this book.

There are more Magical Words projects in the works—we intend to put together an anthology of original short fiction by our regular contributors as well as some of our guests, and at some point we might put together a follow-up to this volume. And of course, the site—MagicalWords.net—goes on.

Through it all, even as we find ourselves moving in new directions and welcoming new faces to the MW family, the fundamental forces that drive us remain the same. Creativity, friendship, our passion for stories and storytelling, and our desire to share with others the joy that we get out of this crazy business. Each is powerful on its own. Blended together they become something truly remarkable.

But don't take our word for it. You have the book in your hand. Turn the page and start reading.

— Faith, Misty, and David
Sept. 2010

Foreword

No matter what genre you're interested in writing, the basics are almost universal. Good dialogue is good dialogue. Proper use of Point of View is proper use of Point Of View. The smartest way to approach an agent or editor is the smartest way to approach an agent or editor. With many aspects of writing, genre truly verges on the irrelevant. If you want proof of that, all you need to look at are the publishing credits of the members of Magical Words. Although each of them has written in various subgenres of fantasy, many have also written mysteries, thrillers, science fiction, romance, non-fiction, and more.

As a compilation of essays, comments, questions, and answers from the Magical Words blog, this book distills almost three years worth of advice into a single, portable volume. It could have been much, *much* longer, and though matters of space may have dictated otherwise for the printed version, the internet is not bound by any such limitations. All of the raw material that went into this book (and much more) is still available online. If you want to read the whole, unedited version of any of these essays, you can. If you want to read more questions, comments, and answers (and you'll find them worthwhile reading), you can. Other essays that the full-length essay referenced but the reference had to be edited out because of space limitations? Links to other sites that are also worth exploring? It's all there at MagicalWords.net.

Although my intention with this book was to create something akin to the experience you would have had if you were a regular reader of the blog, what we actually ended up with was something much like what you would find at a pricey writing conference. About the only thing a traditional writing conference could give you that this book can't is a) the opportunity to network, and b) the privilege of paying as much as $1,500 to get in the front door.

Aside from that, though, what you will find within these pages are essentially workshops and panels covering a wide rage of subjects. The presentations even come complete with counterpoints from other authors, questions from the audience, and, yes, the occasional bad joke. As I said, it's a writing conference on paper, minus the networking and the steep price-tag.

If you're already a MW regular, you know what I mean when I say the blog and the community that has grown up around it is a special place. If, on the other hand, you haven't discovered the site yet, read and enjoy the book; take notes (seriously, we won't mind if you mark it up with a pen or highlighter); and when you're done, come visit us at MagicalWords.net.

We'll look for you there.

— Edmund
Sept. 2010

In The Beginning . . .

They're Not Rules, They're Price Tags

Edmund R. Schubert

Never write in second person.

Always start with a powerful first line.

Never change POVs in the middle of a scene.

Eschew adjectives. And adverbs.

Blah blah blah blah blah blah blah . . .

How To Write Magical Words is devoted to helping people write better, and there's a lot of great advice to be found here.

And it's all negotiable.

Seriously. There isn't a bit of writing advice here that someone, somewhere (probably multiple someones and multitudinous somewheres) hasn't broken, and broken *really damn well.*

So should you listen to what Faith and David and A.J. and Misty and Stuart and Catie and everyone else says about writing? Of course you should. They've been doing this for a long time; they know what they're talking about.

Well, then what the heck are *you* talking about, Edmund?

That would be a logical question.

What I'm talking about is this: I'm replying to a certain question before it's even asked, a question I hear all the time. The minute any writing conversation turns in the direction of "rules" or "guidelines" or even just plain old "advice," it inevitably crops up.

That question is: "Yeah, but what about _____x_____?"

Because yes, there are exceptions to every rule. In fact, those exceptions are usually exceptional. People hold them up as shining examples of why the rules don't apply. They do so wrongly, but that doesn't stop them from doing it.

That's why I want you to stop thinking of them as "rules" and start thinking of them as price tags. Even the rules of grammar and punctuation. They are all price tags.

Why price tags? Because there is a price to be paid for breaking the rules. If the gain outweighs the loss, then it's worth doing. If not . . .

Let's start with the rules of grammar and punctuation; they seem to be the most immutable. You want to break those rules? Generally, the price you pay is a lack of clarity and, as a result, a lack understanding. There's a great book that came out several years ago called *Eats Shoots and Leaves* that talked about the importance of punctuation. Just punctuation. That subject alone filled an entire book. But look at the difference one little comma (or the lack thereof) makes in the title. If you say "eats shoots and leaves" without the comma, you're talking about a panda's diet. What do they eat? Bamboo shoots and leaves. But add one little comma so that it reads, "eats, shoots and leaves," now you're talking about a mafia hit-man who sits down in a restaurant, eats his dinner, kills the guy at the next table, and then walks out. A panda bear and a mafia hit man—and all that differentiates the two is one single comma.

There simply aren't a lot of good reasons to mess with punctuation. Period. But grammar is a little more flexible. Look at the second sentence in this paragraph, the paragraph you're reading right now. That's really not a sentence, is it? "Period." There's no verb, there are no independent or dependent clauses; it's just one word, sitting there, all alone. It's—*gasp*—a sentence fragment. And doggone it, it's not the first one that's been used in this piece.

What price did I pay? Not much of one, because there was no loss of clarity. I knew when, where, and how to use them. What benefit did I gain? That fragment carries extra emphasis. It makes it perfectly clear that I think there are very, very, *very* few reasons to mess with punctuation. And that's what fragments do best: narrow the focus down so as to emphasize a point. But you still have to be careful to construct. Them properly. Because the sloppy. Unintentional use of sentence fragments only causes confusion (see my previous sentence-fragment mess, right before this sentence; yes, that was intentional. And ugly.).

Here's a different example, one that comes up frequently when we're talking about writing: don't write in the present tense, or, heaven forbid, the future tense. Has it been done? Of course. Should it be done? Well, that's really up to you. As always, there's a price to pay.

In this case, because past tense is the tense used in the vast majority of writing today (especially if you disregard "literary writing," which accounts for two-thirds of the uses of other tenses), unless present or future tenses are used seamlessly, it's going to jump out at the reader. *Look at me*, it screams. *I am writing in the present tense. I am going to be writing in the future tense.* If that's the effect you want—if it serves your story somehow—then by all means, go for it. Some writers can do so in a way that's unobtrusive, so you hardly notice it's being done. But here's the thing: most readers want to be swept up in a story and carried away by it. They want to be immersed in the world they're reading about to such a degree that they forget about the real one they're living in. That *can not* happen if the writing is calling attention to itself. Using tenses that scream "look at me" are not going to allow that to happen. Again: "Can it be done" is not the question you should be asking yourself. "*Should it be done*" is the question.

I could go on about this at length, but I'm sure by now you see my point. The bottom line is that the rules are there for a reason. And it's *not* to say you can never, ever, ever do _____x_____. It's to say that if you do _____x_____, make sure you know *why* you're not supposed to do it. Make sure you understand the price tag that comes with doing it. Make sure that you understand that even though great writing breaks a lot of rules, no one breaks the rules *effectively* without thoroughly understanding them.

Once you really, truly understand the rules, then by all means, go ahead and break them. Break them into a million shining pieces that people will hold up and bask in the glory of.

Break them so well that *you're* the one that people are talking about when they come up to me at my next convention or workshop and say, "Yeah, but what about _____x_____?"

Stuart Jaffe
This is the fundamental and only true rule in all art forms: You must *understand* the "rules" in order to break them effectively. Even those few geniuses who break all the rules perfectly at the age of four—I believe they actually understood the rules at some instinctive level. Whenever somebody breaks the rules without any concept of them, it is almost always glaringly evident.

David Jace
I agree, as well. I think I might print this out and post it in my Middle School English classroom. This illustrates and addresses one side of the battle: those who are authoritative about styles and opinions. The other side, however, is equally dangerous: those who don't know enough to do it right, but want to cite the lack of one "right" way as their reason to do it sloppily.

I particularly love the look at punctuation; we so need that second (serial) comma! Lacking it inhibits the clarity of a series.

Here's my example: Make sure that you place siblings, criminals, priests and parishioners, nuns and innocents, warlords, child-molesters and children in separate rooms, or they won't get along.

Each comma sets off a group. The criminals are apart from the siblings, but the priests and parishioners are together. Now, do YOU want that comma between the child-molesters and the children, or not?

Getting Started
David B. Coe

So, you're starting that novel you've been thinking about for all these years. Good for you. Chances are you already have some idea of what you intend to do with your novel. You have characters in mind, a general idea of the plot, some sense of the worldbuilding. That's good. Now—before you actually start writing—is the time to develop those concepts and to plan your book out. Don't worry, all of you seat-of-the-pantsers out there, I'm not going to insist or even suggest that you outline your book. That's a personal choice and you know better than I how much outlining or plotting you'll need to do. But there are others things you should set up ahead of time.

The first thing I would suggest you do is read in your selected subgenre, not so that you copy what others have done or make your work derivative in any way, but so that you familiarize yourself with the tropes of the field, make certain that your work actually fits into the subgenre to which you think it belongs (an important issue later in the process, when you start to pitch your work to agents and editors), and make certain that the book you want to write hasn't already been written by someone else.

If you're writing urban fantasy, you should read Kim Harrison, Rachel Caine, C.E. Murphy, Faith Hunter, and others. If you're writing mystery/fantasy, you should read Jim Butcher. If you're writing epic fantasy, you should know the work of Tolkien, George R.R. Martin, John Marco, Guy Gavriel Kay, and perhaps even David B. Coe. YA books with animals as main characters? You'd better know the work of Brian Jacques. New weird? Read China Mieville. And if you're writing a pirate fantasy, you'd better have read Misty Massey. You wouldn't try to bake a cake without first knowing what a cake looks and tastes like. It's the same with writing a fantasy novel.

While you're reading in the genre, you should also be researching your own book. I use the word "research" a little loosely here, because depending on your book, the amount of actual library/reference research you do might vary. If you're setting your book on a pirate ship, you need to know about pirates. And ships. If you're setting your work in a world with medieval technology, you should familiarize yourself with medieval food and clothing, construction and weaponry. You might want to learn a bit about castles. If your setting is modern and real-world, then learn a bit about whatever city or area you've chosen. If you're writing a historical work, as I am now . . . Well, you get the idea.

To me, research is quite similar to worldbuilding. Both are intended to give shape and texture to the world in which your characters live; both help to set the voice and tone for the books; both give context and weight to the narrative. And both are incredibly time-consuming endeavors that can suck us in and keep us from ever turning to the actual writing of our books.

What is the right amount of research (or worldbuilding)? How much is too much, or, put another way, how do we know when to stop?

The easy answer is that we learn as much as we can about the place and time in which we intend to set our books, not so that we can share every detail with our readers, but rather so that we don't have to. We need to use the iceberg principle: We show our readers what they need to know, while merely hinting at the background lurking beneath the surface. I'll be setting my new series in pre-Revolutionary Boston. I could spend pages upon pages telling my readers about the political, economic, and social phenomena of that time, but they probably didn't buy the book for a history lesson. They bought it for a story. So I'll spare them the extensive discourse, but I'll put in small details—references to historical figures and events, descriptive particulars about the streets of Boston—that will bring the period to life without detracting from the narrative.

As I do my background work for a new novel I also identify whatever sources I think I'll be needing throughout the writing process, and begin to gather them. I buy books, bookmark web sites, draw or collect my maps, etc. Also, if this is your first book, now might be a good time to get certain things you just have to have: an excellent dictionary, a comprehensive thesaurus, a baby name book; stuff like that.

But my idea of research goes beyond what I've just described, to also include the creation of your magic system, the drawing of maps for your alternate world, character background, development of religions, histories, lines of royalty, etc. Some of it will demand that you look stuff up; some of it will happen entirely in your imagination. But in my opinion all of it is "research," and all of it is absolutely necessary for the development of your story.

Now, you'll notice that I've said nothing yet about working out plot points. That's because, for me at least, the research phase (which usually lasts one or two months; no more than three. Get what you need to begin the book, and move on) is an incredibly fertile period for developing plot ideas. As I learn more about my characters, my world, and my magic system, story ideas come to me. So I wait until after the research is mostly done before I brainstorm the finer points of my plot.

The other thing I do in these preparatory stages is come up with a system for keeping track of the information I'm gathering and the ideas that are coming to me. In the past I've used a notebook, index cards, spreadsheets, and combinations of these things along with others. Character Keeper, the program developed by Misty Massey's husband, Todd, might be the perfect computer-based tool for you, if you want to keep track of this stuff on your computer. I hear it's a great program, though it only works for Windows platforms. For Mac users, check out Scrivener.

Finally, if you're the kind of writer who likes to have an outline, this is the point where you should start working on one. Even if you're a dedicated seat-of-the-pantser, you should take this opportunity to make certain that you have at least a general idea of where you're going with your story and how you intend to get there. There is nothing worse than getting half or two-thirds of the way into a book and realizing that you have no sense of how to get from where you are to the ending you've envisioned. If I had a dime for every book idea that had died for lack of planning . . .

All that I've written here is all fairly generalized, because every book is so different, every author's needs so particular, that being more specific wouldn't accomplish much. I should also add that while I described these various stages in a linear sequence, they usually happen for me with a great degree of simultaneity. I read in the subgenre (as I'm doing now for my historical) at the same time I do research. And as I do my research, I develop a system for keeping track of stuff—while also jotting down the plotting ideas that come to me. And while I'm doing all this stuff, I'm thinking about the structure of the book and starting to work on a very general outline. It's an organic process. None of these things is entirely separate from the others. They're all ingredients for that one cake, to return to my metaphor from earlier, and they need to be prepared together so that they can be blended at the appropriate time.

A.J. Hartley

For what it's worth, while I'm doing the kind of research, world-building, and plot-sketching you outline so nicely, I also find myself moving toward some kind of thematic issue. Eventually I open a new document and give it a title which is usually some version of: what is the book about? Over the next few days or weeks I drop in ideas: not plot points, back story, or events, but ideas, themes, political issues, morals, or whatever I need to come to grips with during the course of the book. I won't use all of it, but it helps me flesh out the book at a conceptual level and keep a sense of purpose so that it doesn't get drowned out by the minutia of story.

Faith Hunter

My favorite part of writing a book is the part that takes place in my head. As you said: ". . . the research phase . . . is an incredibly fertile period . . . As I learn more about my characters, my world, my magic system, story ideas come to me. So I wait until after the research is mostly done before I brainstorm the finer points of my plot."

But because I come from the thriller/mystery/hardboiled PI genre of writing and have returned there for the Jane Yellowrock series, I often start a book in a very different way. I start with a germ of an idea, usually character-based, and mate that character to a central conflict, giving the character strengths and weaknesses that will be challenged by that pivotal crisis.

Then I write the first five to ten pages. If my character has a voice I like and can use, and there is an opening that presents character, world, voice, and conflict, *then* I start work on the entire research part, and that is where our pre-writing meshes, with basic-to-finer plot points developing as I research and worldbuild. If those first few pages stink, then I have to find where the character didn't work and refine or start over.

Your way of writing a book is more logical—easier, frankly—than mine. But I am stuck with my process. I need the voice of the character to make me want to write the book in the first place.

And unlike A.J., I never do thematic work, or only vaguely. I have had books (particularly the AKA's DeLande Saga) studied by well educated literati who wanted to dissect the themes and debate them with me. I learned early on that I had to have an answer for them beyond simply wanting to write a good story and punish the bad guys (which was the reality for me). They *expected* to have this lovely discussion (several times; it was over a nice dinner, which ruined the meal for me, of course) on the nature of aggressive violence verses defensive violence, and how I wove that through my plot; the effect of domestic violence on the psyche of women and how I used that concept in my character development; the effect of domestic violence on children in the formative years; the place for the vigilante in situations where the justice system is broken and victims were made to suffer; and the effect of racial and socioeconomic tension in the south as epitomized by the plight of children as victims of incest and abuse.

"I just wanted the bad guy to pay," was never enough.

And the reality for me, is that themes always flow *from* the character and the plot, are resultant aspects of the weaknesses of the character I've grown, and are things that I think about afterward. I envy any writer who has the ability to step back early on and see where society and culture will impinge on the story.

Misty Massey

David said, "If you're setting your book on a pirate ship, you need to know about pirates. And ships. If you're setting your work in a world with medieval technology, you should familiarize yourself with medieval food and clothing, construction and weaponry."

And don't assume you know all there is to know! I knew a good bit about ships before I ever got started, but I still had to research before and while I was working. I'd be plugging away and realize, "Hey, I have no idea what you call the thing that holds the capstan from spinning!"

David B. Coe

A.J., I love that idea. Have never done it, but I will now. I do spend a lot of time thinking about theme as I prepare to write, and also as I actually do the writing. But I tend to keep those thoughts in my head rather than cataloging them in some coherent way. Thanks for this.

Faith, I wouldn't say that one approach is more valid or logical than another—mostly what I wanted to do with this post was point out to people the things I consider as I begin a book or series—a checklist of sorts: things to do and think about as you get started. The order of it is secondary. But I'm reminded by your comment, as well as your subsequent exchange with AJ, that it all comes back to the organic nature of the process. And I think you'll probably agree that this is true for you, too. When the process works—no matter what that process might be in its particulars—there is a synergy to the development of all the elements of the work: theme, character, plot, voice, etc. It all comes together. How we reach that synergy is as individual as DNA, but it happens for all successful projects.

Great point, Misty. When I was working on my first series, which involved birds, I thought it was perfect for me because I knew everything I needed to know about birds already. Wrong! I did a ton of research along the way and learned lots.

Visualizing The Story?

C.E. Murphy

I discovered several years ago that many people see pictures in their heads. When they read, when they listen to music, when they're told stories, they see pictures.

I do not get pictures in my head. Not when I'm reading, not when I'm writing, not when I listen to music. I had *no idea* that people did. It was a stagger-worthy shock when I realized that *Fantasia* was based on the idea that people *saw stories in their heads* when they listened to all that music.

No one in my immediate family had any idea that people did. Dad said he'd have taught many classes differently if he'd known that. I remember a drama class visualization exercise where we were supposed to visualize that we were lying on a white beach with the blue sky above and palm trees and all that sort of thing, and it bent my brain to think that probably two-thirds of the people in the class were *actually seeing that.*

They say to succeed at sports, you have to visualize the win. I had no idea they meant literally. Sure, I can talk myself through it, but actually *see* it? Buh. No.

This clarified something that had been puzzling me for years. There's a scene in *Emily Climbs*, the second book of the Emily of New Moon series by L.M. Montgomery, in which Emily is talking to a man whose son has died. The man can't remember what the boy looks like, because he isn't like other people and can't bring images to mind.

My entire life, I had always thought that was a weird little scene. I mean, not like I spent nights lying awake because of it, but it always bugged me. Like, what did that mean, bringing images to mind? Like people *did* that or something? *snort*

My husband was astounded, because my writing makes clear pictures in his head and he couldn't imagine how I did that if *I* wasn't seeing pictures in my head.

The answer is *by working really, **really** hard.*

Below is a scene from *Urban Shaman*, my first published novel, followed by further commentary on this visualization thing.

> The horse made more sense now, for some nebulous value of the word sense. It had been able to rear up because after it kicked me in the chest it had torn out the entire door structure, and part of the roof had fallen down. The rest of the roof was on fire. I wasn't sure how that had happened, but it didn't seem to bother the horse.

Horse is such a limited word. The beast in the diner had the grace and delicacy of an Arabian and the size of a Clydesdale, multiplied by two. It shimmered a watery grey, bordering on silver, the color so fluid I thought I might be able to dip my hand in it. Despite myself, my gaze jerked up to its forehead. There was no spiral horn sprouting there, but I wouldn't have been surprised if there had been. It was Plato's horse, the ideal upon which all others are based.

It was trying to kill me, and all I could do was admire it.

Then it screamed, shrill and deep all at once. The blonde behind the counter shut up, but I screamed back, a sort of primal response without any thought behind it.

Just for a moment, everything stopped.

There was a rider astride the grey, arrested in motion by my scream. He wore grey himself, so close to the color of the horse I could barely tell where one ended and the other began. The reputed Native American belief that white men on horseback were one exotic creature suddenly seemed very plausible.

The rider turned his head slowly and looked at me. His hair was brown, peppered with starlight, and crackled with life, as if touching it would bring an electric shock. It swept back from a massively sharp widow's peak, and was held in place by a circlet. His face was a pale narrow line, all high cheekbones and deep-set eyes and a long straight nose.

The impression he left was of living silver. I locked eyes with him, expecting to see that liquid silver again. Instead I met wild-fire green, a vicious, inhuman color, promising violence.

He smiled and reached out a hand, inviting me towards him. His mouth was beautiful, thin and expressive, the curve of teeth unnervingly sharp, like a predator's. I pushed up the counter, using it to brace myself, and wet my lips. Marie was right. I was going to die. The rider wanted my soul and I was going to give it to him without a fight because of that smile and those inhuman eyes. I took a step towards him.

That scene, those paragraphs, took me about six hours to write. Not all at once, but going back and staring and thinking and crafting and working as hard as I could to get all the words right. The penultimate and antepenultimate paragraphs took me about four hours of work alone. Remember that I write, on average, about a thousand words an hour. Description is *not easy* for me. And I find it utterly fascinating that apparently something like two-thirds of people see pictures in their heads.

Me, I can't hold an image in my head for more than an instant. Ted, on the other hand, can apparently call up a specific person or thing, hold the image in his mind, do a 3D rotation on it . . . bizarre beyond belief.

(At a con a few years ago I put this question ("Do you visualize?") to the forty people in the room. Every single one of them raised their hands. I said, "You are *weird*," until several people laughed and pointed out I was the oddball there. But being me, I persisted in thinking *they* were weird.)

Faith Hunter

OMG. Catie, I never ever see in pictures. I thought I was the only one in the whole world who can't. I can't bring up pictures of faces, even my own hubby or mother. If I saw a mugger or murderer I could tell someone what they looked like if I started the process right away, but I'd never be able to do it after a few minutes. I'd recognize them if I saw them again, but I couldn't bring up a *picture* of them.

My hubby can do the 3D thing. First time he told me about it, I didn't believe him. So can my mom. We three were eating lunch one day and they were talking about this and I told them they were destined for the loony bin. I *had no idea!!!* (Mom also has the gift of synesthesia, colors and numbers, pictures and numbers, which is weirder.)

When I write, the world disappears, and I suppose there are pictures (of a sort), but more, there are emotions and words. Just wonderful words. The words build a *partial vision*. But if I see a movie of the story later, I am not bothered by it at all. Nothing in my brain to fight with.

And I do not do poetry. I can sometimes see what it needs, if I am critiquing it, but I don't read or write it.

Thank you for being a *word* person!!!

David B. Coe

I do visualize as I write. I see scenes in sometimes minute detail. I'll see a room, say. But I don't just see shape and color and furniture. I'll see things like the post-it note stuck on a desk with something scrawled on it in blue ink. I'll note the way it refuses to lie flat, instead curling up slightly like a dried leaf. Sometimes I can do the 3D thing, but I have to really work at that. But I see stuff as I write. I see people, places, objects, and the images remain in my head until the moment I've committed them to words. Then they vanish, and recalling them without referring to what I wrote can be next to impossible. Weird.

But I don't get poetry at all.

Misty Massey

I'm a movie-in-the-head type. But not really 3D. More like the flat screen of an actual movie.

I hate when I'm reading and I suddenly realize that the character I've been visualizing looks nothing like what I was seeing all along. Blonde instead of dark, or taller than I had imagined. But it's not the writer's fault—it's just me being way too visual.

High Concept Stories

A.J. Hartley

While "high concept" is mainly used for movies, it can be useful in conceptualizing novels. Simply put, a "high concept" story is one in which the hook—that which grabs the reader/audience's attention—is so strong that it drives the engine of the entire story: it's a premise with legs. The core action of the story can thus be summed up very succinctly (and supplies the "log line" used to encapsulate films when they show up in your local TV listings): Giant shark terrorizes Cape Cod resort town (*Jaws*), for instance.

Screenwriters live by these things, reductive though they obviously are, and prominent producers like Steven Spielberg have suggested that if the core of a movie can't be summed up in twenty-six words or fewer, it probably shouldn't be made. To clarify further, most sitcoms are low concept because they depend on character interaction. High concept shows are those like *Buffy* (reluctant high school cheerleader has to slay vampires) or the new program, *Flash Forward*, in which the entire season is driven by the global black-out in which everyone glimpses their part in the same future moment. One of my favorite recent high concept shows was the BBC's *Life on Mars*: a cop injured in a car accident wakes up in 1973—he's in a coma and has to solve cases there to get back home. This is what I mean by a premise with legs. Everything which follows—all the various story arcs, character journeys, the core intrigue of what is going on, what will happen next and what it all means—comes out of that initial hook.

There are, of course, dangers with deriving guides for long fiction from the briefer and more visual forms of film and TV, but a snappy log line can go a long way to piquing the curiosity of an agent or publisher. In fact, I would go so far as to say that—for better or worse—you have a better chance of selling a high concept story which has only mediocre execution than you do a beautifully written story with a lower concept premise. I'm not saying that's a good thing or that a high concept necessarily makes for good art, but I do think that higher concept stories are more marketable. Terry Pratchett's *Night Watch* (in which Sam Vimes is sent back in time to secure the future by teaching his younger self how to be a policeman) is a higher concept story than his *The Fifth Elephant* (which is a convoluted mystery with multiple plot strands), and though I much prefer the latter, I can see how the former would be an easier sell, particularly had it been Pratchett's first book.

And let's not make the mistake of assuming that a high concept story can't have good execution. Just because the premise of a story is particularly arresting doesn't mean it can't have nuanced characters, careful plotting, and emotional depth. Those things will carry the day once your manuscript is in your reader's hands. But the premise will keep them turning the pages, giving your smaller-scale stuff chance to work.

The truth is that editors and agents have to have an eye for how a book will sell, and high concept stories make for good marketing, even if the form that marketing takes is nothing more than the jacket copy or the cocktail party word-of-mouth. When someone is excited about a book and they try to convey that to someone else, a high concept book is easier to describe in ways that might transmit that reader's enthusiasm.

Consider the way these stories immediately raise the collective eyebrow: a beleaguered orphan boy discovers he is a wizard and has to go to a special school for his kind (and no, I don't think Voldemort becomes integral to the series until the [to my mind inferior] fifth book. What initially dominates the story is the school itself). An insignificant person has to save his world by destroying a ring of power deep behind enemy lines (*LOTR*). A "symbologist" races to unravel clues hidden in Leonardo da Vinci's art while being chased by murderous religious fanatics. A prince discovers that his father was murdered by his uncle, the king, who has married his mother (*Hamlet* or, if you prefer, *The Lion King*). In each case, you'll notice, the log-line suggests the story's core conflict.

One of the problems faced by writers of genre fiction is that we are often led to assume that genre replaces the desirability for a strong premise, or that identifying our books as "fantasies" or "mysteries" is all we need to do to make people want to read them. If you have a strong track record as a writer, this indeed may be all you need, but for most of us a high concept story will stir a lot more interest. We have all read work by fledgling writers—including our own—where there's nothing wrong with the prose, the characters are likable and engaging, and there are good scenes of action or suspense, but the whole fails to jell somehow. It's coherent but doesn't excite as a unit. When you try to encapsulate the tale, you find yourself explaining a lot or lapsing into lengthy plot summary. When that is the case, you probably have a low concept story, and while that might not in any way damage the book's chances of success (artistic or commercial) it might also mean that the book is going to struggle to distinguish itself and that its finer points might not be enough to make it work.

I have written entire novels only to discover that while the plot worked, the hook was weak, and the concept low in ways that made the story a tough sell. Sometimes you can go back and rework the story to raise the concept level of the premise, but by the time you've actually written the book it's often too late. As a "pantser" (someone who writes by the seat of his pants rather than planning most or all of the story out ahead of time) this is a particularly difficult truth, because it means that it's very difficult to just dive into a book when you don't know what it's going to be, yet still hope to meander your way to an exciting premise. If your book is to be high concept, you probably need to know what that concept is *right out of the gate*, even if the story evolves some thereafter.

The premise isn't just the conditions of the story as experienced by the reader. It's also the groundwork from which the writer begins, and it's very hard to create this *in media res* without massive rewriting.

So before you start a new project—or before you get too deep into a current one—think about ways you might be able to shape a story whose heart can be encapsulated in a snappy log line. A high concept premise might help you keep the story focused and may even help you sell it. Perhaps people might share log lines of current projects so that we can see which seem particularly compelling. I'll get the ball rolling with the log line for my previous novel, *Act of Will*: a cynical actor joins a band of principled adventurers to investigate a mysterious army of rampaging horsemen. Not incredibly high concept, I'll concede, but it gives you a sense of the conflicts (character and plot) and suggests how the core story will develop.

Kim Harrison
This is a great essay. I love seeing how things we make are marketed. Keeping in mind I'm really bad at this . . .

I've got three. My log line for the first book was "*Buffy* meets *Columbo.*"

For my upcoming release, I went with a very simple, "Wicked Witches Really Do Come From the West" which is kind of lame, but "Rachel pits her magic against her own people for the first time to clear her name" lacks sparkle.

For the piece I'm working on now, (so it will be tweaked as I go) "Rachel puts her big girl panties on and takes care of business."

A.J. Hartley
Kim, these are great log lines, thanks. I'm not (against all my instincts) going to ask too much about the "big girl panties." That way madness lies. ☺ Your "Buffy meets Columbo" is a great, succinct example of how you can evoke a high concept story by drawing on a reader's knowledge of other stories/shows.

Holding Lightning / The Big Bang

Faith Hunter

Before you think I'm nuts (I am, but I get paid for most of it) the following essay is mostly tongue in cheek. Sometimes readers forget that I write fiction, and that means that I have a tendency toward hyperbole. Not that I did that here. Nope. No way. (grins)

Essay starts . . . now.

I like writing. I mean, I do it for a living, so it's important that I like it, right? But a lot of the process of writing isn't exactly fun. A lot isn't exactly creative. Some of it is problem solving, some of it is technical, some is search and replace, some is relationship building, relationship destroying, boring, exhilarating, foot-stomping fun, tedious, and let us not forget, some is exhausting. Most of the time it doesn't pay nearly well enough.

Then there's the more personal side of the job. Strangers give me advice on my hairstyle, clothes, appearance, my love life, my religious life, and my home life, because they think I *am* my characters. People in jail write me love letters. People want to sell me their great ideas. Or better yet, give me their ideas, have me write the books, and put their names on the covers with mine. Fans and other writers (no one here, thank God) fall in love with me, send me love letters, and want to suck out my brain with a straw. No, I am not drunk or stoned. It's true. Misty, stop laughing.

Even with all that, I still love my job. All except one, tiny, miserable part.

I'm not talking about the idea part of writing, though that part is often like an insane treasure hunt. With the idea part of story creation, the problem is that there's no map except the one inside my head, and the treasure, well, it's in the same place, but I can't always get to it from here. I have to go somewhere else to start. It's like being crazy, hallucinating weird things, hearing voices, seeing parts of plays no one ever produced—letting my brain freebase on creativity. You know—the fun part of writing.

This essay is about the *next* step in the creative process. The I-got-an-idea, now-what phase. I'm in it. Oh, baby, I am soooo in it . . . I recently had tea with writer pal, Kim Harrison, and discovered that she is in that phase, too. We compared notes. And here, for both of us, is where the nutso, head-banging part of being a writer lives and breathes and walks the earth and terrorizes small children and dogs and scares our families. I am totally serious. This part of writing is, for me and for my pal, Kim, hair-pulling, sleep-stealing, nerve-grating, and just plain freaking awful.

Why? In my case, it's because: I. Don't. Know. What. To do!

All my life I have needed to know what to do next. As long as I know what

I can do to help or fix a problem, I am content even if the fix and help is painful, exhausting, and difficult. But when I am in idea-land, an idea in one hand but no clue how to control it, where to take it, or how to make it into something wonderful that people might want to read, well . . . I am lost. And half crazy with the excitement and the potential and the possibilities of both utter disaster and complete triumph. Holding onto the idea is like holding onto lightning.

I have an idea and it is churning inside me like a dervish, like a demon on crack, like a Chihuahua on meth. It fills me with explosive energy, and the energy has no outlet. NONE! NO OUTLET! It is stuck inside me, and I don't know what to do with the idea's energy. I can't sleep until I have a direction, a conflict, a character, *and* a plot that pulls it all together like skin on a drum. It has to resonate and have rhythm and life and it has to *feel right*. And for me, it is the worst, most painful part of the creative process. I'm in it now. I have an idea for book three in the Jane Yellowrock series. Just an idea. And it has me in its grip and it is shaking me like a rat in the maw of a fox. Even my skin feels electric and agitated and awaiting . . . something. I lie down to sleep at night and can't because it's racing around inside me, bouncing off the walls of my mind.

But I am not alone in this crazed phase. Kim and I shared about this creative-phase. She too goes through it—no sleep, no rest, just this *IDEA* bouncing around inside, looking for a conflict to ride or a character to conflict. It made me feel so much better to know I am not alone! You have no freaking idea. Kim says it's like a burning bunny tearing through her, around and around, dropping flames everywhere, starting fires, spreading and growing and nowhere to go with it. Hers is so intense that she even created a burning bunny pin for fans, so they could share in the creative carnage. Knowing I was not alone with this particular crazy phase was a huge relief. (Though my family may accuse me of running at the head of the pack when it comes to being nutso.)

This is the Big Bang part of writing. Got a seed, an atom, a whiff of the future. Need some nourishing soil or a cyclotron or a crystal ball. An idea, just waiting, ready to sprout, humming with the potential for conflict or violence or romance or catastrophe. Back when I first started writing, I would have a glass or two of wine to help me live with the insane djinn in the bottle of my mind. That looked to be getting out of hand, so I gave it up in place of just living with the crazed phase, knowing it wouldn't last *too* long. And it usually doesn't. I keep reminding myself of that.

Beatriz
Fabulous post, Faith! It's comforting to know that even pros get that feeling of not knowing what's next—the limitless possibilities can be scary.

David B. Coe

Yeah, every new shiny does this to me, but I have to admit that I relish this part of the process. That new creative energy is like single malt, chocolate, and sex all rolled into one. So, yeah, I know what you're talking about and I remember a wave of new excitement for my Winds of the Forelands series carrying me literally through a book and half of my first trilogy. I struggled with those second and third books and at times wanted to throw up my hands. But the promise of being able to work on the new story once I was done pulled me through.

Faith Hunter

David said, "That new creative energy is like single malt, chocolate, and sex all rolled into one."

David, I wish it was lovely like that for me, all the way through the process. I only start to feel *that* the moment I have an idea *and* a direction. In the Big Bang concept, that lovely sensation you are describing is (for me) the millisecond after the bang starts. That is when the idea takes its first focus, and grows from painful to fabulous. But when I have the about-to-explode atom in my hand, and nothing is happening at all, except pressure is building, it is not so much fun. I can't sleep. Can't rest or have fun or relax. Give me a week though! Then the fun starts.

Storytelling Tropes: Belief
C.E. Murphy

I recently caught a few minutes of one of my favorite early-season *Smallville* episodes, the one where Lex is split into Evil Lex and Good Lex, and Evil Lex utters the line, "You were right all along, Mr. Kent. I *am* the villain of the story."

It got me thinking about storytelling tropes and tragic characters—because in *Smallville* Lex is a tragic character, and it is without question his story in the first four or five seasons that makes the show worth watching. We all know how Clark Kent becomes Superman, but in *Smallville*, the story of how Lex Luthor becomes the villain of the piece is wonderfully tragic. He simply never stood a chance.

But there's one way he might have.

(The remainder of this essay contains some spoilers for early-season *Smallville*, as well as spoilers for *Buffy* with regard to the character Spike.)

A year or two ago (this is tangential, but does come back to the point) I read a great role-playing game write-up done by a father who was running the new D&D4 introduction campaign for his six-year-old son (who played the whole RPG group himself, with Dad as the GM). During the course of the game, the kid's group fought with kobolds, a couple of whom were captured to be pumped for information.

Once the kid had learned what he needed to know, Dad expected the kobolds to be axed. That is, after all, what one does to the bad guys in a role play campaign.

The kid, though, said, "No, Dad, we have to take them with us." Dad spluttered, "But they're bad guys," and the kid said, "I know. But I have to give them the chance to become good guys."

The Dad said, "They're kobolds! They're EVIL!"

The kid said, "But I believe in them, Dad. They can be good."

Dad capitulated. The kobolds got a chance to redeem themselves, and did so. (And apparently in the last encounter of the game, which had obliterated adult gaming groups left and right, the kid sailed through because he'd carefully hoarded all his magic uses and special items throughout the whole campaign and was *totally* prepared.)

But the point is, the kid had picked up on (from his television cartoons, apparently), and made clear to his father, the integral trope that could have saved Lex Luthor: *the good guy believes you can be better*. If, early on, Clark had chosen to trust Lex and reveal his secret—that he's superhuman—that might have cleared the only path Lex ever had to becoming a good man. (Of course, given that it's Superman, ultimately Lex would have to betray Clark anyway.

Though, if he had indeed become a good man he would be doing it to save Clark and at his own personal sacrifice, and the betrayal would be agonizingly poignant. I would love to see a one-shot episode of *that* story.)

This is a trope that was used in the last few seasons of *Buffy the Vampire Slayer*, as well. Spike the vampire, somewhere in season four, gets a chip stuck in his head that prevents him from attacking humans. At some point, Buffy makes the decision to trust Spike, and orders the chip removed.

In the Buffy universe there are some great long-term ramifications of this, but where it ends up being most important is in the last few episodes of the series, when all of Buffy's long-time friends have essentially abandoned her . . . and only Spike remains on her side.

By television storytelling tropes, he *has* to remain on her side. She's his redemption; she's the one who has believed in him, and without her faith, he's left with nothing for himself. Without her belief, all he is is a monster, so he has to stand with her against every last odd, in order to be better than he was.

In novels, I think this trope often manifests as "the love of a good woman," but it doesn't have to stop there. The truth is that people, fictional or not, will frequently rise to the occasion. If you believe they can do better, or more, and say as much to them, they'll often try.

The flip side, of course, is sometimes, or in some way, they'll fail. Lex, ultimately, is always going to be the villain of the piece. Buffy will never fall in love with Spike, no matter how much better he becomes. The good woman may turn out to be a back-stabbing bitch. But then you have all the wonderful juicy material that goes along with the failure—the betrayal, the heartbreak, the excuses, the revenge—and so as a storytelling element, win or lose, it's a trope you can get terrific stories out of.

David B. Coe

I always loved Spike's character. And I didn't watch *Smallville* much, but every time I did, it was Lex who brought me back to the show. Tropes are powerful writing tools; working with them, bending them, turning them upside-down. There will always be new stories to write, because there will always be new ways to play with familiar story elements.

Knowing What You Write

Misty Massey

When I was in high school, I wrote a short story about a catlike alien soldier whose ship crash-landed on a planet under the control of her enemies. She reported her position, but her people ordered her to make her way to a less dangerous spot for retrieval. Along the way, she found a wounded enemy soldier, and together they helped each other survive. (*Give me a break, I was fifteen.* ☺) The teacher graded it and gave it back, with the suggestion that I should write what I knew, and "steer clear of all that daydreamy stuff" (her words). This advice, admittedly, floored me. I wanted to write about magic and space and creatures that couldn't possibly exist. I was at a loss as to how I was supposed to learn such things. Other people were writing about unicorns and time travel and telekinetic aliens, so why couldn't I? It took me years to realize the teacher had been right, though not in the way she thought she was. It's not that we should write what we know—we should know what we write.

We've all run into a situation in which the author clearly had no idea what she was writing about. The questing novel, for example, in which the party stops for the night and eats stew for dinner. Have you ever made stew? Takes ages. A party travelling a long distance would more likely have packed dry meat and bread. If they happen to hunt and catch meat, they won't waste time stewing it when roasting is so much quicker. I have a pet peeve about the way CPR is portrayed in movies and on television, because I've had to be certified in it for the past twenty years. The people on screen are almost always doing it wrong, so wrong that it's a miracle it ever works. Not knowing what you're writing about is a sure way to lose your reader. Luckily there are ways to keep that from happening.

When I was writing the original draft of *Mad Kestrel*, I depended on my writing group to tell me when something didn't sound authentic. I did the same for them. Now and then, though, one or another of us wouldn't listen. Me, for example. I had written a scene in which Kestrel injured her shoulder, and in the beginning, I decided she'd popped it out of joint. Immediately after this happened, she had to fight with two bad guys. Upon hearing these pages, Faith shook her head and said that a dislocated shoulder would have been too painful for Kestrel to do much more than walk to the nearest help. I knew she was right, but I didn't listen. I liked the way the scene played out, and I didn't want to rewrite it. (They call it "killing your darlings" but we'll talk about that another time. ☺)

Several months later, my family and I went to the mountains for the week-end with my best friend. She, my husband, and my son all hit the bunny slopes to try skiing, while I relaxed in the hot tub. (I know my limitations, and strapping long boards on my feet has never sounded appealing!) Suddenly the phone rang. My husband had fallen and dislocated his shoulder. I had to pick him up from the first aid office, and drive, in the dark, on swervy mountain roads, in the snow, to take him to the nearest hospital. My husband has a pretty high pain threshold, but he was in agony. Every bump, every curve of the road made him groan. We reached the hospital, got him settled in with the doctor, and then it hit me. This was exactly what Kestrel would have been feeling. She couldn't have managed to fight anyone. When I got home, I sat down and rewrote the whole scene, making it just a banged-up shoulder instead. Because now I knew what I was writing.

Can you write something without ever seeing or feeling it? Sure. But if you want the authenticity that makes readers connect to your work, you really should dig deep from what you know. If you've suffered loss, or grief, or pain, draw from those feelings to make your characters' behavior honest. If you're sending your adventurers on a long horseback trip, go take a couple of riding lessons so you'll know how it feels to be in the saddle for a while (not to mention getting a handle on how mischievous some horses can be.) You don't have to be a fifteenth level wizard to write about magic. Read what other people have done, and pay close attention to why their magic systems work.

And for goodness' sake, if you have a friend with experience, listen when she tells you to rewrite a scene.

Beatriz

It's the small details, done wrong, that can yank a reader out of the story. Why should I trust an author who is creating some elaborate magical world if they can't even get "normal" details right?

My ex hated most medical dramas because so much of the medicine was wrong. He couldn't just follow the plot because the glaring medical mistakes kept getting in the way of the story.

I've been known to toss a book across the room in frustration because the mundane details were inaccurately portrayed without any reason.

David B. Coe

Yeah, Beatriz, I know exactly what you mean. For more than twenty years now, I've been watching TV shows and movies with a Stanford-trained scientist. It's no picnic. . . .

Great post, Misty. It's amazing how a dose of emotional reality, well-drawn characters, and some well-placed research on background things like smith-work, wheelwrighting, and other medieval crafts can make magic seem perfectly authentic. Knowing what we write. Lovely phrase, that.

On Research

C.E. Murphy

I don't typically do my research—

Hmm. I'd better start this again. ☺

I'd been about to say, "I don't typically do my research until after the fact," except that's wildly untrue. Before I started the Walker Papers, I read every book about shamanism I could get my hands on (and I'm really looking forward to an excuse to buy a few more when I start that series up again in a few weeks! *hahaha!*). I've been an Elizabethan-era buff since I was a little kid, though I've got nothing on many of my friends when it comes to enthusiasm for the topic. So I do groundwork research before I start, but when I get down to the details . . .

Well, my manuscripts have a lot of notes in them. Literally. When I'm writing and I can't, for example, remember what the proper word for the back of a ship is, my manuscript reads, "toward the NOTE: NAME FOR THE BACK OF THE BOAT they went." Injured a character in a modern-world story? NOTE: LOOK UP HARLEM HOSPITALS. Can't remember a character's name? NOTE: FIND OUT HIS NAME AND FOR GOD'S SAKE, CATIE, YOU SHOULD WRITE THIS $#!7 DOWN! I only stop to go find out that it's called the stern if there's some reason I can't continue forward without actually knowing that. There usually isn't.

I have a friend who—when I'm not working quite as close to the wire as I am now—plays unpaid research assistant. She'll read my rough drafts and I get emails back full of answers to my NOTES. I'm *desperately* grateful to her for this and have dreams that someday I'll be rich enough to make her a paid research assistant. But with my last few books I've been tapping into another research resource, which I like to call *Livejournal knows all*.

It's amazing what you can ask the internet and get back instantaneous answers on. For *House of Cards*, I needed, oh, a handful of legal terms that I just didn't even know enough words about to know where to *start* looking, much less get the right ones. Turned out there were lawyers and legal aides on my friend's list. I needed a high-end fountain pen, the kind that runs to silly expensive. *Lots* of pen buffs on my friend's list. I just now needed a couple of translations to Italian and French, and a Latin declamation, and look at that, one of my friends has a Ph.D in Latin, which I had no idea about until now.

I swear it feels like cheating. I don't know why (probably because I'm part of the last generation to grow up using libraries for research instead of Google). I mean, it is not in fact cheating to go to people and say, "Hey, you know more than I do about this, can you tell me about it?" That's precisely what research is. But somehow flinging it out on Livejournal to five hundred people to see if any of them happen to know seems like a shortcut.

Usually what I get back is a barrage of information that I sift through and . . . gosh, use what's appropriate. Just like real research.

So today I've been running back and forth from my work computer to my 'net computer, asking questions and getting answers while I've been doing revisions on my manuscript. It's not the most efficient way to do this—usually I don't address the NOTES until the very last thing before the spell check—but I'm in the revision stages and have been looking things up anyway, so why not. It's all part of the process. ☺

Faith Hunter

I LOVE it when you do the same things I do. It makes me feel a lot less alone and a lot more normal. I type ZZZ when I have something that needs to be fixed later. And I do XXX if it is something I need to check back on fairly quickly. My own personal NOTE code.

I have also left notes to my mystery editor. Like this:

(((((Miranda, Please note that this scene needs a few post mortem details from my forensic guy, who is in France on vacation for three more weeks. Please ignore the spaces and xxxs.)))))

She sends me back smiley faces on them.

David B. Coe

I guess I'm the outlier on this one. I can't leave that one word for later or skip over the details of, say, the wheelwright's shop where the action takes place for one scene. I'd love to, but I can't seem to get myself to do it. Too compulsive, I guess. It makes it harder for me to write subsequent scenes. Too bad. It would probably make my life a bit easier.

I do my research much the same way: lots of books, lots of web searches, and some calling of friends with expertise in a given area. I haven't tried throwing a question out to LJ or WordPress, but I'm sure I will one of these days. It's a great idea.

Metaphors, Similes, and Analogies, Oh My . . .

Edmund R. Schubert

I was reading an article once in *National Geographic* about the intelligence of swarms. It talked about how any large group—everything from bugs to birds to a herd of water-buffalo—can take on an intelligence much greater than that of the individual components of the group, and how scientists were applying some of the principals of swarms to solve human problems. Included in that story was an example of a trucking company that had developed a computer model for routing its trucks based on algorithms inspired by the foraging behavior of Argentine ants, a species of ant known for laying trails by depositing pheromones.

Everybody get that? Let me repeat it: A trucking company developed a computer model for routing trucks based on algorithms inspired by the foraging behavior of Argentine ants, a species known for laying trails by depositing pheromones.

Okay, I like to pretend I'm a reasonably intelligent guy, but my first reaction was, "*What . . . ?*"

But here's the thing: in the next paragraph, the writer of that article gave me something I could sink my teeth into. He gave me an analogy. He said that what the ants (and therefore the trucking company) were doing was like when someone goes into the forest to collect berries. Over time a path is worn in the ground to the best places to find berries.

Now that I understood.

Algorithms and ant pheromones? Not so much. Berries in the woods? Now you're talking my language. And that's kind of ironic, really, because the language we're talking about is pictures. Word pictures.

Writers are all trying to communicate a message, and to do so as clearly and effectively as possible. So what I want to talk about today is the power of metaphors, similes, and analogies. I'm not going to bore you with dictionary definitions of these terms; what you need to know is that the essence of all three is that they describe one thing by comparing it to something else.

There are a lot of ways to do this, and a lot of reasons to do this. First of all, you might be trying to describe something unusual—Argentine ants and their pheromones, for instance—so you compare it to something people are more familiar with. This helps them understand what you're saying.

On the other hand, you might be talking about something very basic, like writing, and want to jazz it up. Writing in and of itself isn't terribly hard; you've all been doing it since the first grade. But you want to make it more interesting, to catch people's attention, so you might describe it using cooking terms. You might say that writing a story is like cooking a meal, and that if all you give people is meat and potatoes, they won't go hungry, but nobody's going to rave about your cooking, either.

If you want to present a meal that really satisfies, you've got to spice it up a little. You've got to throw is some oregano, some thyme, maybe a little parsley on the side. Well, okay, skip the side of parsley. Nobody likes that stuff. Using parsley as a garnish is like using clichés in your writing. Don't waste people's time.

Having said all that, I should also mention that you do have to be careful not to get carried away. As with herbs and spices in cooking, you want to make sure you don't over-do it. A little salt makes everything taste better; too much and it overpowers the meal. Everything in moderation.

Another advantage of using metaphors, similes, and/or analogies is this: they help people remember your keys points. By using one of these comparative devices, you are subliminally telling the reader what your most important points are by placing extra emphasis on them. That helps to reinforce those points in their minds.

By way of (an admittedly silly) example, let's say you're writing a magazine article about gardening, and you're trying to describe the perfect kind of soil to plant rosemary in. And say the perfect soil for planting rosemary is rich but pale and very dry. Well, that's not terribly evocative. But if you say it needs to be rich, pale, and very dry—kind of like Bill Gates . . . Hopefully you'll get a laugh. But more importantly, you've reinforced your point by drawing extra attention to it, making it one people are more likely to remember.

The last thing you want to remember is to make sure your metaphors and similes are appropriate to the subject matter you're trying to describe. I remember a friend telling me about someone who came to his writer's group with a mystery story, and in this story the author had portrayed a particularly gruesome killing. There was a key scene where the police at the crime scene were trying to figure out "who done it," when suddenly the author described the fingerprints the detective found like this: "Detective Spade studied the bloody print on the victim's slashed throat and couldn't help but notice how much the swirling pattern reminded him of the tiny whirlpool his toilet made when it was flushed." That doesn't add anything; in fact, it's a terrible distraction. It's *counter*-productive. You have to make sure your comparative descriptions fit with the tone of the subject matter.

Metaphors. Similes. Analogies. You can call them word pictures if that makes you happy. But I would say that more important than what you call them or the differences between them, is remembering the power they have when used correctly. The power to clarify, the power to enliven, the power to reinforce. The power to make your writing really stand out—as if it were covered with Argentine ant pheromones.

A.J. Hartley

Great point about distracting or overly numerous analogies/metaphors. I read a piece recently for a short story contest and every sentence was laced with these eye-catching metaphors. Some of them were very good, but used en masse it was like being bludgeoned by the writer's cleverness: irritating and distracting. You got so caught up in trying to figure out whether the metaphor worked that you were utterly knocked out of the story. Using metaphors is like sewing seeds: they need space to grow . . . [okay, that was a simile]

David J. Fortier

What I really enjoy in writing, is when the figurative language (metaphors, similes, analogies and other devices) are character specific. For example, when a character with a nautical background compares things to sailing, boats, stars and other things familiar to them. Not only does it help you remember key points of the story, it also is a good way of reminding the reader of characters' backgrounds. Done well, characters really come to life.

Scope
Stuart Jaffe

A week or so ago, I had the joyous experience of finishing the rough draft on my latest novel. And while it sits quietly resting for a few weeks, I've turned my attention to several short stories that I've agreed to write for various anthologies. Looking at the creation process has brought to mind the subject of today's essay: scope.

The scope of your tale, if it is to be a short story, is extremely important. Many of my attempts at short stories failed because the scope was wrong. So, first off, what is "scope"?

Scope refers to the size or range of the tale itself. Not the word count or page count but the size of the story. A tale that covers seven generations of three families has a long, wide scope. A tale that covers the final three seconds of one person's last breath has a short, narrow scope.

In my experience, the best short stories find a place nearer to the middle, but leaning toward the narrow side. This, of course, is easier said than done. Ideas pop in my head and I love the details of the conflict, the grandeur of the idea, the wondrousness of it all. Yes! I've got a Hugo-winner waiting to be put on paper. *Slow down,* my brain says. *This won't work in 5,000 words. Flesh it out and the idea might be a good novel, but it'll never work for a short story.* I lower my head and nod.

So, how exactly can you tell if you're on the right track with the scope of your story? Sadly, as a beginning writer, one of the best ways is trial and error. You have to experience it to understand where that sweet-spot is, so you can recognize it down the road. There are, however, some red flags to look for:

- **Changing Viewpoints:** One of the first shorts I ever wrote dealt with two guys holding up a diner. The story was told in steps by each of the five characters in the diner. Sort of a "Rashomon" thing but forward-moving. The problem is that in a short story there's just not enough time to establish five main characters. Though the "time" aspect of the scope of the overall story is fine (a holdup in a diner), the method of telling the story created too large a scope (five main characters).
- **Too Much Info:** If you find yourself having to explain *a lot* of backstory, do *a lot* of worldbuilding, or perform *a lot* of writing acrobatics just to get readers up to speed enough to understand the story, chances are your scope is too large. A huge world with a complex magic system can be wonderful fodder for short stories,

just narrow the one particular tale down so that the world and its magic don't need full explanations to work.

- **Filler:** Most problems in scope fall in the "too large" category, but on occasion you can have an idea that is so narrow, it boarders on flash fiction. The biggest red flag is that you find yourself struggling for something to happen in order to fill out the tale or you're putting in unimportant details to pad out the pacing before you get to the end too quickly.
- **Sub-plots:** This is a *short* story. Where did you think there was room for a sub-plot?

Of course, these are merely red flags, not hard and fast rules. I'm sure there are plenty of examples of award-winning stories that pull off these scope issues and thumb their fictitious noses at me. But the way they succeed is by knowing what the problem is and working around it.

So this post is meant to be nothing more than a way to help you identify potential problems. Beginners, if you see those red flags, start adjusting your tale and save yourself a lot of anguish. For the more advanced writers, if you see those red flags, you know the fire you're playing with and the risks you take.

> **Ryl Mandus**
>
> Stuart, you must be psychic—"scope" is *exactly* what I've been agonizing over for the last week. It seems that whenever I get a nifty idea for a short story or a novelette, it wants to "grow up" and become a novel—or worse, a series. Makes it bloody hard to complete that first draft.
>
> You've just shown me it's a matter of mindset, not material, offering a way to possibly apply the brakes so I don't have to go downhill like a juggernaut into the bay in a van full of beer: No point in steering, now, eh?
>
> Thanks! I'll be giving these boundaries a serious try.

Short Fiction Revisited

David B. Coe

I was recently asked to write the introduction for an upcoming fantasy anthology (*Blood and Devotion: Tales of Epic Fantasy*, edited by W.H. Horner, from Fantasist Enterprises Books). In writing the introduction, I spent a good deal of time thinking about short fiction and how writing it differs from writing novels. This has been on my mind anyway recently, because I've been asked to submit to two anthologies in the next couple of months and I'm working on the first of my stories right now.

Here's an excerpt from my introduction:

> Think of a novel as one of those towers of amethyst crystals that one sees in a mall nature shop or mineral store. It's huge, it sparkles; looking at it, one can't help but be impressed. But if a novel is such a tower, then a short story is a single crystal. It doesn't need to be part of the larger piece; it shines on its own. It's small, but multifaceted; simple, but brilliant and captivating.

I truly believe this. I'm awed by successful short-story writers. Most of the books I've published have been parts of larger projects—we call them extended story arcs, which is really just another way of saying that I take several hundred thousand words to create my worlds, establish my characters, and resolve my plot points. Writing a successful short story is, at least for me, far more difficult than writing a successful novel. I sold my first short story back in 2002, and I was every bit as proud of that sale as I was of my first book contract. In many ways more so. Until then I had felt that my failure to sell a short story reflected poorly on my skill as a writer. Selling that first short piece confirmed for me that I had finally begun to master my craft.

The clearest difference for me is that a short piece is simply more directed. The story focuses on one narrative conflict and follows it to its resolution. One also has to be more subtle and concise in conveying background material, be it for character development, worldbuilding, or the explanation of some dynamic in the narrative. For me, this might be the greatest challenge in short story writing. Worlds and magic systems need to be drawn with broad strokes—much of what the reader needs to know has to be implied rather than explicitly stated. In many ways, I believe that when I'm writing short fiction I wind up placing more trust in my reader, having faith in her/his ability to catch the subtle hints, the narrative breadcrumbs that I leave along the way as I write.

Other differences: I find that I write slower when I write shorter. Lately I've been shooting for 2,000 words a day when working on my novels; while working on a short piece, I'm satisfied with half that amount. I take greater care with each passage; I work harder to make the most of every sentence, every word. I think I also keep my characters on a slightly shorter leash. If a character begins to lead me in a direction I hadn't anticipated, I'll follow for a while. But I won't be as indulgent as I would be in the midst of a novel or series. In part, this is because with the shorter work, I have a better idea from the outset of where I intend to wind up. But I also know that I don't have the time or space for the more leisurely pace of storytelling that one can establish in a novel.

A lot of novelists I know don't write much short fiction. There is far less money in it. Selling a short story can get you some exposure and help you sell a novel, but short story pubs are no longer the near-prerequisite for selling a novel that they once were. And there are fewer markets now, so selling the short work is that much harder.

But there are benefits to writing short fiction that all writers should consider. For one thing, they offer a venue for exploring themes, developing characters, and discovering more about one's world that can prove enormously helpful in the writing of a novel. But even more important, those differences I catalogued earlier improve one's writing for all forms. Learning to be more directed, more concise, more subtle in the conveyance of background infor-mation, more careful in the crafting of each passage, more trusting of my readers—all of these things improve my writing overall.

I don't think it's a coincidence that as I've written and sold more short fiction, my novels have improved. Nor do I think it's a coincidence that as I've become a better novelist I've grown better at writing short work. The two skill-sets reinforce one another. And maybe that's the best reason of all for writing short stories. Learning to do different things as a writer can only serve to make us more versatile, more comfortable with the written word. In the end, that's the most important goal we can have. The market is unpredictable; what sells one month might languish the next. But good writing is its own reward, and so I'll continue to write short work as long as it's still fun, and as long as I feel that it's making me better at the writing I do.

Charles E. Dunkley

Every now and then I try my hand at short stories, but more often than not they end up being scenes instead, especially if they are related to my second-world fantasy setting.

I'd like to try to hone my short story writing skills, but as I'm concentrating on writing novels, it is hard to make the time. I find I need a very different mind set for short story writing than the one I have for novels.

My writing at the moment is all epic fantasy, and yet I've had this urban fantasy idea rolling around for about a year. I think the short story format would be quite useful there.

I think writing a short story to get to know the main character and his situation will be quite helpful. Now, whether I could shape that into a publishable short story is something else altogether. I have a lot of respect for the short story author. I'd love to be able to write with that level of focus and sharpness. All I can do is work at it when I can.

David B. Coe

CE, I understand completely, because I was exactly the same way for a long time. When we're writing our novels it's hard to shift focus to short pieces that a) feel like something of a distraction, and b) have little potential for making money. But I've come to love the time I spend writing short fiction, and I think it has improved my writing a good deal. Yes, do it when you can, when it doesn't detract from the novel writing. My problem was always that I SAID I'd handle it that way, but then, even when I had the time, I avoided short stories because I found them far more challenging. I hope you'll avoid that trap.

Juggling
Stuart Jaffe

Research. Plot. Character. Worldbuilding. Story. Voice. Theme. Scene. Conflict. Revisions. Rising action.

The list goes on and on. The question for today's essay is: "How do I juggle all of this?"

Well, like everything in writing there is no one, simple, easy answer. We are all unique, and we all deal with the challenges of writing in our own unique way. However, there are a few things I can suggest that may help you at least get started.

For the supremely disorganized, I suggest a simple checklist. In fact, I suggest two simple checklists. The first checklist is for the work as a whole. This is not necessarily to be done in order, but rather to make sure you have included the crucial elements to a successful story. Here is where you list plot, protagonist, antagonist, worldbuilding, theme, etc. Most of the items on this list should be checked off before you actually start writing the work. Depending on your writing style, items such as plot may not get checked off until the very end. It will alter as you go. I've never had a story finish exactly as I envisioned it, but making sure you have the basics in place will make the exploration of writing a bit easier.

The second list is for your daily writing. Here is the checklist to handle your actual approach to getting words on the page. Some authors like to warm up before tackling the actual WIP. John Steinbeck often used a writing diary in which he would lay down his thoughts about the WIP, the current scene, as well as the mundane events of the day. Others prefer a simple writing exercise, whether it be to describe the scene or character or moment. Still others warm up using a short story (this has the added benefit of producing a short story when you finish). If you're a warm-up type, then make that the first item on your checklist. If you prefer to jump right in, then do so. The daily writing checklist also includes items after the day's words are finished, such as reminding yourself to backup files, research that seafaring lingo you thought you knew, and plot revisions you've made along the way (and you will make them).

For the moderately organized, perhaps some computer software will help. As I haven't used any such software myself, I cannot speak to their effectiveness. However, even a simple spreadsheet might help. The idea is simply to find a secure place to organize your thoughts so that they're not bouncing around in your head all the time. You need to get that stuff out in order to make room for the new thoughts.

Finally, for those of you already organized or those of you who really like to fly by the seat of your pants, I return your attention to a suggestion made by David a short while back. Write some short stories. Write stories about events your characters have dealt with before those of your WIP. I tried this method with my current work and discovered it to be of great value. I learned more about my characters and the world they live in than in any world I ever created before. It's not just the practical side of things either. Not just the names of flora and fauna or the placement of buildings in the town or the history of one of my characters. I learned about the textures, the aromas, the tastes of the world I had created. In writing a few short stories (I wrote three), I was able to take all the research I had been juggling in my head and stir it together in the cauldron of writing. When I actually began my novel, I had already lived in its world.

What works for each of us is, of course, different. The more you write, the more you go through the process, the easier the juggling act becomes. Well, all right, not really easier, but rather you'll develop a method that eventually will work for you.

David B. Coe
We offer so much advice on this site, and I can see where some would find it overwhelming. Offering a way to keep track of it all and reduce it to useable information is great. As for starting out each day: One piece of advice my grad school advisor gave me for writing my dissertation was to finish each day in the middle of a sentence. That way, the first thing you write the following morning is the completion of that thought. In a way, it primes the pump and gets things moving. I use this periodically, when I find myself struggling in the mornings.

Characters, Dialogue & Point of View

A Rose By Any Other Name . . .

A.J. Hartley

I was fortunate enough to get a round of notes on my new YA adult novel from no less an author than R.L. Stine (of *Goosebumps* fame) and he pointed out that I had to rename one of my major characters. Her name was Isabella, often simply "Bella," which, he pointed out, was the same as the heroine of the ubiquitous *Twilight* series. I had realized the coincidence before, but a better name hadn't leaped to mind so I left it as it was. But Mr. Stine was (unsurprisingly) clearly right. I had time to change it, and doing a quick find/replace in my Word document was no sweat. All I needed was a new name.

This is where things got tough. The problem was that I had finished the first draft of the book almost five months earlier and had been tinkering with it ever since. I now knew this girl and her name was Bella. I tried inserting alternatives and they wouldn't work or didn't fit. The search for a replacement— which took several agonizing days and produced only a provisional solution— made me acutely aware of how difficult naming characters can be. Today I offer a few things to bear in mind as you dish out monikers.

Things to be aware of:

1. Real or made up? If you make up a name (i.e. if you invent a new word, or invent a name from a regular word like Neil Gaiman's Door) remember the way we respond to real people who have odd names. And if you do start making up words, ensure that it fits the world of your story, that the pronunciation is clear and that the word feels right without unfortunate associations or echoes (see below).

2. Associations. If you choose a conventional name, test it out on your friends to see what associations it generates. I wanted to call my new character Angelina, but since I see a real Angelina looking at me from every supermarket tabloid (not to mention Angelina Ballerina) I decided I didn't want to battle whatever baggage that name might evoke for a reader.

3. Ethnicity. Few names can be found in all cultures, so choose what fits your real or imaginary world. I wanted to call my African-American girl Danika (partly because I liked its abbreviations, Danny/Danni or Dan), but my wife (a pediatrician who knows these things) pointed out that the name has northern European roots and is rare outside Caucasian families. And right now it's particularly associated with a race car driver, which wasn't the right association either.

4. Meaning. The web is jammed with sites offering baby names, and these are an obvious resource when you are assigning names. Most give a short explanation of what the name means, and such information can help determine whether it's right for your character. Some of these definitions are a bit shaky, however, so once you've identified a name you like, look it up in some more reliable source.

5. The irrelevance of point #4 (!) Appealing though it is to have a character name with a cool meaning, remember how little we think of people we know in terms of what their names actually mean—even if we know. Unless you find a way to explain it in the narrative (which has to be handled carefully), the meaning may not be much of a factor in determining the impact of the name in your story.

6. Feel. More likely to shape the impact is the *feel* of the name: what it sounds like when spoken aloud, whether it's driven by hard consonants or broad, open vowels, how many syllables it has, or whether it ends with something tight and closing (like a "t") or flippant—even trivial—(like a "y" or "i"). What does the name weigh? Is it light like Pippin (note the child-like repetition of the vowel) or simple and earthy like Sam (with the tell-tale honorific "wise" tacked to the end?) Does it have an onomatopoeic quality, like Grond (Tolkien's *orkish* battering ram) which is the sound of its iron head against the doors of Minas Tirith?

7. Appearance. How does it look on the page? The appearance of a word is slightly different from its sound and can have implications for feel, too. If you make up a name full of Ks and apostrophes, ask if it is ever going to feel familiar—like a real name—to a reader, no matter how many times they read it.

8. In Combination. How does it combine with other names, particularly a surname or title, but also with other names in the book? All of these concerns about feel come back into play when the name is paired with another proper noun, both of which might be good alone, but dreadful together.

9. Sound. An extension of that: is it different enough from the other names in your book that it won't get confusing for your reader? I once had a book where it seemed like every minor character's name began with H. Maybe I'd been thumbing through the phone book and got stuck there. It was very confusing. I also had two characters who were together a lot and both had names beginning with D. I had to change one so they didn't sound like a nightclub act.

10. How does it abbreviate? Only in the highest fantasy do four syllable names not get contracted by the people who are supposed to be their friends. Plan this out.

11. Friend Factor. Is it—or might someone think it is—close enough to the name of someone you actually know that a reader might think they recognize them from reality? If so, change it. You don't want your sense of a real person to dictate your character (for you or your readers), and you certainly don't want to face a lawsuit over perceived defamation of character.

I'm over-thinking, right? Well, maybe. But readers recognize these things at least subconsciously, and the name has to feel right if you are going to write the character well. Sometimes it's good to wait, let the character emerge in the writing before giving her a name. If I give a character a name arbitrarily right out of the gate I find she will be shaped by the name I picked, and that's a pretty random way to write a story. One dodge I use is to assign the character a generic tag like XXXX until I have written enough to know what the character feels like. A simple find/replace search can then be made.

Faith Hunter

A.J., you said, "If I give a character a name arbitrarily right out of the gate I find she will be shaped by the name I picked, and that's a pretty random way to write a story."

I had that exact problem with Jane Yellowrock. I had no name to start out with, wanting some cool AmIn Cherokee chick name, that meant war-woman, and ending with a real surname like Man Killer or SixManKiller. So I named her Jane Doe. Random. But then my hind brain came up with a story to match and Jane was born. I like the random creativity that my mind applied to the name. But next time I'll go back to the XXXX method, which is my more common method of character not-naming-until-I-find-the-right-one.

Ordinary People

Misty Massey

"I wonder if it's possible to write a ripping good yarn with a hero or heroine who is ordinary in every way."

A reader emailed this question a few days ago. It's a good question. Why do novels tend to be about unusually skilled people in extraordinary circumstances? Why do they have tortured pasts? Why are they always better-than-average looking? What about middle-aged Jim Johnson, the married car salesman who lives on the corner? Why can't he be a fantasy hero?

When I read a book, I want to be transported. I want to enter a world I can't possibly find by driving my SUV across town. I want to share the experiences of people I could never, ever be. Heroes who discover they can perform magic, or are related to a fabled line of martial artists, or cause the weather to change just by staring at clouds long enough. Those people are interesting. I want to be near them. I want to be along for the ride as they learn what they're capable of, and overcome the dilemmas facing them. I want to root for them, and I want to turn the last page with a satisfied sigh that once again, the good guys succeeded in the face of overwhelming odds.

Does this mean I want to read stories about characters who are so magnificent they can do it all? Naah. That's boring. An invincible hero is certainly nice to have around, but after he's saved the busload of orphans from falling over the cliff and stopped the asteroid from smashing the town, I'll probably wander off to find something else to do. He can't be beaten, so why should I bother paying attention? That's where that tortured past thing comes into play. We're all slaves to the mistakes of our pasts, and a book's characters shouldn't be any different. An unbeatable character is dull, but a hero who's afraid of snakes is fascinating. What if he has to wade through a snake pit to save his friend from certain death? Will he? The sword-warrior who can't sleep because she has nightmares about the father who beat her will have to make a decision when he turns out to be the evil duke she's been hired to guard. We want to read about their worries and triumphs, because in a way, they are ours as well.

I just finished reading a very good book called *World's End*, by Mark Chadbourn. The main characters are ordinary people, living lives not unlike any of ours, when they are swept into the events that drive the story. Church is grieving a lost love, Ruth is worrying that she might lose her job. But when the ancient gods of Celtic myth start chasing them through the countryside, they have to become more than they are. They have to become heroes.

So there's your answer. Even when a story begins with someone going about his boring old life, he has to change, to transform into someone who can solve the mystery, find the magic, save the world. Otherwise, it wouldn't be a story anyone would want to read.

And if they're good-looking, too . . . well that just makes it more fun to imagine while I'm writing. ☺

David B. Coe

". . . they have to become more than they are. They have to become heroes."

Yes, that's my favorite kind of story. One of the things that made *The Hobbit* so effective the first time I read it so many, many years ago, was the fact that Bilbo was utterly ordinary. Not particularly brave, not strong, small and quick, but no more so than any other hobbit. But as the story unfolds and he's forced into his adventure, he has to become more than he was, more than his neighbors back in the Shire would like him to be. I love that.

Neil Gaiman excels at this kind of character—check out *Neverwhere* or *Ananzi Boys* or even *American Gods*. He handles the ordinary hero beautifully.

Faith Hunter

"Ordinary" gets my vote (says the girl currently writing about a skin-walker and a stone-mage/battle-mage.) Okay, I lied a little. When I write mystery/thrillers, I like ordinary people forced to evolve strengths by the conflict of the plotline. When I write fantasy, I like the odd, quirky, got-a-few-tricks-in-his/her-bag character. And I'm not even a Gemini!

C.E. Murphy

Everybody's extraordinary in some way. My dad likes looking at orchestra performers and then imagining them on the street, just walking along in regular clothes, and you'd never know that that guy was a trombone virtuoso, or whatever. So I think most people have something in them that they're extraordinarily good at. Those things are frequently the basis for character's careers.

Margrit in the Negotiator trilogy, for example, is a Very Good Lawyer. But Margrit's also very grounded in the real world. Her ambitions and goals are very concrete, unlike Joanne in the Walker Papers, who essentially wants a quiet, unambitious life working on cars, because it's what she loves. So when Margrit's pulled into the extraordinary world of the Old Races, she behaves very differently than when Jo discovers she's a shaman. They're both heroes, but they come into it in completely different ways.

The Importance of Wanting in Fiction

Edmund R. Schubert

This may sound odd, but after years of editing, I have found that frequently, if I find your story to be wanting, it is because I find your main character wants for nothing.

Let me elaborate. Having the advantage of reading a lot of awful, bad, mediocre, and not-quite-right stories on a regular basis is always educational; there is much to be learned from fiction that's less than stellar. It's the number one reason why I tell people that if they get a chance to read slush for any magazine, volunteer without hesitation. The education will be well worth the time you invest.

Now, the really bad stuff is as obvious as the really good stuff, and doesn't require much thought. It's the stuff in between—especially at the upper-end of the not-quite-right spectrum—that I study and learn from. It was close, but not quite right: Why? It was interesting and well-written, but not compelling. Again: why? The reasons for near-misses can often be hard to nail down, but when you do, it's like finding a small treasure.

One of the things that has become more and more clear to me lately is the power of Vonnegut's third rule of writing (you can Google "Vonnegut's Eight Rules of Writing" if you want to see his complete list, which I highly recommend). You may have heard of this third rule before, but if you haven't it reads thus: "Every character should want something, even if it is only a glass of water." It sounds silly, but then, that was always one of Vonnegut's special skills; making important things sound silly (and vice versa).

The only thing I'll disagree with Vonnegut about is that I think this should be Rule #1, not #3. Wanting something is the most powerful thing an author can give to a character. And it's usually most effective when it is something simple. It's extremely difficult to relate to someone who wants to save the world: how many of us have ever been in, or ever expect to be in, that situation? But two people who are in love and want to be together? You'd be hard-pressed to find anyone who hasn't been in that position at some point in their life.

That makes not just the situation relatable, but renders the characters relatable, too. When the main character wants something, we usually start wondering how they're going to get it, and rooting for them to succeed. Often the rooting is unconscious, but it happens just the same. Which means you've hooked your reader into siding with your character. It takes more than that to get readers to *like* the character, but frankly I consider *hooking* readers to be more important.

Two characters who want something—to be together, for instance—is a simple premise, but one that is behind some of the most beloved stories of all time. Take, for instance, one of my own favorite movies (and a great book, too): *The Princess Bride*. What is that story about? At its core you'll find nothing more than a man and a woman who fall in love and want to be together. Everything else is details. Kidnapping, torture, revenge; giants and screaming eels and Rodents of Unusual Size; the albino, his cart, and the holocaust cloak: they're all rich, fun details, but they're still just details. The *story* is about two people who want to be together.

Having your characters want something is, for a number of reasons, also an effective tool for constructing a story. First, it makes it easy to identify your antagonists. Antagonists don't have to be mean, horrible people. In fact, mean, horrible people are boring. But a nice, well-intentioned character who wants the exact opposite of what your main character wants? Now you've got a believable antagonist you can work with, who can do some real damage without being reduced to a cliché.

Second, knowing what your main character wants is useful because it makes it clear what the ending has to be. Not "ought" to be, or "might" be; what it *has* to be. Make the character's wants or needs as difficult to attain as you like (the more difficult, the better), and the number and severity of the obstacles will go a long way toward determining the length of your story. But once the character gets what they want, the story is over. Period. There might be an epilogue to tie up a few loose ends, but for all intents and purposes your story is over.

Third, knowing where your story ends is one of the most valuable things a writer can have because it gives you a target to aim at. The difference between knowing your ending and not knowing your ending is the difference between getting in your car and driving from New York to California, vs. simply getting in your car and driving. You might visit some interesting places if you simply drive around, but how do you know when you've *arrived* if there's no destination?

Finally, knowing what your character wants (and focusing on it) goes a long way to keeping your story character-driven instead of event-driven. I like stories where things *happen*—in fact, I vastly prefer action over characters who sit around contemplating the meaning of the universe—but fiction that resonates with readers is about people first. Action is the best way to reveal character, but if the cool "stuff" that happens in your story is the main focus, you are not going to connect with nearly as many readers as you will if the people are the heart of your work.

Part of the reason I'm bringing this up now is that I've read a slew of stories lately (everything from novels to short stories) where the author starts with a bit of a mystery or a bit of action (or even a lot of action), but the minute the action or the mystery eases up, my interest in the story dwindles, frequently to next-to-nothing. Even when the writing is professional-level, the voice resonates, the setting is interesting, and the characters are rich and alive, when it hits me that there's nothing that the main character really wants, I lose interest. The character has no goal, no objective, no unmet need. They simply got swept up in events around them; nothing more.

Even if the situation that the writer puts the character in *remains* hazardous, I can only stay interested in a leaf that's blowing in the wind but for so long. That leaf might be blowing inside a hurricane or a tornado, but it's still an inert object. And inert is just another word for lifeless.

There's a saying: "Where there is life, there is hope," and that saying applies to this situation in many ways. The bottom line, however, is this: If you want editors to buy your stories, make sure there is life. And you accomplish that by making sure your characters—protagonists and antagonists alike—*want* something.

Even if it's just a glass of water.

A.J. Hartley

Great point, Ed. As Stuart will, I'm sure, agree (as my fellow MW writer with a foot in the theatre) this is one of those notes which overlaps literary and performance arts. Stanislavski is great on this for actors: characters always want something, large scale "super objectives" and moment to moment wants (which might conceal less conscious "needs": the stuff of the much ridiculed but essential "motivation" which is the core of how good actors function on stage and screen. Just as crucial to writing as well.

Carrie Ryan

Excellent post and something that's always great to be reminded of! Recently I was listening to a lecture on craft where they distinguished between what the MC thinks s/he wants and what s/he really wants/ needs. Their idea was that you should give the character what he most wants in the beginning of the book and force them to face the "oh, now what?" because they then face the real possibility that they were wrong about what they wanted or needed.

Of course, I'm also someone who rarely figures out what the characters want or need until the end of the first draft (if then) so that's always a big part of my revising.

Befriending Your Characters
David B. Coe

How do we make our characters work? What is the secret to creating believable, compelling characters who will capture our readers' hearts and make our stories more than a set of plot points? I'm of the opinion that good characters are the single most important element of effective storytelling. There's nothing earth-shattering about this; lots of people would agree with that. But while most of us might agree on the things that make for good characters, we would probably have a harder time explaining how one goes about creating them. How do you teach character development?

I've written before about the background work I do on my major characters. I try to establish a history for each of them, much as I would for a world I create: upbringing, family life, major events from childhood, adolescence, and early adulthood (assuming the character is an adult). I gather as much detail as I can on the circumstances of his/her current life: profession, friendships, romantic relationships, etc. And I establish personality traits: easygoing or prickly, even tempered or moody, social adept or awkward, gregarious or a loner; confident or insecure.

Naturally, the choices are not always as clear-cut as that list implies; there are gradations. But you get the idea. I do everything I can to get to know my characters so that when I start writing about them or narrating from their point of view, I can get the voice right and make each character something more than a list of attributes. Ideally, I want my characters to come alive, to begin to carry the story and even change the story to fit his/her needs.

But there is more to character than developing this portrait and then animating it in prose. I believe that ultimately the creation and development of an effective character is an act of empathy. I begin by gauging what my own emotional responses would be to the situations I throw at my characters, and drawing on my own emotional experiences, the good and the bad. We all carry this stuff within us. At one point or another in our lives we've felt a tremendous range of emotions. When I was a younger man, I was prone to terrible bouts of jealousy—not admirable, and not conducive to healthy relationships. But though I've learned to tame my inner green-eyed beast, I haven't forgotten what it felt like. And thank goodness! I can write jealousy quite well now, thank you very much.

Many years back, I lost both of my parents within a year of each other. It was a difficult time but one that made me a stronger person, and that has given me insights into emotional pain that have served me well in the years since.

So we draw upon our own emotional responses, and impart them to our characters. But first we also have to blend those personal emotional responses with our understanding of the character herself. We all respond to things differently depending on our temperament, our experiences, our upbringing, our moods at a given time, etc.—all that stuff we learned about our characters when doing that background work. Good character work takes all of these things into account.

Let me put this another way. In my mind, my characters are real people. They have distinct voices. They have needs and desires and impulses. I write them, but I don't control them. They surprise me all the time, doing things as I write about them that I don't expect, sometimes taking my stories places I didn't foresee. Now, you can argue that they are part of my subconscious and that on some level I AM controlling them. But that's not how it feels. When my creative juices are flowing, they feel like independent beings and I listen to them and give them consideration the way I would my real world friends.

And that's what it comes down to. When we deal with our friends, we don't deal with them in exactly the way we would want to be dealt with ourselves because we understand that each friend is different. We try to put ourselves in their shoes, to see the world from their perspective, so that we can help them with a problem or share their outrage or their joy or their excitement. That's where the empathy comes in, and that's what we all need to learn to do with our characters.

I have lots of insecurities, but there are a few things I feel confident about. I believe that I'm a good husband, a good father, and a good friend. I listen well, and I'm good at anticipating the emotional needs of the people I love. I also write good characters. There are other things that writers do better than I do, but I feel that my character work is pretty strong. And I believe that the things that make me a good dad and husband and friend are the same things that make me a good writer. I listen to my characters. I step out of myself and into their minds and hearts, and I feel what they feel.

Befriend your characters; treat them as you would the people in your life who mean the most to you. It will make you a better writer. And—this has certainly been the case for me—it might also make you a better friend.

Chris Branch

David, the trap I've fallen into is to empathize with characters so much that they're often too nice to each other. Because when I'm in the head of each character—even the bad guys—I try to think "How would I behave here?" But sometimes you need your character to be rude and nasty, and the problem I have is: in my mind there's never any excuse to act this way—regardless of your childhood, current circumstances, strongly held beliefs, whatever. So let's just say I have a lot of trouble justifying the behavior of the antagonists!

David B. Coe

Chris, what a great comment. I know exactly what you mean, and have the same problem, though it's most troublesome for me with my good guys who have prickly personalities. They do and say things I would never think of doing or saying myself. But when I'm writing them I have to turn off my own filters and speak with their voices. Very hard to do. And yes, it can be just as hard with my "bad guys." Again, great comment.

I Know Who That Is!

Misty Massey

Last Friday morning, I had the delightful pleasure of being interviewed via webcam by the Dutch Fork High School "Beyond the Best Sellers" class. I was nervous—I'd never been interviewed that way before! When the connection went through, several of the students growled "Arrrrr!" in their most terrifying piratical fashion, and suddenly I was at ease. They asked me interesting questions about writing, about pirates and about my characters. There was one question that stuck with me. It wasn't all that unusual of a question, but it stayed with me for days. The student asked me, "Where did you come up with the character of Philip McAvery?"

For those of you who have not read *Mad Kestrel* (and why not? It's available in all sorts of places, so run on out and buy a copy. I'll wait.) McAvery is a good-looking rogue who could be Kestrel's dream man or her worst nightmare. Maybe both. People are always assuming I based him on my own husband. Part of the confusion lies in the names—McAvery is my husband's faire name, which he came up with for a gaming character long ago. I used it in the book because I liked it. And yes, my husband is nice-looking and a pin-wearing, card-carrying rogue. But the character of McAvery is very different from my husband. Philip's a little bit my husband, a little bit of that old gaming character and a little bit someone else entirely. When you see him on the page, he's his own person.

But it doesn't just happen with McAvery. I've had friends insist they know who Shadd really is, or Olympia, or even Kestrel. The thing is, they're right, after a fashion. Just not in the way they think.

It's hard to write a compelling novel without characters who come alive for the reader. The characters are our storytellers, our guides through the world of the book. If the reader doesn't connect somehow with the character, he'll never care about the story. So writers have to create characters who live and breathe and suffer and rejoice just like real people. It's not enough to give them different colors of hair and eyes, or to let one like country music while another prefers Beethoven. It's the little things that make us unique. Small characteristics that you probably don't always notice are the best.

But if you don't always notice them, how are you supposed to figure out what traits to write in?

The easiest way to do this, of course, is to watch real people. Try to do this when they don't know you're watching. Look around at a meeting sometime. One man is bouncing his leg so hard he could tip his chair over. Another seems to be listening intently, but if you look closer, his eyes are far away and he hasn't blinked in five minutes. A woman at the end of the table is humming so quietly that you can hardly hear it. She may not know she's doing it. Heck, I have a tic myself. When I'm nervous or stressed, I'll start tearing at the skin of my fingers, and unless someone brings it to my attention, I won't stop until I draw blood. These are all tiny, insignificant behaviors, yet adding them to your writing will grant your characters a layer of texture you wouldn't have had before. They're the things that make a character an individual.

I've heard of some writers hanging out in malls, sitting in the food courts with a notebook and a pen, making notes all day about the behaviors they see. I'd be afraid of someone deciding I was a stalker, but if you like this method, go for it. I tend to draw from people around me. I'm lucky enough to work in a place with lots of people around. One person I know always walks with her head down, as if she's charging through the crowd like a bulldozer. She's perfectly friendly at all other times, so this is odd. Another friend always blushes during ordinary conversations with me. Yet another person lifts her chin and closes her eyes when she's talking, only opening her eyes again when she finishes what she is saying. And of course there are two people I know with hazel eyes that change color with their moods, clothing, and location. It's a perfectly natural phenomenon, but I lifted that for the character of McAvery because it has always enchanted me.

So okay, sure, maybe you *do* know who my inspiration for McAvery was, because of how he looks. Maybe you know me well enough to think you've figured out all the characters. But remember that I also took traits from other people to make each one his own person. There may be a little of you in there, too, something small you did when you didn't think I was paying attention. Be careful when you're in the company of writers, because you never know when we'll be writing you into our next novel.

David B. Coe

I've always found that the characters I write from scratch (as opposed to those who I base on people I know) are the ones who come out best. Maybe it's because when I base a character on someone I wind up limiting my creativity and preventing that character from becoming his or her own person. That said, you're totally right: basing a character on someone is one way to go, though I rarely do it myself, drawing on the quirks, habits, mannerisms, etc. of people we encounter can be enormously helpful in making each character we create unique and recognizable.

Creating Characters in Small Spaces

Stuart Jaffe

So, there I was, hard at work on my WIP, barreling down the final stretch, feeling the light at the end warming my skin, when all of a sudden my team of heroes comes up against the Big Bad. The Big Bad has been talked about throughout the whole book. We've heard about him from other characters and seen the devastating results of his handiwork. We've come to know him as the dark specter lurking in the shadows waiting to strike.

But now we actually meet him. For the first time. As a writer, I had to create a full, three-dimensional character with very little space left in the book. The big question: how?

For the answer, I turned to my training as a short story writer. In short stories, you face this question with every character. From the beginning to the end, you have limited space and must learn to convey large amounts of information as concisely as possible. The tools at your disposal are the same as that of the novel writer—description, dialogue, action, thoughts, etc. The only real difference is the space allotted.

Below is the opening page of my short story "A Final Battle" (from the *Rum and Runestones* anthology), in which I must create the two main characters and establish the world in less than 200 words:

> George Worthington groaned as he clambered back to his feet, his ears ringing with the echoes of cannon fire. Remnants of the battle covered the ocean in a milky fog and the familiar tang of gunpowder filled the air. A blood splotch near the staysails marked where Captain Taggart fell—his body had been removed to his cabin. Straightening his red waistcoat, the short, stout Worthington headed toward the foredeck.
>
> Butler rushed up beside him and said, "Sir, sir, they've run. They're gone."
>
> "Of course they're gone, Mr. Butler. They're lucky if they don't sink by sundown."
>
> "Aye, sir," Butler said, moving back and forth on his feet like a child that has to pee. "Um, a question, sir."
>
> Worthington ignored the man and stared at the fog. Their enemy, His Majesty's frigate *Osprey*, had not suffered serious damage and would not be sinking anytime soon—it just left. Why? They had killed Captain Taggart. They had blasted an enormous hole in the *Annabelle's* side—a little

lower and the brigantine would have sunk. Why leave with victory so close?

Now, let's go through it again, this time with notes:

George Worthington groaned as he clambered back to his feet, his ears ringing with the echoes of cannon fire. Remnants of the battle covered the ocean in a milky fog and the familiar tang of gunpowder filled the air. A blood splotch near the staysails marked where Captain Taggart fell—his body had been removed to his cabin. Straightening his red waistcoat, the short, stout Worthington headed toward the foredeck. *This paragraph clues us into the world (one of cannon fire, staysails, and foredecks) and two crucial events (a battle has just ended and the Captain is dead). We also learn the name of our main character and get a bit of description—short, stout. But the key item is "Straightening his red waistcoat". While the cannon fire is still echoing, Worthington is not running around screaming orders or hiding or anything big—he's making sure he looks proper. The reader may not consciously pick up on that, but she will visualize the moment and in doing so, she starts to see Worthington. That's how to use an action to create a character.*
Butler rushed up beside him and said, "Sir, sir, they've run. They're gone." *Butler, the other major character, is introduced in contrast. Contrasting characters gives us information about both at the same time—two for one! By having Butler rush up, it underscores the previous waistcoat bit showing both Butler's panic and Worthington's calm. Next, I use dialogue to further both characters. Butler speaks in unsure and stumbling ways ("Sir, Sir" or later "Um") while Worthington is very proper and confident.*
"Of course they're gone, Mr. Butler. They're lucky if they don't sink by sundown."
"Aye, sir," Butler said, moving back and forth on his feet like a child that has to pee. *Here again is an action that shows us more of Butler. In explaining the action, I not only create a visual that adds to the character but I use it to describe both action and character—"like a child."* "Um, a question, sir."
Worthington ignored the man and stared at the fog. *Worthington's reaction to Butler establishes their relationship and adds to both characters—he is capable of ignoring Butler and Butler doesn't appear to take offense.* Their enemy, His Majesty's frigate Osprey, had not suffered serious damage and would not be sinking anytime soon—it just left. Why? They had killed Captain Taggart. They had blasted an enormous hole in the Annabelle's side—a little lower and the brigantine would have sunk. Why leave with victory so close? *This last paragraph*

gives us Worthington's thoughts. Like contrasting, showing thoughts can serve more than one purpose. Here, we get more of Worthington's character by seeing how the man thinks in contrast with how he has spoken, but we also receive worldbuilding and even get a bit of plot.

The key, then, is to make each sentence carry as much weight as possible, and to realize that the readers will fill-in enormous chunks of detail if you point them in the right direction. Look at that excerpt again and pay particular attention to the character of Butler. Nowhere is he physically described. All we get is a little voice and two actions—all showing, not telling. The more he appears in the story the more opportunities exist to flesh him out further, but by placing him in contrast to Worthington and by carefully crafting his speech, he is already real enough to imagine. If the reader can imagine him, the reader starts filling in the details. Pretty soon, between the two of you, a full character is born. And that's the ultimate goal.

Faith Hunter

I totally agree. Character description info dumps work only seldom, as in police procedurals, where you know the main character has been trained to view all people in a specific manner, as if taking down details of a crime scene or criminal suspect. And even then I get sooo tired of, "He was five-five, blonde and green, and walked with a limp."

"She was six-two, dark-skinned, mixed African, close-cropped hair, maybe a skinny 150."

"She was average height, two hundred pounds overweight, black and brown, and breathed like she had a leak somewhere."

Oy . . .

Edmund R. Schubert

I'll add to this conversation by mentioning that Stuart's point about the reader filling in their own images is SO true that you have to be careful with it. Precisely *because* they fill in their own image so quickly, if you add physical description of the character too late in the story, it frequently ends up contradicting the reader's mental image, which is jarring and counter-productive.

David B. Coe

This is a terrific essay, Stuart, and I love the story opening. You manage to convey so much so quickly. Well done. I could use that kind of economy in my own writing. That said, I would like to respond to Faith by rising in defense of detailed character descriptions. I love reading them and I love writing them. I have a description of a key character in the new book that goes on for a while, and I think it is absolutely essential in filling out who she is and how she figures into my MC's life. A good character introduction can make the difference between a person readers visualize and one they carry around with them all day long, even when they're not reading the book.

Hello, Mary Sue! Goodbye, Plot

Misty Massey

Perfect characters are boring as hell.

Really, they are. Think about it . . . when the main character is physically gorgeous, runs faster, jumps higher, knows every trick, can pick a lock with his nose while blindfolded and never loses a fight, why bother reading any further? The excitement of reading a good story is the thrill of not knowing what's around the corner.

The trouble for some writers, in the beginning, is the love we have for our characters. "Look at this fabulous person I created!" we think. "She's so amazing, she must be able to do everything I wish I could do in real life." It's okay to feel that way. Ask any mother if her baby isn't the most perfect creature ever born. *laughs* But loving your character isn't what makes a story great. The best characters aren't the ones who sail through the events of the story as easily as they might walk down their hallway. No, the characters we stick with are the ones who make mistakes, trip over branches, lose their way, get thrown in prison for crimes they didn't commit and worry about whether they'll live through the night. A character who has no flaws can't change and grow. Did you read *Gone With the Wind*? Whose story was more compelling—Scarlet's or Melanie's?

I fell into the trap myself, some years ago. I was writing Kestrel as a Mary Sue—a character who could do everything better than everyone else, and couldn't be defeated. When I finally started digging deeper, looking for the feelings Kestrel must have been feeling to drive her on her journey, I was amazed at how much better the story became. These days, I watch carefully to make sure none of my characters are superpeople. They're jealous, quick to anger, grumpy in the morning, superstitious, impatient and greedy. My friend, writer Lisa Mantchev, was talking about this very thing, and challenged us to share our character's flaws. So today I challenge you—and I'll begin.

Kestrel, a pirate, a fighter and a beginner in the use of magic, is FLAWED.
- She is slow to trust, and quick to believe the worst in people
- She is fearful of magic, even though it's a natural part of her.
- She is stubborn, sometimes to her detriment.
- She doesn't believe she's worthy of love or admiration.

David B. Coe
Besh, one of the lead characters in *The Sorcerer's Plague* and *The Horsemen's Gambit*, is an older man, widowed, drawn out of the

comfort of his final years by a catastrophe that he can't ignore. His faults?

- He's terribly stubborn.
- He's judgmental and has allowed this trait to create a rift between himself and his daughter's husband.
- He refuses to accept that he is limited by his age and the decline of his physical strength.
- He is moody and not very good at concealing his temper from those he cares about.

Faith Hunter

You are an evil woman, which is why I love you.

Hmmm. Character flaws.

Thorn St. Croix, stone mage:

- Her gift makes her open to the minds of all other mages, and therefore incapable of being near any of them without hating them all and probably going insane
- She is lazy and hasn't bothered to attend to her mage education or her swordplay.
- Self pitying, self destructive, little twerp
- Raised with humans she fears and, though she has won the love and friendship of several humans, she has hidden her true nature from them.

Man. She's a mess at the start of the series.

C.E. Murphy

Oh, jeez. Well, Joanne Walker is terrified of commitment and responsibility and caring about people, and Margrit Knight thinks she can take on the world without ever asking for help, and Belinda Primrose . . . well. She's a psychopath. If you want to call that a flaw.

The Great Satan: Part 1
(Antagonists We Love to Hate)

Faith Hunter

Subtitles:

> . . . The Axis of Evil
>
> Or . . . The enemy of my enemy is my friend
>
> Or . . . The BBUs (Big Bad Uglies)

Despite the subtitles, this is not a post about religion or politics. I was brought up Southern and as my mawmaw used to say, "We don't talk about things like that, Punkin . . ."

(Which is one reason why slavery, the genocide of the American Indian, and government approved racism were permitted, and a thousand lesser evils took/take place. No one talked about the pink elephant in the room. But really. That is not what this post is about.) This post is about the believable bad guy, the antagonist, the "quiet guy next door" who keeps to himself, grows beautiful azaleas, and kills children on weekends. Bad Guys in my world are referred to as Big Bad Uglies (BBUs). These antagonists are taken from the concept of conflict: man against nature, man against man, himself, etc.

Culture shapes how we see evil. The evil character as viewed by someone in ancient Greece is going to be different from the evil character as viewed by someone from the same time period but living in Central America. Their cultures were vastly different so their vision of good and evil (right and wrong, social and antisocial) were different. Similarly, albeit not quite so spectacularly, the readers of different genres will view antagonists differently. The overall literary market leads and/or follows current culture and shapes what kind of BBUs will and won't work in our books.

Why should writers of fantasy and UF (urban fantasy) and other fantasy subgenres care about the BBUs of other genres? Because they all have attributes in common, and understanding some of the aspects of other genre's antagonists create a clearer vision of the antagonist in fantasy.

Mainstream literary fiction may have no human BBUs. The antagonist in the novel can be mother nature, diamond mines in Africa, ghosts from the beyond, current culture, some aspect of the MC's personality (the refusal to give up anger, hatred) etc. The antagonist in literary novels can also be the darkness in a human soul, not an entity outside of the MC (main character). Less often is the conflict between humans: man against man.

My AKA, Gwen, writes mysteries and thrillers. The antagonist in mysteries are formulaic only from the standpoint that they remain unknown to the reader until the end of the novel. One quick note—there are as many subgenres in mystery as there are subgenres in fantasy. I'll concentrate on the traditional mystery, which is well encapsulated by Agatha Christie novels and the TV show, *Murder She Wrote*. Someone dies and the non-police sleuth solves the crime. It's a simple formula where keeping the reader guessing is paramount.

If we look at the traditional mystery BBU in terms of four specific questions we get:

1. What makes them work? The traditional mystery BBU may have several motives for the crime committed, but he *needs* only one motivation. Of course, he must also have opportunity, means, and the will to do evil. Usually this motive is simplistic—money, revenge, money, romance, power, and money. The genre of traditional mystery is perfect for television because the plot isn't heavily layered and the BBU isn't multifaceted. A lot of the individual *Buffy the Vampire Slayer* shows were mysteries cloaked in urban fantasy (UF) clothes. A crime was committed (a human was drained of blood, for instance) and Buffy had to find and dispatch the evil one.

2. How do we keep them from becoming formulaic? To keep the BBUs from being formulaic, murder mystery writers use two main devices: an unusual form of a murder (being pickled in vinegar, drowning in a vat of beer, exposure to a rare poison, accidentally falling on a stake meant for another vampire), and bait and switch. In bait and switch, they offer the reader two or more possibilities of characters who might be the BBU. All are eliminated through the course of the story, leaving the one guilty BBU. Then they sometimes do one last bait and switch and reveal the *true* BBU. It's a puzzle shared by writer and reader.

3. What mistakes do we as writers make that allow them to become formulaic? BBUs are characters who believe they deserve all the goodies. In traditional mysteries, they believe they have the right to perpetrate whatever crime has been committed. When we writers make it too obvious who the BBU is, and/or make his motivation too multifaceted, the mystery is no longer just a mystery. It is the *simple* nature of the conflict that makes a novel a traditional mystery.

4. How do we as readers contribute to the success or failure of the BBU? By picking up a mystery, the reader accepts the premise that a crime will be/has been committed and the bad guy will be identified and caught (sometimes punished) by the book's end. The genre tells us this will happen. If we read a mystery we are therefore partly responsible for our own willingness to accept the crime committed, no matter how bizarre, and our own suspension of disbelief. If we are smarter than the writer and figure out the puzzle, we won't enjoy the ride nearly as much. That said, figuring out who the BBU is and beating the writer at his own game is half the mystery's fun! So it's up to the reader to play the game that was set in motion by the writer and be willing to be led along his literary puzzle path. If you are thinking about this suspension of disbelief in terms of fantasy, you begin see to why the BBUs in all literary forms have some similar characteristics.

Thriller BBUs are tougher to write and tougher to analyze because:
- The level of inherent violence is higher.
- The BBU often is known to the reader.
- The BBU often is known to the MC.
- The pace must be tighter and the BBU is usually on a deadline to achieve his evil ends.

Thriller BBUs must have strong, believable motivation(s) for the reader to accept the rising suspense and the rising level of violence. I like writing and reading thrillers because the plot can take such delicious twists and turns and the BBU can be fully fleshed out. He becomes a well-rounded, four-dimensional character, unlike a lot of traditional mysteries where the BBU is often a two dimensional character, known mostly by his motivation. Like the MC, the BBU in thrillers can have a past, a current life, personal needs, personal failings and strengths, good and bad aspects to his character. He may rescue cats on Saturday and kidnap the children of politicos in Argentina on Sunday. He may be married, attend religious services, work a fulltime job as a doctor, veterinarian, town councilman, or any other upstanding job.

And yet he is a BBU. His need to do the evil in the book must be clearly laid out and justified (to him at least), though the reader has to believe the BBU will act in a way contrary to society. If the BBU is a contract-killer, he needs to be humanized, even in the face of the crimes he commits. Hannibal Lector's justification was that he was smarter than anyone else, so he belonged at the top of the food chain. He was clearly a psychopath with a taste for human flesh. It was enough for the time. But current readers have had a belly full (I know, I can hear the groans) of Hannibal look-alikes. Today's thriller BBUs have to be more. And this is where the characteristics of thriller BBUs begin to cross the lines into some subgenres of fantasy.

Stuart Jaffe
Wow. This is a lot to digest. Thank you for taking the time to write this up.

At one point you were discussing how time/location/culture/etc can alter the nature of a BBU. That made me think of the Russians. Growing up in the 70s and 80s in America, the Russians were often depicted as the BBU (in thrillers especially). But when the Cold War ended, there was no unifying BBU. That lasted for several years until 9/11. Nowadays, Muslim terrorists tend to be the BBU, but because they lack the structured organization that the Russians had (no KGB, for one), modern thrillers have had to alter the way they approach telling the tale. You can't just "find & replace" the word Russian with Muslim terrorist. The entire story has to be restructured—particularly because of #4—what the reader brings to the experience.

Faith Hunter
Stuart, that is so true, and it meant an entire subgenre of mystery disappeared over night. Robert Ludlam went from absolute king of the thriller genre to nobody. Until that time he was the highest paid thriller writer in the biz. It took him years to figure out how to write in the new world.

The Great Satan: Part 2

Faith Hunter

BBUs of mysteries and of thrillers share many similarities, yet have some distinct differences. Many of the differences can be said to apply to other genres, like the traditional romance genre. The romance BBU usually tends to the simplistic bad guy, the BBU with one motive for his evil and not a lot of character development. As in: "I want the castle and lands and will kill your intended to get them!" Or: "I must have an heir and I have chosen you for the vessel. Mwahahahahaha."

The plot in romantic *suspense* is more layered, similar to thrillers, though it's usually pretty easy to pick apart by an astute reader. Romantic suspense tends more toward the thriller BBU: a lot more development, though seldom is he quite as layered or as developed as in thrillers. After all, the reader wants a little excitement with his cup of romance, not the other way around.

SciFi, from space opera to first-contact stories like the TV series *V*, tends to fit into one of the mystery categories. It may be the more simplistic BBUs like in the Vorkosigan series by Lois McMaster Bujold or the BBUs attacking the Earth in *Independence Day*, or they can be the more multifaceted BBUs of *Lost*, with its concomitant multilayered (can we say five-dimensional?) plotting. We can start the argument about *Lost* later. What argument? The: *Lost* is *not* SciFi! Yes, it is! No, it isn't! Yes, it is! . . . that argument.

Fantasy has its own BBU possibilities, taking us into new realms, with new species and new potential for conflict. (Conflict is what makes a book work. We read for character, but if the character doesn't have conflict(s) to resolve, it's not a story. And only conflict creates the emotion reader's crave). Let's look at traditional fantasy, which can cover swords and sorcery, epic, coming of age fantasy (the "Look ma! I can do magic! Oops. What's THAT? Oh, crap! RUN!" books like the first *Harry Potter*).

If we look at the traditional fantasy BBUs and urban fantasy BBUs in terms of the original four questions we get:

1. What makes them work? Traditional fantasy and UF BBUs can *literally* be big bad uglies—the troll under the bridge, the evil knight, the wicked witch of the west with a cauldron, huge hairy moles, bad attitude, and flying monkeys. (I'm not tossing aspersions on Wicca or goddess worshippers, or others. Some of them are friends, and none of them have hairy moles so far as I know. I am referring to the practitioners of black arts and human sacrifice. *None* of them are friends!)

The closest thing I ever wrote to a traditional fantasy was the *Thorn St.*

Croix, Rogue Mage series. These books were a crossover between traditional fantasy and urban fantasy. In the Rogue Mage series, the biggest BBUs were—literally—the dragons of the Revelation. Not the devil (it wasn't a religious series) but the monsters and the backstories of the monsters were stolen (plagiarized? fanfic?) from the Bible, Apocryphal writings, and other sources, to include the BBUs of many old religions, cultures, and histories, but with twists from both older and modern fantasy work, including vampires (daywalkers in the series). This was a huge change from my mystery/thriller BBUs. It was the mixture of the old and the new that made the BBUs work. So, for traditional fantasy to work, the BBUs need motivation or dependable (evolving is okay as long as the reader knows it might happen) characteristics. When the BBU is a sentient being, the writer should make clear that the BBU has (several?) motivations, even if the reader doesn't know what they are at first.

2. How do we keep them from becoming formulaic? It is the motivation that is necessary—and often missing from traditional fantasy—to keep the BBU fresh and believable. *Why* does the evil overlord want to lay waste to the land? *Why* does he want to kill all the inhabitants? What parts about a dark, lifeless, gloomy world where only the rats and buzzards are happy could possibly make *him* happy? If he wanted a lifeless habitat, why not just take over the moon? His motivations for his evil deeds *matter*. They make the BBU work in a genre of fiction that often forgets he needs this motivation. Older fantasy-BBUs were seldom described in terms of motivation but that won't work as well in today's market. Today's reader is market savvy. This is why the human-like BBU/antagonist is so successful. He is an equal to the MC. They want the same things, they fight an equal battle with equal weapons. In urban fantasy we edge back over to the thriller description of BBUs. In fact, you can go back and reread the thriller BBUs, add in magic or uber-paranormal, and you have the UF BBU.

3. What mistakes do we writers make that allow them to become formulaic? I think there are several common mistakes. We copy bits and parts from other BBUs, parts that make them identifiable and closely associated with existing work. Or we make the BBU so foreign to our culture that he is either silly (*Attack of the Killer Tomatoes* comes to mind, though that was scifi) or in-comprehensible. Or we don't describe him well enough for the reader to picture him. (The big dark cloud is on the horizon! Run for your lives!) Or, most important, we forget that unless the conflict is man against nature, the BBU needs motivation. The well defined sentient-being-BBU must have weaknesses and strengths, just like the MC. He needs to grow through problems, find new strengths, and evolve. Even in the Pern books, Anne McCaffrey gave the fire-fall BBU an elliptic orbit, so it was dependably undependable.

Today's traditional fantasy *and* UF BBU must fit into the story like any other character. It helps for the BBU to be on a timetable, one that makes sense to the reader, just like the thriller BBU. A short time-frame means the MC must act now or fail utterly. In the Pern books, the world, the crops, the people, everything, will be destroyed unless the humans and the dragons unite and fight together. It is man against nature and man against man. Even if the BBU is a dragon, he *must* want something. Writers need to balance on the blade of a sword in terms of creating non-formulaic BBUs, yet let them be culturally recognizable, bringing a level of uniqueness with an identifiable element that makes the BBU feel culturally familiar.

4. And how do we as readers contribute to the success or failure of the BBU?
That suspension of belief required by the simple mystery has its place here. Maybe more so! We have to believe in (or want to believe in) magic, other-worldly power, cosmic war, the bigger-than-life battle between good and evil. We have to believe that right wins in the end, when we *know* it doesn't always. We have to be willing to root for the underdog, a character often lacking in training, ability, and power. We have to believe in the main character as a human being, associate with him on some human level. And we have to believe he can win.

Sarah Adams
Thank you for the discussion, it's very helpful.

I'm running up against the lazy author issue (me) in my WIP. At bottom my BBU is just a petty jerk. He's bad because he chooses to care more about himself and his power/ego than anything else and so he's blown up a series of minor sibling grievances into a sense of massive grievance. It's an "Everybody wants to rule the world" sort of situation, except that the "world" he wants to rule is just his own little corner of Buffalo, NY. And he'll kill his own sister and unleash a new Ice Age to do it.

When I put it that way he sounds rather interesting, at least to me. But on the page I find him very flat. His motives seem obscure and insufficient for what he's doing. He's not insane—I'm not using that cop out. In real life, people will do idiotically destructive things over an exaggerated sense of offended rights. But I'm having a very difficult time making that work on the page in an emotionally satisfying, cohesive way.

Faith Hunter
Sarah, that is exactly what I am talking about! The BBU has to make sense to the reader on an emotional plane and, if possible, on a rea-

sonable (logical) plane within the confines of the conflict you have set up.

You have described a selfish bastard as BBU. Selfish bastards only make sense to themselves, but they work in family sagas, especially as you track back to the seminal event or originating events, which is what you need to do—give the backstory in small chunks so the reader accepts the development of the child-to-selfish-bastard character.

Selfish bastards don't work so well in bigger-than-life scenarios.

It sounds as if you are writing a family saga that goes wildly out of control (assuming that the Ice Age comment was for real and applied to the plot). If the premeditated murder and the Ice Age comment *are* real, then your bigger-than-life scenario needs motivations and thinking that are bigger than life too. Your BBU has to have the skills to pull off the Ice Age, the will to do so, *and* the motivation.

On Writing Dialogue
C.E. Murphy

Dialogue Introduction

There are constraints on fiction that real life doesn't have to hold to. Wild coincidences have to be explained in fiction, whereas in real life, coincidences happen all the time, without apology or rationality.

Dialogue in prose is a great deal like that, really: it has to sound real, without actually being real. The truth is that if we record ourselves holding a conversation, there are an appalling number of half-finished sentences, our speech is littered with "Um" and "well" and "but-but-but." But we all know we do that, right? That we use filler words—um and uh and well—pretty much constantly. It's a natural assumption to believe that if our writing reflects those vocal idiosyncrasies, that it's going to sound authentic.

Unfortunately, it's not true. Writing dialogue that sounds like we *actually* speak comes across as awkward at best, because we sound awkward when our speech patterns are analyzed. Are any of you familiar with David Mamet?

Mamet, for those who aren't familiar with him, is a playwright whose thing, his gig, is writing natural speech. I think people essentially either love or hate Mamet. I personally find his plays excruciating to watch, because to my ear the language is so incredibly inept. It's unquestionably how we really speak, but listening to lines scripted that way sets me on edge.

However, having said that, I'd hugely recommend actually watching one of his plays—several have been made into films, including one that Steve Martin starred in several years ago, called *The Spanish Prisoner*. I think every writer should watch at least some Mamet—and it's more important to watch than to read, because watching and hearing those deliberately scripted lines really helps the ear to understand how we talk, and how inept it is. It's an object lesson in how *not* to write dialogue.

(Yeah, it's worked for Mamet, but the problem is that once one person makes a name with that kind of dialogue scripting, for the rest of eternity anybody else who tries it is going to be referred to as "Mamet-esque." You can't win.)

Generally, what we as writers want to do is write dialogue that mimics reality. We want to actually impart information, to show emotion, and to do it in a way that tricks the reader into accepting it as natural speech. Fortunately, there are a lot of ways to do this.

Dialect: A Useful and Dangerous Tool

Listen to people. Listen to young people, to old people, to immigrants, to attorneys and to surfer boys. Listen to word choice and sentence cadence. Strip away the filler words—"um" and "oh" and "well"—and pay attention to the rhythm of their speech. It's all going to sound different: a 75-year-old man is not going to sound like a 17-year-old girl, and an upper-crust British woman isn't going to sound like a New York stock broker.

Go to Starbucks and just sit and listen. Go to Starbucks in every city you can visit, and just sit and listen. Write down phrases that catch your ear. Study how people speak. You're going to have to strip a lot of it away when you use it in your actual writing, but listening will help you develop an ear for dialogue.

A few years ago I saw an interview with Ben Kingsley, who is of Indian heritage, but he changed his name from a traditional Indian name to a recognizably English one so he could get work as an actor. Quite some time after that, he was cast as Gandhi in the Richard Atwood film, and he said the response from the Indian government and people was, "Who is this English man, this Ben Kingsley, who is playing our beloved Mahatma Gandhi?"

It's almost impossible to get that down phonetically. It's easier to evoke Texas by having a character say "Y'all" than it is to invoke India with dialogue alone. As a writer, what you're reaching for in trying to capture an Indian accent is the way all the words are spoken: the breaks between words and phrases shown by punctuation, and you may be counting, a little, on the reader being familiar with the Indian accent.

An American asking that same question might say, "Ben King—who's Ben Kingsley, and why's he playing Gandhi?" or even just, "Who is this guy?" It's a completely different sentence structure.

You can do this with nearly any language or dialect. It takes work. You've got to develop a fundamental grasp of the differences in sentence structure. We all know Russian accents, right? We know that it has heavy sound, with round words in your mouth. And we know if you are Russian and you are speaking English, there are words you drop, words you add: you say, "I am thinking that we should do this," not "I think we should do this."

These changes have to do with the speaker's original language. I've been living in Ireland the past three years, and it's grand fun listening to the way they use words. Order a piece of apple pie, and they'll say, "Will I be heatin' it up for ye?" Twist a kid's arm and he cries, "It's me arm yer breakin'!" One that I cannot quite get the cadence of is a filler word that they put at the *end* of sentences: "so," so the sentence is something like, "I'm after visitin' me mother so."

All of those idiosyncrasies are born from the fact that the Irish version of English is basically structured on Irish-language sentence structure. They don't have a word for "yes" or "no" in Irish, so if you say, "Are you going to the store," the answer is almost always, "I am," or "I am not." Now, as a writer, you don't have to know the base languages. You just need to learn to listen for the differences in how a sentence is put together, and then learn to apply it in your writing. You can do the same thing with American regional accents, from Southern accents to upper peninsula Michigan, to California golden boys and to New York City socialites.

Here's where it gets dangerous: over-using dialect. Sometimes as a writer, you're going to want to spell out the phonetic sound of the words used when it's a different accent. Done sparingly, that can work really well. It can remind a Pacific Northwest reader that the story is set in Atlanta, or set in the highlands of Scotland. But I really truly believe it should be done *sparingly*. I've read stories in which all the dialogue was dialect, and . . . okay, "read" is an overstatement, because I couldn't get through them. It's easy to do too much. Dialect, particularly if you're writing out the sound of an accent, should be a spice, not the flavor.

Punctuation

I cannot emphasize enough how important punctuation is in dialogue. Actually, in general, but since we're talking about dialogue . . . ☺

I could do an entire class on punctuation alone, but that's not what we're doing here. I'd mostly like to say that if you have even the slightest suspicion that you might not be absolutely solid on the rules of punctuation, please consider taking an English 101 writing class, either at a local college or online, in order to study that.

You just don't want an editor running up against that kind of mental block when she's reading your writing. Learn punctuation. It's worth it.

Dialogue Tags

Dialogue tags are a bugbear for most writers. I want to tell you what may be the most important thing:

"Said" is an *invisible* word. Like "the" and "and," readers do not notice "said." This means that ninety percent of the time, if "said" will do as the dialogue tag, then "said" is the word you *should* use. The reader will notice if you use "stated" or "declared" or "observed" or "noted", and again, ninety percent of the time, you don't want the reader to be noticing those words.

A story along those lines: a writer of whom I was quite fond put out a new book a while ago, something co-authored with another writer. It had an introduction, in which it mentioned that the author's idiosyncrasies had been kept intact, including the fact that he never used the word "said" when another word would do.

Now, I'd read about fifteen books by this guy. I'd noticed that he often used other words when "said" would do, and I found it vaguely annoying. I had not noticed that he *always* used another word if it was at all possible.

Having had it pointed out to me, I was so distracted and annoyed by it that I got maybe forty pages into the book and put it down and not only never picked it up again, but will never pick *any* of that writer's books up again.

This is not the end result you're after. ☺

This isn't to say you can't use other words to great effect. Just bear in mind, as writers, that "said" will essentially never offend.

One Thing At A Time

One of the things we do in real life is let conversations flow back and forth over each other. In prose, you almost always have to keep your dialogue to one topic at a time. What works for our ears doesn't necessarily work for our eyes. In dialogue, a conversation can flow from one topic to a second to a third and then back to the first, but most of the time you don't want to have all three threads going on at once. If you can pull it off as a writer, more power to you, but even so, don't overdo it.

"As You Know, Bob"

Dialogue is often used as an "As you know, Bob". What that means is Scotty suddenly stands up and begins lecturing to Engineer Bob: "As you know, Bob, the dilithium crystals store energy which permits our warp engines to carry us beyond the speed of light. Without these engines and those crystals, we would be stuck in low Earth orbit, waving wistfully at the Vulcans as they zoomed by."

Bob already knows this. If the reader needs to know it, then the last way you should want to inform the reader is by having Scotty tell Bob something he already knows. It's far better to have an action scene where the dilithium crystals are suddenly drained and the Enterprise drops out of warp, thus *showing* us the crystals' importance rather than telling us about them.

Virtually any time there's an "As you know, Bob" or an information dump—and, in fact, whether it's in dialogue or in the text—as a writer you should want to have a look at that and see if you can't work it into the story.

David B. Coe

Last year I did a dialogue workshop and hit many of the same points, particularly with respect to said-bookisms. I had my group do an exercise: write a scene/conversation between two people without using "said," "asked," "stated," or any other direct form of attribution. It was a challenge for the people in the workshop. I made myself do it at the same time as my "students," and I found it challenging, too. But that little scene wound up being one of the best things I've ever written. I need to work it into a story.

He Said, She Said: Thoughts On Dialogue

A.J. Hartley

Dialogue is where a book comes to life, where its characters seem to breathe, where we can feel the basic human reality beneath the most outrageous or fantastical storyline or setting. It's not surprising, then, that few things knock me out of a story more completely than poorly executed conversation, and though these aren't exhaustive by any means, I'd like to offer a few observations on why some dialogue doesn't work, with the usual caveat that this is a personal opinion.

1. Too often the characters don't have distinctive voices. They all sound the same, so that if you covered the name, you couldn't possibly guess who was speaking. I'm not suggesting that every single utterance should be stamped with the individual character's personality (that can quickly get irritating), but as a rule, all the characters should have slightly different ways of speaking, not in terms of dialect necessarily (another thing which quickly feels hokey) but in terms of those things which mark out all speakers: word choice, rhythm, whether they speak in complete sentences, what kinds of metaphors they use. You can describe a character's eyes a thousand times, but nothing will communicate him better than his own words.

2. Don't make the mistake of thinking that good dialogue is necessarily naturalistic. Dialogue grows out of reality, but is shaped—like everything in your book—by art. Characters can be kept distinct and individual while still staying within the range dictated by the style (sleek and cynical for Chandler; modulated, even metrical for Tolkien; lavishly purple for Anne Rice; etc.)

3. And (of course) the opposite of that, don't forget that these are supposed to be real people even in the most outlandish piece of fiction, so you shouldn't overstretch your reader's suspension of disbelief in your characters. Balance is all. This can be tricky in fantasy, particularly in high fantasy where naturalism in speech can be at odds with its surroundings. Try reading it aloud, or even (if you have a thick skin) drafting it like a scene from a play and having some friends or family read it with you. It's amazing how often what seems acceptable on the page sounds contrived, jarring, or just plain fake to the ear.

4. I read some work by a novice writer recently and was struck by how much the mood shifted in the course of a few lines. In a single page the two characters talking had taken offense at each other, fought, reconciled, lost their tempers again and made up. It was bizarre. But I remembered having a similar problem with my own stuff once and asked the author what his typing speed was like. "Miserable," he said. And there it was. If you write dialogue too slowly, you can lose track of how brief the exchange actually is, so you start overloading it with shifts, forgetting that what took you ten minutes to write will take thirty seconds to read. Idiotic though it may sound, my own dialogue improved exponentially when I became a faster typist, because I was then able to get down on paper what was going through my head in something close to real time. If that doesn't work for you but you want the dialogue to feel quick and spontaneous, consider dictating the conversation into a recorder then transcribing it. It may come through lighter and more naturally when you aren't fumbling around on the keyboard while trying to compose.

5. Though people sometimes advise burying exposition in dialogue, be wary of this because it's often glaringly obvious and takes the conversation into utterly implausible directions. "Remember that time we went fishing, Jimmy?" "Down at the pond by the old barn? I sure do, Bob." "That would be five years ago now, isn't that right, Jimmy?" "About that, Bob, yes. I'd just bought the shotgun that Old Man Whosit used to kill Mrs. Jenkins in the barn up on Whimpole Street." Please. If you need to tell us something, tell us. Don't make your characters sound like idiots in the process.

6. Related to that (and point 4), don't over explain how your character feels in response to every word which is said. Good dialogue should carry the mood and the impression it makes on those involved. Disrupt the conversation with too much reflection on how each bit felt to the protagonist and the whole exchange gets bogged down. Again, a degree of naturalism is usually key: most of us don't articulate to ourselves how we feel about every beat in a conversation. We might feel things during the exchange, but we are rarely able to process precisely what those feelings are till later (which is why we always think of the perfect come-back ten minutes after a fight).

7. Similarly, good dialogue doesn't need explanation about delivery, so while you should always be wary of adverbs in general (because they tend to over-explain), banish them entirely from the little tags that show who's talking. A good writer should never have to write "he said sarcastically." If the sarcasm isn't evident, there's a problem with the utterance. If it is evident, your little pointer makes the reader feel condescended to.

There are, of course, more points I could make, but I'll leave it at that for now. With one final bit of advice. If you suspect your dialogue needs work, force yourself to listen more deliberately to the way people talk, perhaps even transcribing conversations you've had from memory as a play, then cutting down to a few pithy exchanges which you might actually use, and—as always—look for good dialogue in novels and study how it works.

Faith Hunter

Based on a book I am working on now, I'll add a dialogue problem I see often: not enough stage direction and scene setting for characters. If a conversation is taking place in a car at night, there should be headlights and traffic lights and oncoming cars with bright lights. Not a lot, but enough to remind the reader where they are and that they are going somewhere. If they are in a restaurant, they need to interrupted once by a server, call for more drinks, and when the pithy part of the conversation ends, there needs to be a transition (for time to pass as they finish their meal) before they jump up and leave. (And BTW, I have an editor pal who says "Find another place to meet for dialogue than in a restaurant or bar. Booooring!")

Oh No, She Didn't!

Misty Massey

Last weekend I was talking with a good friend about a book we'd both recently finished reading. The writing was brilliant, and the first half of the book had promised glorious results. But somewhere along the way, something went wrong. The main character's behavior changed, suddenly, and for no discernible reason. Changed so much that I didn't like her any longer, and didn't want to waste any more time reading about her. The character no longer felt real to me, as if the author forced the character to do the things that were not in her nature, but just to drive the story in a certain direction. At that point, it didn't matter what nifty surprise the next chapter might have held. I had stopped believing.

While working on *Kestrel's Dance* (the sequel to *Mad Kestrel*), I discovered I'd gone three full chapters with nothing happening except talk. Different characters talking to each other, and tons of internal monologues, but no action. Don't misunderstand—dialogue is vital. No one wants to read a story in which characters don't talk to each other. But when you realize your characters have done nothing but yack at each other for the last three chapters, something's wrong. Time for a little action to ramp things up, make those pages turn.

It's not just a question of throwing something into the mix, though. The action you choose has to be reasonable to what's happened thus far in your story. It has to make sense. If your character has spent fifteen chapters being afraid of water, she won't suddenly decide in chapter 16 to go whitewater rafting. How many times have you watched a scary movie and wondered why on earth the victims, who are standing on the main floor of a home, run *upstairs* to escape the villain? Whatever you choose to do to your characters needs to have a logical progression, a flow from prior events so that readers aren't bounced out of the story and back into the real world.

Now's the point where new writers will shake their heads at me and say, "But people are unreasonable! They do crazy-stupid things every day, for no reason at all. Doesn't it make sense that people don't make sense?" Sure it does. People are nuts. But stop right there for just a second . . . when people do foolish things with clearly no forethought, think how frustrating it is. It's confusing and a little frightening, and we don't particularly like it. As parents, the first thing we ask a misbehaving child is "Why did you do that?" Shucks, we stand around the water cooler at work asking the same thing about stories we saw on the news the night before.

We like to understand what drives people to do what they do. We can't control that in real life, but in fiction, we can. As writers, we must. Just because we need excitement in chapter 12 doesn't mean it should be random and pointless.

David had an excellent suggestion— *"Gee, character X is trying to do this right now; what would be the worst thing from her perspective that could happen at this very moment?"* If that doesn't work for you, or you just can't think of what that horrible thing might be, reach out to the world around your character. What could upset the balance enough to affect the character and change things? If you're still stuck, find a beta reader or a trusted friend, ask him to read your pages and tell you what happens next. My husband loves when I come strolling into his computer room with that look on my face. I don't always use what he suggests, but sometimes an opinion from outside of my own head is all I need to knock the ideas loose.

Luckily for my problem with the endless-dialogue, I had some action-events I'd held in reserve, things that would fit appropriately into an ocean-going adventure, so the change wasn't all that complicated. And I hope that when readers get to that point, none of them will stop reading, furrow their brows, and say out loud, "What the hell?" Because the only thing I like more than people buying my book is for people to read all the way through to the end.

David B. Coe

". . . when people do foolish things with clearly no forethought, think how frustrating it is."

Spot on, Misty.

Tom Clancy (of *Hunt For Red October* and *Patriot Games* fame) once said that the biggest difference between fiction and reality is that fiction has to make sense. Think of it this way: I have lots of friends who are also named David. A couple who Nancy and I are incredibly close with have a daughter the same age as my older daughter, and they named their girl the same thing we named ours. My brother and my best friend from college married women with the same first names and then named their first-born sons the same thing.

Stuff like that happens all the time. But not in books. You simply can't have people with the same name in a book (unless it is a specific plot point) because of how confusing it would be. As writers we sometimes have to sacrifice on the "realistic" side in order to make the story work. Same thing with irrationality. Yes, people do strange inexplicable things every day, but our narratives have to follow a logical path in order to be readable. We're not writing reality; we're writing fiction, which is an artistic and imperfect mirror of reality.

Beatriz

As a reader, I find it distracting when a character suddenly does something not in keeping with the character. It will yank me out of the story PDQ. Sometimes I'm left with the feeling that I'm a dummy, that I missed the foreshadowing that allowed Character X to do Y. After all, the author is All Knowing, isn't (s)he?

I don't enjoy feeling like a dummy. Odds are, I won't buy another one of the author's books if that's how I feel.

Binding Character and Narrative: Point of View

David B. Coe

Let me begin by saying that I have a pet peeve when it comes to reading fiction. I find it very distracting when a story is being told from one character's viewpoint and then suddenly shifts—without some kind of visual clue to the reader—either to another character's POV or to omniscient voice. There are things about the Harry Potter books that I don't like, places where I feel that J. K. Rowling has not done a great job. But one thing she does superbly is maintain a consistent voice for her books. We are almost always in Harry's point of view, and when we're not, she makes it absolutely clear where we are. Her POV never wanders in the middle of a chapter; she never tells her reader something that Harry can't know. Rather, she allows us to figure things out right along with him, and that's what makes the books work so well.

That's how point of view should work. We should see the story through the eyes of a character and know only as much as he or she can know at any particular time. If you want to use multiple POVs—if you want to tell the story from the perspective of several characters in order to weave together plot lines—great. But make certain that your reader knows exactly when you are shifting from one character to the other.

Why? Because point of view at its best should be the nexus of character and narrative. Point of view is more than a way to tell a story. It is how we imbue our storytelling with emotion. Harry Potter's voice works because he's not just telling us the story; he's sharing his fears, his desires, his teen angst, his loneliness. His voice gives the story its dramatic impact. That's what point of view is about.

Maintaining a consistent point of view is not just a matter of keeping your storytelling clear (though that is important); constantly shifting POV without warning can confuse and frustrate readers. Good use of POV is about remembering whose story you're telling. Sure, Rowling could have shifted from Harry's POV to Voldemort's during one of their confrontations in order to tell us what Voldemort was thinking at that moment, or what he knew about what was going to happen. But we weren't reading Tom Riddle's story. We were reading Harry's. The meat of the story is in Harry's head and heart. That's where the focus needed to be, and that's exactly where Rowling left it.

Point of view is what binds character development to plot development; it's what allows a story and its main character to grow and change and resolve together. When that bond is broken, even briefly, character and narrative both suffer. The storytelling becomes confused; the reader's identification with your lead character is compromised.

I don't mean this to sound quite so dogmatic—I know that the Magical Words mantra is "There's no *single* right way to do any of this." But I would suggest that you think about point of view not as a rule, but rather as a tool. Used consistently and carefully, it can make storytelling easier, more effective. Used haphazardly and it can undermine much of the good work you've done in other aspects of your writing.

L. Jagi Lamplighter

Interesting that you posted this just the day after I saw an editor on another website list "head hopping" as first among the reasons why he rejects manuscripts.

Do you think it is more common to make mistakes in this area than it used to be? I don't remember ever having a problem with this as a child, but nowadays, I read books where it shifts point of view without a line of white space, and I can't figure out who is who.

David B. Coe

That is interesting, Jagi. I hadn't seen the article, but it doesn't surprise me that an editor would find this annoying. To answer your question, I think it's not that the mistake has become more common, but rather that omniscient voice has become less accepted. It's a trend, like the falling out of favor of said-bookisms, which were much more accepted three or four decades ago. One of my favorite books by one of my favorite authors is filled with instances of head-hopping (love that term, by the way), but the book was written twenty years ago, and it probably didn't raise any eyebrows at the time. I think it would today.

Point of View: Single vs. Multiple
David B. Coe

Those of you who have read any of my books know that I like to tell a story from the perspective of several different point of view characters. A point of view—POV—character is simply the character whose head we're inside as we write or read a book. For the Harry Potter books the POV character is always Harry. For a book like *Tigana*, by Guy Gavriel Kay, or with my Winds of the Forelands books, the POV shifts from character to character, with each new chapter or chapter section. The alternative to writing with POV characters is writing with an omniscient narrative voice, which I just hate. Why? Because I find, as a reader, that it distances me from the characters, and it's just not as interesting. I read—and write—because I like to get inside people's minds, to see what makes them tick. An omniscient voice doesn't really allow that.

Writing in multiple points of view has many advantages. It allows an author to piece together a complex story without requiring a single character to know and see everything. It makes it possible to give more information to your reader than you've given to your main character, which in turn makes it possible to ratchet up the tension and the sense that your beloved protagonist is in danger. And finally, as my comments about omniscient voice imply, it helps with character development, by putting your reader inside the thoughts and emotions of several characters.

And yet, with my new project I've chosen to limit myself to a single POV, and I'm finding it challenging. Why would I do this? After all the things I just said about how much I like writing in multiple POV, why would I choose to write from the viewpoint of a single character? Well, because this has certain advantages, too. With a single POV character, readers tend to grow quite attached to that character, and since this new project revolves around this one character, this is a good thing. Also, this new series has a strong mystery component, and by writing from a single POV, and keeping that character in the dark about certain things, I heighten the sense of mystery and perhaps make the implied but unseen threats faced by my character seem that much more frightening. So again, my POV choice is designed to increase the narrative tension.

The challenges I'm encountering relate back to the benefits of multiple POV. From the standpoint of narrative, giving my readers necessary information is complicated by the fact that I'm writing from the viewpoint of only the one character. I don't want him to know too much, because I need to preserve certain aspects of the mystery. And logistically I simply can't have him everywhere my readers might need him to be. So I have to keep my readers in the dark about certain things. I have to balance the need to maintain the sense of mystery with my desire not to tick readers off by telling them too little.

From the standpoint of character development, the challenge is in making the characters around my protagonist come to life. I can't be in their heads, so I have to rely upon my POV character to "tell" my readers about them through his observations and the interactions he has with them.

Clearly, these challenges can be overcome, and I think that what I've written thus far works quite well. But this is new for me, and I'm finding that I'm having to learn some of the basics of good storytelling all over again. That's not a complaint; not at all. I think I decided to go with single character POV, in part, because after writing eleven books in multiple POV, I was looking for new challenges.

But I'd be interested in hearing from readers and writers alike. Which do you prefer: multiple character point of view or single character POV? Why? What do you get from one that you miss in the other?

David B. Coe

I should point out that omniscient voice used to be the standard and that it was used to great effect to get into people's thoughts and emotions. I shouldn't have been so quick to dismiss it. Omniscient voice used carelessly is what I object to—done well, it can be great.

Mark Wise

David, I think I like multiple POVs in enormous Fantasy Epics, but single POV in mystery/suspense. I think it depends on what you want to do in your story. Can you write a huge story like Winds of the Forelands from only one POV? I think you could, but who would want to read it? There is only so much character-building to carry through five books.

I have a question as a writer . . . How do you know how often to switch POVs in a multi book? Is there a rule or hint as to how often a POV switch is *too* often? I always fear switching it too often and confusing the reader. Then I worry about sticking with one too long and missing some great viewpoint.

David B. Coe

Mark, excellent point about POV fitting the type and scope of the story being told. You're right. I couldn't possibly have written Winds, or even the LonTobyn books, from one POV.

As to how often to switch, I really think it's as individual as anything else, and often it depends on where you are in the story.

There are parts of Winds where I remain in one character's head for a whole chapter and other parts where I'm in two or three people's POV in a chapter of the same length. In my final chapters of the last book in the series, I jumped around A LOT, but that matched the pacing at that point in the story.

I treat multiple POV as a conversation of a sort. When it seems that one character has "talked" for too long, or when the narrative seems to demand that someone else do the talking, I switch. It's a pacing question. And if I have written an entire chapter in one character's POV, I will generally switch as I begin the next chapter, even if the action stays in the same place. If I'm writing Grinsa and Tavis chapters and one's from Grinsa's POV, I'll switch to Tavis with the next chapter, just to keep that story-thread fresh.

Again With the Point of View Stuff . . .

David B. Coe

My last essay focused on point of view, specifically on the choice between multiple person point of view—using several different characters to tell the story—and single person point of view, which is what I'm using in my current work in progress. Today I'd like to continue the discussion of point of view by comparing single third person point of view—telling a story through the eyes of a single character who is referred to in the third person ("he" or "she")—and first person point of view.

Once again, this is something I've been thinking about a great deal with respect to my current project because having made the decision to write the book in third person, I've been finding myself unintentionally slipping into first person as I write. There's a part of me that feels that this story needs to be told in that "I," "Me," "My" voice. So why don't I just write it that way? Well, let's talk about what lies behind making such a choice.

The use of first person narrative is actually somewhat hard to find in fantasy. I've had fantasy readers tell me that they won't read a book if they pick it up and find that it's in first person. I've heard writers say that they hate writing first person, and I've had editors say that they are less likely to buy books that are written in that voice. The reasons for this are hard to state with any certainty, but I'm going to try anyway.

Worldbuilding and the description of the worlds we create are crucial elements of successful fantasy. There's a lot of background information that fantasy authors have to convey to our readers, and doing that through a first person narrator can be difficult. When we use third person narration instead of first, we place just a bit of distance between ourselves and our readers. Instead of having the lead character telling our story, we have what's referred to as a "hidden narrator" telling the story through the eyes of our protagonist. That little bit of distance allows us to give crucial information without it seeming forced or awkward.

Let me put it this way: As we go through our day, we don't think discursively. When someone tells us that they're going to Washington and will see the Lincoln Memorial, we don't stop to think, "Ah, Abraham Lincoln, the 16th President of the United States who led our nation through the Civil War, gave one of the most famous speeches in American history at Gettysburg in 1863, and was assassinated soon after his second inauguration in 1865." We know all this stuff and there's no need to think about it. In fact, it would be odd if we were to stop and ponder it. In the same way, it reads as contrived if we have our first-person narrator stop and think about such things. But if we use third-person point of view, if we rely on that "hidden narrator" and put some distance between our voice and the reader, we can explain what needs to be explained without it feeling forced and unnatural. This is not to say that third-person narration makes huge data dumps okay—far from it. But it does allow us to convey a bit more background in a way that reads well.

This is also not to say that first person narration is not without certain advantages. First person narrators are quite common in mainstream literature and also in mystery. Just as in fantasy you sometimes want that distance between reader and point of view character, sometimes in other literary circumstances you don't. Removing that distance can heighten the emotional impact of your plot points. Again to use an example: Having someone tell you about a friend who lost a loved one is sad. Having a friend tell you that he or she lost a loved one is devastating.

In mystery writing, being inside the lead character's mind as he or she pieces together the clues allows your readers to feel that they're solving the puzzle right along with your hero. By removing that narrative distance, you allow your reader to relate more thoroughly to the main character and his or her story.

As authors, we have to choose if we want that distance or the immediacy that comes when we remove it. I think that one of the reasons I've been drawn to both approaches as I work on my new project is that the story revolves around a murder mystery, but is set in a different historical era. Sometimes I need that distance; sometimes I want that immediacy. If I could write the book in both voices, I would, but that won't work, and ultimately I've decided that I need that hidden narrator to convey certain story elements.

What about you? Which voice works best for your current project? Is it possible that a change in narrative approach might help you get past a problem you're having?

L. Jagi Lamplighter
"The use of first person narrative is actually somewhat hard to find in fantasy."

Except for noir fantasy, of course. (*Nine Princes of Amber*, the *Dresden Files*, etc.) The fantasies that copy noir mysteries in their mood are in first person (which is why I did my Prospero books that way.)

But you are right about the fact that other fantasies usually are not, and I think your ideas as to why are pretty good ones. Third person allows the author to include a good deal of stuff the main character might generally know, but not think about . . . which is quite necessary for a fantasy story!

David B. Coe

That's a great point, Jagi: There is indeed that strain of fantasy that crosses over into noir or mystery. This project I'm working on straddles the line a bit. Hence my confusion about which to use. And I should also add that the first-person voice in *Prospero Lost* (Jagi's book from Tor, for those who don't know) worked very well.

Butt In Chair

Deadlines

David B. Coe

"Butt in Chair."

Over the past couple of years BIC has become something of a mantra here at Magical Words, and it remains some of the best advice we as a group have given. If you want to be a writer, you have to write. Simple as that. Except . . .

Writing professionally is not only about writing, but often about writing to a deadline, writing on demand, churning out content on a regular basis. Every Sunday, I write my Monday post for Magical Words, and quite often it takes me a while to come up with a topic for my post. It's hard, after literally hundreds of posts about writing, to come up with something original and relevant and, we hope, entertaining.

But as writers, this is something we have to do. Like creating characters and developing narrative flow and building tension, writing on demand and to deadline is a skill to be honed. And there are great ways to teach oneself to do it.

I first learned to write creatively to a deadline when I was in seventh grade. Really. We had a class assignment for the second half of the school year to write just about every night (maybe five nights a week) in a journal. We could write anything we wanted—diary-type entries, poems, stories; whatever. This was a school assignment, but there is no reason why you can't give yourself the same assignment now. It's a great way to make writing a habit.

There are other things we can do, of course, to make ourselves write on demand—join a writing group, start a blog, or merely resolve to turn out a story every other week, or some such thing. The point is to force yourself not only to write, but to finish pieces by a certain time and date. Deadlines are a fact of life for writers, and while many publishers will forgive the occasional late book, no writer—and in particular no new writer—wants to develop a reputation for turning in work late. One of the other things we say often here at Magical Words is that writers need to comport themselves professionally. This means, in part, making certain that manuscripts look clean and neat, that they are free of typos and grammatical problems, and, yes, that they are turned in on time.

But wait, you might say. Writing a short story in two weeks is one thing; turning in a manuscript of 100,000 words on time is quite another. To which I'd reply, yes and no. Writing a book is a larger, more complex undertaking. But when I'm working on a book, I break down that larger project into a series of discreet tasks—chapters are very handy in this regard. If I were to start a book in the beginning of October and give myself a January 31 deadline for finishing it, I'd approach it this way: the book is going to be about 100,000 words, and I have four months to finish it. I'll want to give myself a couple of weeks at the end to polish and revise. So the actual writing is actually going to have to take about fifteen weeks. The way I work, that means that I'll have (allowing for Christmas, Thanksgiving, and New Year's) about 70 writing days. That's a shade under 1,500 words a day; definitely doable. In fact, what it comes out to is a chapter every three to four days—a brisk pace, but not a terrible one.

Now, your chapters might be longer than mine, or shorter. Your book length might be longer or shorter (although in today's market, as a new writer, you don't want to try to sell books that are too far off of that number in either direction). And you might have more time than I gave myself, or you might work weekends, or you might think that 1,500 words per day is way too slow or way too fast a pace. These are decisions you have to make for yourself. And then you have to adjust your math accordingly.

But the process works. Some might ask if I really think of my book writing in these terms, and the answer is yes, I really do. As I said, writing a book is a big thing. It can be intimidating, especially early on. I've been doing this for a long time; I've written more than a dozen novels, and I still find it a bit daunting to start that first page of something that will eventually be 400 or 500 pages long. But if I look at it as starting the first page of a chapter that might be fifteen pages long, it doesn't seem so huge. And if I can break down the process and see ahead of time exactly how I'm going to meet my deadline, it forestalls any panic I might feel.

To be honest with you, when I was working on that hypothetical example above, and I typed in that January 31 deadline, I paused for a moment, wondering if I was being realistic. As soon as I did the math, though, I realized that I was. That's happened to me with actual book projects, too. I've looked at a deadline, and thought, "There is no way I can meet this deadline. No way at all." But then, after breaking down the project into its component parts, and plotting them out on a calendar, I've realized that in fact I can.

A deadline doesn't have to be a burden. Instead, it can be a tool, a way of carving up a project into manageable pieces. Learning to use your time constraints that way can make you a more efficient writer. It can also preserve your sanity.

Chris Branch

David, I think the most impressive part of your post is the throwaway line where you say you'll need *"a couple of weeks"* to polish and revise your 100K-word ms. So that's all it takes when you're a pro, huh? ☺

One question, is it really accurate that 100K words translates roughly to 400 or 500 pages? I was thinking it would be more like 300, but never having had a manuscript transformed into an actual book (yet), I never think in terms of pages.

David B. Coe

Chris, don't be impressed. Really. Because that two-week polishing period that you find impressive is linked directly to the very un-impressive writing pace of 1,500 words per day. Now, these days I'm a bit faster than that—maybe 2,000 words a day—but this is a new pace for me and I don't like to plan for it yet. But my point is this: I write slowly because I tend to polish and revise as I go along. That's just the way I work. My first drafts tend to be very clean and, thus, they tend to need relatively little work. Plus, I factor in that the book is going off to my editor, who is going to help me revise and polish as part of the publication process.

Other authors, whose books are every bit as good as mine, might work very differently. They might write 3,000 words a day and thus finish their books in only thirty-five or forty days, but they might do all of their polishing in the revision stage, in which case they'll need those extra weeks at the end. Does that make sense? It's not that I'm a professional, or that I don't need as much revising as others. It's just a matter of where in my creative process I do that polishing work. I do it along the way, so that I only need a bit of time at the end to do some last minute work. I hope I'm being clear.

As for your page count/word count question: Yes, 100K words is about 400 pages give or take a few. Industry standard for man-uscript pages is as follows: double spaced, 1 inch margins all around, and somewhere around a 10 or 12 pitch font. The end result is about 250 words per page. Now this number tends to fluctuate a bit: more words per page when you're doing lots of exposition; fewer when you're writing lots of dialogue. But that's the standard. Me? I use Courier New font at 11 pitch because it just looks right to me. And I get about 240-260 words per page, which is right where I should be.

The Great Plot Synopsis Project
C.E. Murphy

A couple of weeks ago I got email from Joshua Palmatier inviting me to participate in the Great Plot Synopsis Project, wherein he asked a bunch of published writers to post a book synopsis in order to help show aspiring writers how they're done. (Joshua keeps having good ideas like this and then *following through on them*. I think he's an alien.) So today is the Great Plot Synopsis Project Day. ☺

I have blatantly stolen the Synopsis Q&A Joshua posted. Please note that there are *SPOILERS* for *Urban Shaman* beyond this point. The book synopsis is replicated in its entirety. As it happens, because of how this particular synopsis is written, it's not *very* spoilery, but it is spoilery! So be warned, and now you can, if you wish, read:

How did you sell your first book: agent, slush pile, alien intervention?
Slush pile. Luna was the third house I'd sent *Urban Shaman* to. I dashed out and got myself an agent (the incomparable Jennifer Jackson) that weekend. Luna, at the time, was looking for traditional fantasy with a strong female protagonist and a strong romantic subplot. I sent them a contemporary fantasy with a strong female protagonist and almost no romantic subplot. They bought it. This is my way of saying "Let them tell you no." I mean, don't send a romance novel to Baen Books, let's be reasonable, but also don't assume that because your book doesn't exactly fit what a publisher says they're looking for that they're going to reject you.

Was a synopsis involved, and if so what did it look like? (seriously: page length, spacing, font, straight-up story or broken down by character/setting/plot, etc.)
There was a synopsis: it was a two page, 25pt spaced, .3" tabbed, 12pt Courier New font, *extremely basic* synopsis that incorporated the entire story at once, without breaking things down into character/setting/plot. I can't even imagine how you'd do that, in fact. Here's the *Urban Shaman* synopsis:

> Joanne Walker is a Seattle cop with no use for the mystical. When she sees a woman running for her life, she has to get involved—even when the woman, Marie, claims to be hunted by Cernunnos, an ancient Celtic god who leads the Wild Hunt.
>
> Jo's solid, real world explodes when Cernunnos tramples through a local diner and calls her out. The fight ends with

Jo's near-death, and in a hazy experience between life and death, she's greeted by the Native-American trickster Coyote. He gives her a choice: death, or life as a shaman. Jo chooses the healer's path, forced to acknowledge an aspect of the universe she's never seen before.

Marie is murdered a few hours later. Jo, stunned, throws caution to the wind and seeks out guidance on a psychic plane. Half a dozen shamans, all of them dead in an apparently unconnected series of recent murders, respond. They charge her with finding the man who murdered them, unable to give her a greater clue than "he seeks the child."

The next morning Jo wakes up to news that four children have been murdered at a local high school. She arrives at the school to discover a ritualized death scene. She speaks with the class teacher and, through a healing trance, learns the killer's identity—Herne the Hunter, Cernunnos' son.

Jo begins tracking Herne; Cernunnos, in turn, hunts Jo. Her newborn shamanic powers are the key to his ability to stay on Earth rather than be pulled back into shadow with the turn of the seasons. Their final confrontation takes place on an astral level, a very physical battle that leaves them both worn and battered, and binds Cernunnos to the cycle of time once more.

Another fight still remains, though: Jo tracks down Herne and with him, his daughter, whom Herne intends to sacrifice in a blood ritual that will permit him to take Cernunnos' place as leader of the Hunt.

As she battles Herne, Jo comes to better understand the path she's chosen, finally accepting her fate as a warrior and a healer in a world full of ignored mysticism. With her new understanding, she finds herself able to guide Herne to his own place in that mystical world, righting an error made centuries earlier.

When do you write a synopsis (before, during, after the novel)?
Well, that synopsis I wrote after the book was written. I wrote the original synopses for *Thunderbird Falls* and *Heart of Stone* while the books were in progress. These days I sell on proposal, so I write the synopsis before I write the book.

Then I ignore it.

How do you go about doing it?
With a great deal of pain and agony, usually.

Actually, I've found the best way to write a synopsis is to log onto a chat room, seize someone, and tell them what happens in the book. Then I take the log of the file and convert it into a synopsis. For some reason I get a huge mental block about having to Figure It Out in a formal fashion, but it's a lot easier to just say, "Oh, yeah, and, crap, I forgot that back toward the beginning Jo did this which sets this up, okay?" and then keep going.

The problem with doing this, of course, is it means whomever I've seized gets spoiled for the book I'm writing, at least in the general sense. I don't write a lot of details into my synopses, so they remain a mystery until the book's written (to me as well as to whomever I've blurted at).

I still haven't learned to get enough emotional content into synopses, particularly in the form of motivation. I tend to focus on the plot, the whole plot, and nothing but the plot, which, to me, *is* the story, and leave out emotional ramifications and "er, why exactly did she do that?" "Because I NEEDED HER TO" sorts of things. I'm more aware of it than I used to be, and I'm better than I was, but that's still an area I fall down in.

Does this change depending on circumstances (genre, adult/YA, publisher, time of year, whether it's raining, etc.)?

Not really. Everything I've done a synopsis for has been the same amount of agony, except one synopsis that flowed in its creation and which I was proud of and liked a lot and which the publisher responded to with, "Well, okay, but what about these problems?" and made me have to reconsider the whole book. She was right, too, dammit. They usually are.

Did your approach, or the final product (the synopsis), change as you got publishing experience? Does your agent or editor want something different from you now than when they were pulling you out of the slush?

My agent pretty much always says the same thing when I turn in a proposal: "Not bad, I think maybe you've put too much information in the first few chapters, a little too front-loaded maybe," and I always have. One of my editors responds to the proposal with ideas for changing things around, for improving the story, etc; the other one does not, unless the synopsis I've turned in is absolute crap, in which case she says, in much nicer words, "This is crap. Do it again." (That's only happened once. And she was right. I knew it was crap when I turned it in, but I sort of hoped she wouldn't notice. She did. ☺)

As for myself . . . I'm trying to learn to incorporate the things I'm not good at, and eventually they'll become second nature. I hope. I'm better at them than I used to be; I'm better at considering long-term ramifications and I'm better at seeing when I, for example, have forgotten to put a plot point in. But it's still incredibly, incredibly helpful to have an editor respond, because even though it makes me sulk, the truth is that all writers have blind spots. Having someone else illuminate those areas is critical.

We've been debating the eternal question of how much to include or leave out. When *you* write a synopsis, how closely does the synopsis match the book?
Oh, God. Well, the *Urban Shaman* synopsis is practically just High Concept, because it was written after the book. I really just took all the high ideas and wrote them down.

I've got the basic shape of the book in my head, and it usually does come out more or less like what I wrote in the synopsis, although never exactly. But what I find them useful for is when I get slowed down or stuck and don't know what I should be doing next. I go look at the synopsis and go, "Oh! What a cool idea that is! Now how can I get my characters to that point so I can do it?" which certainly unsticks me.

The problem with doing that is that in re-reading the synopsis I sometimes find that I forgot something REALLY COOL that would now require rewriting half the book to work in. So I've begun keeping a copy of the synopsis open along with the other doc files I'm working on so I can take a peek now and then and see if I've forgotten any cool ideas.

Ideally my synopses cover the action thread, the emotional thread, hit a few scene highlights that I know or expect to be seeing, and resolve the book. This is easier with the Walker Papers, say, which have one POV character, than with the Inheritors' Cycle, which has . . . one main POV character, but six or something minor ones. On a high story level the books almost always do what the synopses say they will. It's just that my details frequently change, and that, I don't worry very much about.

And how do you introduce/explain an SF/F setting in the short space of a synopsis?
Looking at a synopsis I wrote for an unfinished SF novel, I took about a page (as described above with formatting) to set up the world. It's a four page synopsis (I think it had to be four pages for some contest or something I submitted it to), so that's a lot of space dedicated to the setup, but it was also the bare minimum I thought I could get away with.

Is writing a synopsis a difficult process for you? Enjoyable/detestable? Any tips for making it easier?
The only person I know who likes writing synopses is Judith Tarr, who says something like, "But it's so easy, that's just how it all has to go in order to make the story work!" This is probably why she can write books that leave me staggering around in awe of her skill, and wide-eyed with moments of, *oh, *that's* how you do that . . .*

For those of us who are merely mortal, writing synopses generally seems to be a teeth-grinding, hair-pulling kind of experience. As I said above, the best way *I've* found to do it is to sit down and tell someone in a chat room how the story goes. (It doesn't work out loud, because I need the text to build the actual synopsis from.) I don't know if that would work for anybody else, but it helps me.

But here's something I haven't mentioned: having the damned things helps. It *does* give me something to refer back to and say, "Uh, what next?" and it gives me ideas of, well, what next. I've been writing . . . a lot, these last few years. My first book came out in June 2005; my eighth is out this month, my ninth will be out in May, and my 10th in September, with two more coming out in the first half of next year. Out of those, one (*Urban Shaman*) was fully written before 2005. (*Heart of Stone* was as well, but underwent such massive revisions that it may as well have been from scratch.)

There is no way I could have written ten books in three years without synopses. They help guide me away from false starts, they help get me back on track, they give me a *structure*. It might not be exactly right, but it's something to at least lean on. Writing them forces me to consider where the story is going and how it's going to get to the end scene I have in mind. Doing what I've done the last three years, that's critical. Much as I hate writing them, I seriously doubt I'll ever write another book *without* writing a synopsis: they are, in the end, too useful.

How To Title Your Story — Or Not

Edmund R. Schubert

As Misty Massey once said, "Despite the old adage 'You can't judge a book by its cover,' we happily judge just the same." She's absolutely correct. The title of your book or short story is your opportunity to make a good first impression on a reader; it will either establish a promising tone—or not. Writing fantasy (or SF) opens up additional worlds of creative possibility, but "creative possibility" is a double-edged sword and you have to wield it carefully.

As an editor, a bad title has never (consciously) caused me *not* to buy a story, nor have I ever heard any editor say they failed to buy a book or story specifically because of the title. However, it does set certain expectations regarding what I'm likely to encounter once I start reading, and obviously it's in your best interests to have an editor start reading with the best possible impressions.

If a title doesn't work and I want to buy the story, I won't unilaterally decide to change it; I'll point out what I consider the specific flaws in the current title and suggest some alternatives. At that point the author and I will discuss it, come to an agreement, and we're set. However, I do know that many book publishers will (and frequently do) tell their authors what the title of their novel is going to be when it's published, and it's not just first-time authors that this happens to. I once had a conversation with Orson Scott Card about one of the books in his Ender's Game series, and even he had one of his titles changed. It was early in his career, but well after his huge success with the original Ender book. The point is, it can happen to anyone, and you should be neither surprised nor insulted if it happens to you.

The reason why book titles are *so* important to publishers is they know that titles are one of the top three factors in a customer's decision to pick up a book off the shelf and look at it—or not. (The other two factors are the cover art and the reader's familiarity with the author's name.) The title may not make a reader decide to actually *buy* the book, but they can't possibly buy it if they don't pick it up, can they?

With short stories you have a little more room for fun, creativity, and, quite simply, words. But with a novel, titles needs to be catchy, punchy, and short enough to fit on the spine of the book (and still be readable). Are there exceptions? Always. But consider these excellent titles: *A Game of Thrones*, *The Sorcerers Plague*, *Enders Game*, *Skinwalker*, *Fahrenheit 451*, *Mad Kestrel*, *Act of Will*. All are generally one to three words long, and all contain either uncommon words or uncommon combinations of words.

That brings me to one of the biggest problems I see in titles: incredibly overused words and/or painfully common words used *in isolation*. The word "game" is a common one, yet there are two hugely successful books with that word in the title (just in the list I gave you; I'll bet there are others). The difference is that in both cases the word is closely paired with another word that it normally has nothing to do with.

On the other side of the coin, look at these titles from my pile of submissions at *IGMS*: "The Long Fall," "Human Child," "The Chorus," "Rationalized," "It's Not You, It's Me."

What do these titles tell you? Nothing. What questions do they raise? None. This is the essence of a bad title. Common and overused words (and expressions) used *in isolation*.

On the other end of the spectrum, you can also easily over-do it. "ORANGE AGBADA JACQUARD," "Photon-Card from Delteron-9," and "Gray as a Moth, Scarlet as Sumac" are all real titles that were submitted to *IGMS*. And in my opinion (with apologies to the authors), they are all trying *way* too hard.

Yet another thing to avoid is titles that are only clever, or only make sense, *after* you've read the story. If you need the context of the story to understand the title, you have a bad title. If the title takes on additional meaning after the story has been read, that's great. But it has to work beforehand, too.

I mentioned earlier that I occasionally work with authors to change the title of a story I want to publish. Let me give you a few examples, so you can see my logic:

"An Early Ford Mustang" by Eric James Stone was originally titled "Brad Decides To Be Early." The story is about a guy named Brad who inherits a Ford Mustang from his uncle. This car has the ability to influence the flow of time, but that ability comes with a price. The original title only made sense after you'd read the story (strike one), but even then, it is incredibly bland (strike two). Not that the new title is stellar, but it's a big step up from "Brad."

"Judgment of Swords and Souls" by Saladin Ahmed was originally titled "Red Silk In The Lodge of God." "Red Silk" isn't necessarily a bad title, but the climax of the story centers around a ceremonial battle called—you guessed it—the Judgment of Swords and Souls. As a title, it's tighter, has more drama to it, and brings the added benefit of taking on additional meaning with the reading of the story. Bonus.

"The End-of-the-World Pool" by Scott Roberts is actually just a trimmed-down version of the original title, but I think the difference is an important one. I thought the original title, "Horseplay at The End-of-the-World Pool" set the reader up with expectations of something with a lighthearted tone. And though the story does open with two boys fooling around at the edge of a swimming pool, it quickly takes on a much darker tone that it maintains throughout the story. The tale reads like something Bradbury would have written in his early days and is a favorite of mine, but it required a title that didn't mislead the reader.

"Horus Ascending" by Aliette de Bodard was originally titled "Aten's Fall." This is another example of a title that had the right *basic* idea, but this one needed to be turned around one-hundred eighty degrees. The story is about an interstellar ship called the *Horus*, which is run by an artificial intelligence named Aten. The problem as I saw it was two-fold. First, the story is about the *ship* after it crash-lands, is separated from the AI, and learns to survive on its own, so it's not even about the entity named in the original title. And second, although both names come from Egyptian mythology, a lot more people have heard of Horus than Aten. My concern was that "Aten" was going to leave a lot of readers scratching their heads in bewilderment.

So there you have it: a crash course on what makes one title effective and another not, along with some specific example of titles that were changed and why.

A.J. Hartley

Great, specific examples, Ed. Thanks. I happened to look over my contract from Razorbill the other day. I sold them the first of a new YA series a few months ago. The book was then called *The Olde Mirror Shoppe*. When they first expressed interest in the book they said they would want a different title, something less Dickensian which conveyed a sense of mystery and intrigue in terms suitable for a kids' book. I offered lots of titles, and though we had several close calls, they eventually opted to go with something that emerged from their own meetings: *Darwen Arkwright and the Peregrine Pact*. I was okay with it, but the contract language made it clear: the title is "Subject to author's consultation. However it is understood that this is a right of consultation, not approval, and in the event of a disagreement, the Publisher shall prevail."

Great Expectations — No, Not Dickens

Edmund R. Schubert

Earlier I wrote about the importance of having the characters in your stories *want* something, and about how "wanting" gives shape and direction and a sense of purpose to your story. I'd like to expand on that idea and say that in an even more sweeping sense, the difference between good, publishable fiction, and pretty, wandering words that no one cares about is determined by whether or not the writer can create a sense of expectations in the reader and then meet those expectations. "Wanting" is just the simplest way of setting that sense of expectation in motion.

To be blunt, a lack of expectations is *the* most common reasons that I reject a lot of otherwise serviceable fiction. Most of the submissions I read for *InterGalactic Medicine Show* have already gone through the hands of at least two, and sometimes up to as many as four assistant editors, so there are no painfully terrible stories left by time the pile reaches me. But time after time what I do find is wonderful prose with no sense of purpose. Without that sense of purpose, fiction is just words wandering aimlessly around the page. No matter how beautifully composed the words may be, if there's no purpose, there's no story.

A sense of purpose helps the reader to know where to focus, what to pay attention to, what's important and what's not. It makes them susceptible to red-herrings. Without it, the reader is drifting through your story aimlessly, hoping for the best. Or more likely, getting bored and losing interest. And that is the kiss of death.

An author I've worked with for a long time at *IGMS* emailed me once about a story I had rejected, saying that every editor who had seen the story had said nice things about it, but ultimately rejected it, and could I give him an idea of what about his story had turned me off. (Let me say right away that the only reason I replied to his email was because we have a long-standing relationship. Don't write to editors with this kind of question and expect to get an answer unless you know them *very* well.)

My answer to him was this:

"There were other factors, but the knife in the heart was that I was six or eight pages into the story and still didn't have a sense of what the story was supposed to be about. The story lacked a specific focus and direction. To give you an example of the kind of thing I *am* looking for, go back to issue four of *IGMS*, to Eric James Stone's story, "Tabloid Reporter To The Stars." You know within the first 500 words that the main character is a disgraced science reporter who has been given an opportunity to redeem himself. A lot of other stuff happens in that story, but at its heart, it's about that character's quest for redemption. To me, every successful story has to have that kind of engine. And to get back to *your* story, if it had that kind of driving engine, I didn't see it, or it didn't show up soon enough."

A story's purpose can be established in a variety of ways. It's not hard to do; you just need to be intentional about it. One way is the classic mystery structure. Lay a corpse out for all the world to see, let us know who's responsible for bringing the murderer to justice, and let the fun begin. Simplistic? Yes. But it's so effective that people have been doing it for a hundred years and there's still a market for it.

Another way to approach this is what Orson Scott Card refers to as the M.I.C.E. quotient. It's detailed in his book, *Characters and Viewpoint* (which I highly recommend), but in a nutshell, here's how it works: M.I.C.E. stand for Milieu, Idea, Character, and Event, and each of those terms represent a different kind of story structure.

With each structure, the kind of story you are telling is clearly defined. A Milieu story is any of the fantasy-type stories where the main character gets taken away from his normal life (usually here on Earth) and inserted into a very foreign realm. One of the earliest examples of this kind of story is *Gulliver's Travels*. When Gulliver first arrives in either of the strange worlds he ends up in, the immediate question he (and the reader) asks is "Where the heck am I, and how do I get home again?" This question should arise within the first few pages of any short story, or within the first chapter or two of any novel. Once the question is asked, the necessary sense of purpose has been established. Once it is answered, the story is over.

The next kind of story, the Idea story, is one where the driving force behind the story is an idea of some sort. The classic mystery structure I talked about earlier is one example of an Idea story. Anything, really, that involves solving a puzzle is an Idea story. The movie, *Close Encounters of the Third Kind*, is an example of an Idea story that isn't a murder mystery. Various characters in that movie start having strange experiences and visions, and they all want/need to find out what's going on. When they finally do understand what's happening—aliens are visiting Earth—the story is essentially over. Idea explored, story done.

The most common kind of story today is the Character story. Character stories are often blended with other kinds of stories, which is fine as long as the author keeps in mind which is the primary structure and which is secondary. You can't start by emphasizing the mystery and end by emphasizing the character's personal growth; you have to pick one primary and stick with it throughout. Sadly, the Character story has become so prevalent that many people argue that it is the only one worth telling. While I enjoy Character stories very much, I strongly disagree with the idea that it, and it alone, is worthwhile.

The essence of the Character story is showing the main character in their current life-situation, making it clear that that situation is difficult or challenging for them, and then showing their quest to create a new situation. If they succeed, you have the traditional happy ending. If they fail, you have the traditional tragedy. But the key here is to show right away that the way they are living *at that moment* (the beginning) is intolerable and has to change. That sets everything else in motion.

The last kind of story in the M.I.C.E. quotient is the Event story. This is your basic disaster story. Think *Poseidon Adventure*. The characters' world is literally turned upside-down, and the story is about what they have to do to adapt to their new world (or return it to the way it was before the Event), and about who survives the experience and who does not.

All of these structures can be used to establish expectations for the reader, to tell them what kind of story they are going to be reading. But really, these structures still all boil down to one single question, the one I asked earlier, and the one I ask you again now: What does your character want? Whether it's to know "who done it," or to know why their world has been turned upside-down, or to know why all the people around them are three-inches tall, establishing expectations by making plain the character's greatest desire remains *the single most important thing* an author can do in their story. Its absence is, without a doubt, the single most common reason why I reject stories that are otherwise wonderfully written.

When Kurt Vonnegut talks about having your characters wanting some-thing as simple as a glass of water, it's a fine starting point. But opening up your characters' souls and showing us their hopes and dreams is what great story-telling is made of. Of course, once you get the ball of yarn rolling properly, pulling all the threads together successfully is another project, requiring a host of other skills. But it is, without a doubt, *the* place to begin.

Faith Hunter

Edmund, I've studied writing for years, trying to see why some stories work and why some don't, why some grab me by the throat and why others leave me dangling or, worse, bored. Bait and hook got me close to that understanding, and bait and hook fit nicely into what the character wants/needs/fears. But I still find books, stories, where I am properly baited and hooked, but not involved in the story.

These lines explain the problem so well. "Without that sense of purpose, fiction is just words wandering aimlessly around the page. No matter how beautifully composed the words may be, if there's no purpose, there's no story."

Spot on!

Eric James Stone

This is something I didn't really learn until a few years after writing "Tabloid Reporter to the Stars." Sometimes I would get it right by accident, like I did in that story, but I didn't really understand why my characters worked so much better in some stories than in others. I still have trouble with it sometimes, so this is a good reminder.

Trusting Your Reader
David B. Coe

Over the course of twelve novels and twelve sets of revisions, my editor and I have touched on one topic again and again: Trusting our readers.

What does that even mean? Trusting our readers . . . to what? To not steal our books from the stores? To not read them while taking care to keep the spine uncracked, so that the book can be returned to the bookstore for a refund? To not trash our books in Amazon reviews just for the fun of it?

No, this is actually a writing issue. Trusting our readers, is, in some ways, similar to the familiar saying "Show don't tell," and it is particularly important for beginning writers. Certainly it was for me when I was starting out. Basically it means not giving your readers too much information. Or, put another way, giving them enough information to understand what's happening, but not so much that you preempt their sense of discovery. My editor scrawled "Trust your reader!" again and again when reading through my first couple of manuscripts because I tended to explain too much. I was writing what I thought were complicated story lines and describing the motivations of complex characters. I wanted to be certain that my readers knew where I was going with each twist and turn of my plot, and so I left markers to make sure they "got it."

My editor's response was to say, as gently as he could, that while my plot was clever and my characters multidimensional, what I had written was not nuclear physics. The average reader would understand where I was taking him or her. More to the point, by explaining too much, by using those markers, I was denying my readers one of the great joys of reading: that feeling of epiphany that comes when we figure things out along with the characters we're following.

In what specific ways did my failure to trust my readers manifest itself? Well, for one thing, I described tone of voice too often. "She said, her tone suddenly urgent . . ." "He explained, obviously trying to sound comforting . . ." "She said with compassion . . ." All of those are dialogue attributions lifted directly from my first novel in its published form—these are the ones that slipped by my editor, or that he chose to ignore because some of my other passages were so egregious they needed more work. None of them needed to be more than "She said . . ." "He said . . ." The actual dialogue and the context were enough to convey the emotions and thoughts behind the dialogue. I should have trusted my readers to get the rest. But I was young and new to the craft and I felt that I needed to explain it all.

Another example, also from that first novel: In discussing my main character's struggle to learn to ride a horse, I describe how he overcomes the initial aches and pains of a long journey on horseback.

As they remounted and rode on, he also realized that his horsemanship had improved. He was being jolted less; he felt himself moving more in concert with the animal beneath him; and he sensed that his horse now labored less than it had, no doubt in response to his growing comfort and confidence.

Here's how I'd write that passage today:

As they remounted and rode on, he also realized that his horsemanship had improved. He was being jolted less; he felt himself moving in concert with his animal; and he sensed that his horse now labored less than it had.

The stuff I cut was extraneous. Of course the horse is laboring less because he's a better rider. My readers get that; they don't need to have it explained. Trust the reader! Here's a little trick I learned early on: when I find myself introducing or qualifying a passage with words like "No doubt" and "Obviously," chances are the passage isn't necessary.

As you can see, this really is a "Show, don't tell" issue. By trusting the reader we rely less on explication; we allow our characters and dialogue and action to tell the tale. Our storytelling becomes leaner, more direct. Because while the phrase we use is "Trust the reader," what we're really saying is "Trust yourself—trust your character development, your storytelling, your worldbuilding, your descriptions, your dialogue."

These days, when I find myself explaining too much, my own internal editor kicks in and tells me that this is a symptom of a deeper problem. If I'm explaining too much it probably means that the plot lines aren't clear enough in my own mind, or that I'm making my characters do things that are . . . well . . . out of character. In other words, it probably means that I've temporarily lost faith in the way I'm telling my story.

So how do we avoid these "trust" issues? To begin with, I do my best to know as much about my characters, my world, and my plot as I can before I start writing. Some of you may say, "Hey, I'm a seat-of-the-pants writer and it almost sounds like you're telling me to outline." Not at all. Pantsers can write a book without an outline but still know the story they're telling. They can be familiar with all the background, the world they've built, the characters they've created, and they can know where a story is headed. Knowing all of that, having a clear vision of your project, can give you the confidence to trust your writing, even if you haven't outlined your plot points.

I also try to keep my prose directed and strong. When I slip into passive writing or start using vague filler words—"a bit," "somewhat," "obviously," etc.—that is usually a sign that I've lost my way and need to rethink where the story is going. Finally, I look for redundant passages. If I'm saying things more than once in order to drive home a point it probably means that something is wrong with what I'm writing.

So trust yourself, trust your reader. Have enough faith in your craft to believe that the story you're telling is clear and compelling enough that your readers are paying attention. You'll wind up with a better book. In the end, trusting your reader is self-fulfilling and reciprocal. If you write a book that's lean and clear, you'll have justified the trust your reader placed in you when she took it off the bookstore shelf and spent her hard-earned cash to buy it.

Kenneth Mark Hoover

Just wanted to elaborate. This was probably the single hardest lesson I had to learn in my growth as a writer. It's difficult to believe because it's not intuitive. When you're starting out in this business you figure you gotta make things obvious and apparent for the reader. So in my case that meant a lot of over-writing.

I look at really old stuff I did twenty years ago that's 10K words and realize I could write the same story at 5K or 6K. It's hard to believe, but when you finally buckle down and "trust the reader" the writing improves immeasurably. Anyway, it did for me.

David B. Coe

Mark is an accomplished writer, and his comments are spot on. It is counterintuitive—you want readers to understand. The last thing you want is for your work to seem too obscure, too difficult to follow. But over-writing is just that. Trust yourself; trust the reader—it's a good mantra. Thanks very much, Mark.

Developing Your Voice
C.E. Murphy

What Is Voice?

Voice is the distinctive style that tells you who wrote the book you're reading as much as the name on the cover does. It's not terribly likely, for example, that a reader would mistake Hemingway for Dickens: they're very nearly the antitheses of one another.

A friend of mine often says that she thinks people who grow up to be professional writers usually come to the table with a couple of cards in their hands. Voice, dialogue, description, character-development, plot, motivation—whatever your couple of cards might be, chances are you're going to have to work hard to learn the rest.

I came to the table with two cards: voice and dialogue. My writing sounded like me right from the get-go: take a pile of essays or stories from a class and if you knew me at all, you could tell which one I'd written. So in retrospect, when I sat down to prepare a lecture on this topic, I realized that perhaps I'd chosen poorly. This wasn't something I'd studied on my writer's journey; it came naturally. On the other hand, I also realized that having a strong, natural voice meant I'd had a lot of leg-work to do when I stepped outside of what came most easily to me.

How do you develop your voice?

In all honesty, it's the same way you get to Carnegie Hall: practice, practice, practice. But it's also about trust. I know a lot of writers who have been screwed up by listening to people telling them how they "should" write, and trying to do that for years and years rather than trusting themselves and their own style.

This actually comes down to something I think is a little ironic: I think trying to teach someone how to develop their voice can be dangerous. I figure there's an equally good chance of me screwing you up entirely as there is of me helping you.

Really, though, a significant part of developing your own voice is trusting yourself. As a professional writer, I passionately believe that the only way to succeed is to be true to yourself. Don't try to write to the market because the market's going to change by the time you're done writing, much less by the time your book gets published. Don't try to sound like Nora Roberts or Michael Connelly just because you think that's what's going to make a novel sell. Your passion and your talent are going to make it sell.

Okay, so I just said don't try to sound like Nora Roberts or Michael Connelly. Now I'm going to say, "Well, *except*..."

If you want to write chick lit, for pity's sake, read Jennifer Crusie. Read Meg Cabot. Read Stephanie Plum, for that matter. If you want to write romance, read Nora and Kat Martin and Teresa Medeiros. If you want to write crime, read Michael Connelly and John Grisham and Raymond Chandler. *Learn* from them. Discover what you love about their writing. Absorb what they do: their wordplay, their methods of showing emotion or description, their cadence as storytellers. Then write. Don't try to ape them, but take what you've learned—and this isn't even necessarily a conscious learning process—and write. We all know what a Sam Spade noir detective sounds like. The important thing is that we don't know what *your* Sam Spade detective sounds like. He's not going to sound like Dashiell Hammett's Spade, because you're not Hammett.

I have a great quote from Louis L'Amour: "I took a number of stories by popular writers as well as others by Maupassant, O. Henry, Stevenson, etc., and studied them carefully. Modifying what I learned over the next few years, I began to sell."

This is exactly what I'm talking about. L'Amour apparently took a very deliberate approach, where as I tend to be a bit more haphazard myself. But what he's saying here, I think, is the crux of developing your own voice. Read, learn, adapt. This is the first step, and I imagine most Magical Words readers are avid readers already, so I'm going to assume the groundwork's already been done.

Finding Your Voice
David B. Coe

Recently Catie also wrote an essay about "voice," so potentially there is going to be some overlap between us. Catie and I might reinforce each other's points. We might disagree. That's okay. Getting more than one perspective on any of these writing issues can be a good thing.

I have long believed that "voice" is something that works on several levels. Let me offer my definition. Basically voice is the distinctive tone, mood, and style that makes any book unique. For me voice exists on four levels, and I like to distinguish between 1) Authorial Voice, 2) Genre Voice; 3) Book Voice, and 4) Narrative Voice. What do I mean by each of these? Let's take each one in turn.

Catie offered this definition: "Voice is the distinctive style that tells you who wrote the book you're reading." That is a perfect description of Authorial Voice. Every author writes differently. Clearly. You can read Raymond Chandler and Ernest Hemingway and William Faulkner, and identify stylistic quirks and tendencies that set each one of them apart. You can do the same with fantasy authors. An Anne McCaffrey book is going to read differently from a novel by Guy Gavriel Kay. They can write high fantasy, contemporary fantasy, YA fantasy, and you'll still be able to tell one from another. (Yes, I know, McCaffrey has always said that she writes science fiction and not fantasy; work with me here . . .)

An author who is just starting out might have a harder time establishing a unique Authorial Voice, for the simple reason that he or she is new at this. When we first start writing we tend to mimic others. I know I did it as I was working on short fiction and early drafts of my first couple of books. I admired Kay, and so I wanted to write like him. But I also admired the simpler, more direct style of Ursula LeGuin, and so at times I imitated her. I had read a good deal of McCaffrey and Donaldson, Card and Herbert, and I'm sure I brought elements of their writing to my own. I also had things that I liked to do that were more idiosyncratic—they were mine. And with time, what began as an amalgam of stylistic mimicry became something entirely my own. I don't think I'm unusual in this regard. Writers are readers. We learn what we like and dislike; and inevitably the styles that emerge as our own are actually alloys of individual preferences and chosen influences.

Like Authorial Voice, Genre Voice is an outside influence of a sort. Lets go back to the example I used earlier. Guy Kay and Anne McCaffrey have individual styles. But they also are guided in part by what they write. If they're both working on high fantasy, their books are going to reflect what I would call the "received culture" of that subgenre. The prose and dialogue might be somewhat more ornate than it would be for, say, a contemporary urban fantasy. The pacing might be somewhat slower. There might be more threads to the plotting. If for their next books, Kay and McCaffrey wrote urban fantasies, their books, while still distinctive, would reflect that subgenre: tight prose; terse dialogue; fast pacing. Just as an epic movie feels different from a "noir," different types of books read in certain ways. This is Genre Voice. As beginning authors move into one subgenre or another, they should familiarize themselves not only with tropes and trends of that field, but also with its voice, so that their work reads as it should. It's not that you want your work to sound like everyone else's, but rather that you want your stylistic choices to reinforce your pacing and plotting.

Book Voice might be the hardest of my four voice levels to explain. I find that every project I work on has a different feel, a different mood. Usually the Book Voice is a blend of plotting and character and worldbuilding; put another way, it is the sum of all the storytelling elements that I draw upon to write the book. I've often found that the first 50-75 pages of my own books are the ones that need to be reworked most extensively in rewrites. And I think this is because it takes me several chapters to find the right voice for the book. With time, I grow more comfortable with the characters, I start to see exactly how the plot is unfolding, what themes are developing. If the book is one of a series, I get a better sense of how this volume fits into the larger work. And so, by page 100, I have found the right tone for my writing; I have established my Book Voice for this particular novel. If I was smart, I would stop there and go back to rewrite those first fifty pages. But usually I save that for revisions.

For me, the importance of Book Voice is greatest in a series. Every series has its own style and mood (I suppose I could have created a fifth level: Series Voice). Book Voice ensures that you don't write the same book three times in a trilogy. Each book within a series should stand apart from the others. Yes, the characters and the world are the same—it might even be one extended story line—but each book should be unique. Book Voice makes that happen. One way to establish Book Voice early on is to write short fiction about characters or situations that are going to appear in the book. They don't have to be stories you send out for publication, though it's great if they are. But simply writing character studies and vignettes can help you establish that Book Voice, so that you don't have the 50-page lag I describe above.

Finally, we have Character Voice. If you're writing a book from a single point of view, then Character Voice is going to be quite similar to Book Voice. Your point of view character—your narrator—is going to establish the mood of the novel with her personality, her humanity. And yet, if you're writing a series of books all with the same POV Character, you will still have to distinguish between Book Voice and Character Voice. You want your narrator's style to be distinctive, but you don't want it to be static. Remember, every book should be different from the previous one; otherwise readers have no reason to keep reading.

It's in books with multiple point-of-view characters that Character Voice really takes on importance. If you're switching narrators, your goal as a writer should be to make each Character Voice distinctive enough that your readers don't need to be told whose point of view they're in. Again, writing short fiction about your characters can be enormously helpful in establishing Character Voice. So can taking the time to learn as much as you can about your character's background.

Finally, I find it helpful to give some of my characters (definitely not all of them) distinctive ways of speaking—a verbal tick ("ya know?"), a speech impediment (I have one character with a lisp and another who has a nervous habit of clearing his throat quite often), or even something weirder. One of my characters in my urban fantasy always talks about himself in the third person, and sometimes, for no reason, he speaks in verse. These are things that can help establish unique Character Voice. Ultimately, though, Character Voice is made by the character him or herself. It's not verbal tics, but established attributes that make a character, and his or her Voice, unique.

Getting Started: First Lines

Misty Massey

First lines in a novel are a lot like the first words you say to an attractive person at a party. You want to get it right, say the words that will make those eyes light up. If you're dull, you've lost his attention. If you're obnoxious, you've chased her away. You want that in-between spot, the phrase that's just right to draw in your reader and keep him around for the next line and the next. But how?

Alas, I can't tell you. I can't, because there's no one answer. There are suggestions, certainly. But the perfect first line is as individual as the person writing it. If you take a class or attend a workshop or conference, you'll probably be told never to begin with a phone call. Or a dream, or weather. They tell you this because amateur writers tend to choose those devices so often that editors have seen them a hundred times in every search through the slush pile. The last thing you as a writer want to do is bore the prospective buyer of your work.

When I was a kid, my mom would make baked chicken every Sunday for lunch. Every Sunday. After a long while of this, we finally begged her to make something else. Anything would do, just not the same thing we were used to. Baked chicken had become dull and uninteresting. The same thing happens to editors with story openings. If they've seen forty stories beginning with a dream this week, they aren't going to pay attention to yours. Yes, the big names can get away with it, but they've already proved to an editor that they can produce a story worth reading. Until you've done that, it's better to stick with the rules.

So no phone calls, no dreams, no weather. What's left? Well, a lot of things. When I'm beginning a story, I sit down for a while, close my eyes and envision the opening as if it's a movie. Who shows up first? Where is he? What is he holding? Who's with him? I'm fond of opening with dialogue. Think about it . . . people talking is always an attention-draw in the real world, isn't it? But dialogue can fall into that phone call category if the writer's not careful, so be sure it's the right way for your story. One of the best pieces of advice I ever received came from a rejection letter after I submitted to *Marion Zimmer Bradley's Fantasy Magazine*. "Always start your story where things begin to go wrong." If your protagonist's life turns upside down because of a car accident, try beginning with the accident. The best first lines have a hint of what's to come, even if it's the tiniest hint of all. That hint has to make me curious. It's like people whispering over the water cooler—you hear just enough to know that you want to know more. That's the job of the first line. Let's look at a few.

"With almost ludicrous care, the old man carried the pitcher of beer across the sunlit room toward the older man

who reclined propped up in a bed by the window."
—Ti m Powers, *The Drawing of the Dark*

This one's easy. Why is one man giving an invalid beer? I'm already curious on that alone. The Dark in the title refers to dark beer, and as one reads further, it becomes clear that the beer was being honored more than either of the men in the scene. It's subtle, but it's there.

"Dion Welch read auguries in rock-and-roll like some people read Tarot cards, and in very much the same manner."
—Tom Deitz, *Soulsmith*

Using songs on the radio to tell the future? How nifty was that? I was hooked, because I wanted to know how that worked. The story is about a young man destined to become the magical leader of a contemporary county in Georgia. The magic and the setting are displayed in the first line, in an easy way that gets the reader's attention.

"She wondered what it would have been like to be perfect."
—Robin Hobb, *Ship of Destiny*

Who hasn't wondered this? This time we're attracted because we can all relate to this feeling. If she's wondering how perfection would feel, what is it that makes her less? Is it the same thing that makes me imperfect? I'll keep reading just to find out what's wrong.

So now that we've talked about it a little, and maybe we're feeling brave . . . tell me your first lines. Don't share anything else about the story than that. See what people think might be going on, whether we can guess the tale from the hint of the line. Ready?

Go.

David B. Coe

My best first line is probably the opening of my most recent book, *The Horsemen's Gambit*. The story begins in the middle of a battle tournament, so it was a natural:

First blood, the rules said. Beyond that, they didn't specify. A nick of the skin, the severing of a limb, a fatal strike to the breast; any of these would do. First blood.

Charles E. Dunkley
Well, the opening line of my WIP is one I've shared here before. It's internal dialogue:

Cast! I'm bleeding.

However, I've been thinking for a while now that the novel might actually benefit from having a "pre-scene" as Faith once mentioned her editor had requested. And for similar reasons: worldbuilding among them.

At the moment, here is the first line of this pre-scene:

The prince watched, eyes widening in growing horror, as the prow of his glorious war ship was slowly swallowed in mist.

Kim Harrison
Okay, I'll play!

First line in my WIP Madison Avery III:

The hot fall sun seemed to go right through me, bouncing up from the aluminum bleachers to warm me from my feet up as I stood beside Nakita and cheered Josh on.

Not magical at all, so my editor and I agreed that we ought to stick our neck out and have a two paragraph prologue, so the very first words a reader will see are: "I'm Madison Avery, dark timekeeper in charge of heaven's hit squad . . . and fighting it all the way." Last sentence in the prologue to keep them reading: "It would be a lot easier if my own people weren't working against me."

The Opening Pages
David B. Coe

I often refer to myself as "an inertial writer." [Inertia: a body at rest will remain at rest, and a body in motion will remain in motion, unless acted upon by an outside force.] I write very slowly at the beginning of a new book or story—sometimes even at the start of a new chapter. The first day of actually writing a new book, I might only get a paragraph or two. On the second day, I'll be lucky to get two pages. The third day is a little better, and by the end of the first week, I'm usually writing at close to my normal daily pace of eight pages, or about 2,000 words. It's like getting a big rock rolling—it takes a while to kick my creativity into motion, but once it gets going, it moves along pretty well.

I have no secrets or tips for overcoming this initial inertia; if I did, I'd use them myself. I've come to see it as a natural part of my creative process. I don't fight it anymore. And I'd suggest the same approach if you find that your first few days of writing are equally slow, or even if you encounter the same problem as you start a new chapter or part of your book. Creativity is not linear, it's not always logical or consistent. Sometimes we have to be patient with ourselves and accept that some parts of writing a book are harder than others. If, after a couple of weeks, your output hasn't improved, then you might want to consider a different approach. But for those first pages, even the first chapter or two, give yourself room to grow accustomed to your new project.

What about content? I want my opening lines to reach out and grab my reader by the collar. A novel, as opposed to a short story, can move at a leisurely pace. It doesn't necessarily have to be nonstop action. Like a piece of music—be it a symphony or your favorite rock album—a good book (in my opinion) will have varying dynamics and rhythms: *Vivace* for some sections; *adagio* for others. *Forte* and then *pianissimo*. At times a book should leave a reader breathless with excitement and suspense. It should shock and frighten and arouse. But at other times, a reader should have a chance to catch his breath and regroup a little. There should be humor and quiet romance and time for a character (and the reader) to reflect. That said, I don't believe that the opening pages are a time for reflection and calm. Like the first notes of Beethoven's Fifth Symphony, they should smack you in the forehead.

I try to come up with opening sentences and graphs that will catch a reader's attention. Sometimes this means putting in action or at least suspense. Sometimes this means trying something unusual, unexpected, even strange. In my second book, I wrote of the interaction between two societies: one without technology, one with. I wanted to convey immediately the sense among those without technology that they were out of their depth. And I imagined what it would be like to know only parchment and then encounter a written message from a society like ours. My opening:

> The paper itself was a message. Immaculately white, its edges were as straight as sunbeams, its corners so sharp that they seemed capable of drawing blood.

It's a bit odd to speak of a piece of paper in those terms, but "odd" was exactly what I was going for. Another example: In one of the Forelands books, I opened in the point of view of my villain:

> What did it mean to be a God? Was it simply immortality that separated the great ones from those who lived on Elined's earth? Was it their power to bend others to their will, their ability to shape the future and remake the world as they desired? Did he not possess those powers as well? Had he not made himself a god?

In this case, I wanted his voice to be the first that my readers encountered, because he was the character who was going to drive the story throughout the book.

Which leads us to this: in composing your opening, you need to decide a few things. First, who is your point of view character for this first passage? If you only have one for the book, that's easy. If you have several, whose is the most compelling voice? Which character is most likely to intrigue and seduce your reader? For the purposes of the story, who is the most logical choice? Sometimes this will be the lead character. Sometimes it might be a secondary character who doesn't even survive the chapter. I often start my books with a killing. I establish a point of view character and then promptly kill him off. Why? Because murders can be intriguing and exciting. And also because this quickly establishes in my reader's mind that no character is safe. Even a POV character can die. When I threaten a character it might not be for effect; it might be for keeps.

Second, where in the narrative do you begin your story? This probably seems like a pretty basic question, but it's more complicated than you might think. At times I like to jump right in to the action that drives the plot. Other times I like to introduce a character, and so will place him or her in a situation that's only tangentially related to the main story line, but that establishes certain talents or abilities he/she might have that are essential to the story. And at still other times, I like to play with time and chronology.

Third, you also have to decide the setting for that first scene—not just the where (inside a castle, out on a city street, in a space ship) but also the atmospherics: night or day, sunny or stormy, raucous or quiet.

Finally, you need to make sure that the opening works with the stylistic choices you made in your planning stage. Are the voices we talked about last week still right for what you're writing, and does your opening begin to establish them? Will you write in first person or third? Will the ambiance you create be light or dark or somewhere in between? Are you writing in the noir voice of an urban fantasy, or in a style more appropriate for high fantasy?

I'm in the process of finishing the first chapter of the first Thieftaker book. My first sentence isn't really strange or innovative, but it does put the reader right into the first action, which is what I was after. The first few pages offer insights into my lead character—his past, his strengths and weaknesses. They also tell us where we are and when, they set the mood for much of what follows, and they introduce the magic system. By the end of that first chapter, which is only about 2,500 words, my reader should be informed enough to understand where they are, and intrigued enough to start reading chapter two. And ultimately, that's what the book's opening should do.

A.J. Hartley

As a "pantser," the first section is hard for me because I often don't know where the story is going when I set out. What that means, of course, is that at some point (when I DO know where the story is going) I have to take all those questions you raise about opening pages and apply them. The result is often a massive edit—even a new start, or a heavy cut. My beginnings are usually too slow and saturated with back story, so I have to find ways to cut that stuff, start with a bang and then work in the essential parts of what I cut later. I find this very difficult.

Stuart Jaffe

While I do try to plan quite a bit before I write, I find the best approach for openings to be "jump right in." I don't mean the opening must be a "jump right in" opening, I mean as the author, I have to just jump in, start writing, and see what develops. Like A.J., this approach means a hefty rewrite, but it does help figure out what works and what doesn't for an opening. However, in my latest WIP I used your method of writing short stories first. As a result, I was on a more solid footing when I began the novel and have found less problems with the opening. So, thanks!

David B. Coe

A.J., I think that the deeper I go into this series of essays, the more idiosyncratic my advice is bound to be, and probably the same will be true of people's responses to my posts. Writing is a highly individualized endeavor; everyone works his or her own way. The advice I set forth here is probably far less useful to a "pantser" than to someone who works from at least a rudimentary outline. Which is not to say that one way is right and the other way isn't. But I suppose I'm thinking that I should cast things more in terms of "this is what I do" and less in terms of "this is what you should do." If that makes any sense . . . I also believe that, for me, beginning a book is the hardest part of the writing process. Even with an outline and all the planning I try to do, I still need to rework my opening chapters pretty extensively.

You know, Stuart, that might be the best (and most succinct) advice we could offer here: just jump in. There comes a time when we have to stop thinking and rethinking, and planning, and outlining, etc., and just write. Yes, maybe it will lead to rewrites, but better that than not getting anything down on the page, right? And wow! You mean I offered advice and not only did someone take it, but it actually worked! I'm amazed. Someone should tell my kids . . . But not me; they wouldn't believe it coming from me . . .

Wave Formula

Faith Hunter

As writers, we often look for new devices to improve/change/grow our skills. Some writers refer to this is adding tools to our writing tool boxes. One of my favorite devices is the elegant Wave Formula.

The wave formula was first described by Edith Wharton and quickly became a standard for writers in the mid- and late-twentieth century, though it has fallen out of favor more recently. While it has fallen from fashion, it still works as a good writing exercise, especially teaching you (forcing you to find ways) to show instead of tell. Wave Formula appears in three parts, to solve a writer's common problem: how to introduce a character to the reader quickly and succinctly.

The presentation in three parts:
1. Feelings of the character
2. Actions of the character, or gestures
3. Dialogue of the character

Ms. Wharton said this device was like a wave making its way to the shore.
1. The motive or feelings is the power of the wind driving the wave.
2. Action or gesture is like the wave as it suddenly appears, rising, rolling up the beach.
3. The dialogue or speech is like the foam on the crest of the wave as it breaks and spills over.

It's a fluid, smooth, effective introduction of a character, and with little twists, it still works.

Here are a few Waves I've done over the years to keep my skills sharp.

Angrily, Josh tossed the picnic basket to the sand, scattering sandwiches and the lovely grapes he'd chosen with such care. "I didn't ask you here to talk about Robert. I asked you to lunch to talk about us."

Amused, Cheryl laughed, the sound oddly chilling. She stood from the sunny yellow picnic blanket and propped a hand on her hip. "Us? There is no us, Josh. Never has been. Never will be."

Confusion swept through him, followed quickly by embarrassed warmth which he knew showed on his fair features. Tommy wiped his damp palms down his dress slacks, the gesture wrinkling the fine fabric, unlike the denim he usually wore. "Good morning, Mrs. Robinson. Um. I really like that, um, outfit. Ma'am."

Pleased with the effect of the blood red polish on her nails, Emily held out all ten to admire them. "I do declare, there is something about red nail polish that is purely decadent, don't you think?"

Do you *have* to introduce a scene or character in this order and with this presentation? No. Of course not. As we've said many times before, there isn't just one way to write. A writer can introduce a character, emotion, and dialogue any way he wishes. This is the Wave Formula, and it stimulates us to write with the active voice.

Swing Thoughts + Writing Tips = Swing Tips

Faith Hunter

Swing thoughts are the few, important, special things a golfer keeps at the front of his brain before and during each shot. It might be, "Pick a target, let it happen." (That's a real swing thought as said by a caddy with a lovely accent, caught by a mic, and sent out over the airwaves.) So what do swing thoughts have to do with writing? A lot, as a matter of fact, especially when they get twisted up with writing tips. For the purpose of this group of essays I'll be blending the concept of swing thoughts with writing tips and I'll call them swing tips, just because I like the way it sounds.

These are more than just concepts and rules of writing. These are things (tips and goals) I keep close to the forefront of my mind when I write a scene, any scene, be it battle, fighting, sex, discord, discussion, fire, drowning, internal dialogue, whatever. I keep these swing tips close to my heart, like a golfer will keep his swing thoughts in mind with every swing. Why? Because I have goals for every single scene I write.

I'm a commercial writer, not an artiste. I don't expect people to agonize over my work, teach philosophy or ethics classes with my work, nor do I expect to win a Pulitzer. I'm a genre writer who wants to create heroes and stories well enough to make a living at my craft, well enough to have loyal readers who will pay for my work. I'd like that number to grow to bestseller-dom, that's the goal, but I know my limits.

Because I want people to pay their hard-earned money for my books, I want to give them the best *bang for their buck* that I can. That is my credo, oft said, though I can't remember using it here, oddly enough. *Bang for your buck.* I want readers to say, "Holy hot dang!" when they finish my books. (Or something along that vein. Be creative. I'm open to suggestions.) Swing tips help me accomplish that.

Writing, for me, is a commercial process, so as the market changes, my focus changes. For the next couple of essays, I'll be enlarging on the swing tips and on the explanations, giving reasons why keeping them in mind works for me, and reasons why they might work for others. The list below represents my current swing tips. Explanations of the first few follow.

SWING (WRITING) TIPS

BIC. Hero? Intensity and POF. Kill Off a Character. No Duh. BS (not what you are thinking). Ruthless Words. Transitions. Five Senses. Immediacy. No Excuses. No Fear.

1. BIC: The movie *Finding Forrester* has this great line: "Thinking? No thinking! Later is for thinking! Now is for writing!" More than anything else, a writer must write. I call it BIC—Butt in Chair (a phrase used at MW for years now). The same tip holds true for any creative endeavor. You're a painter? POC— Paint on canvas. You're a dancer? SSS—Stretch, stretch, stretch. You're a singer? ETVC—Exercise Those Vocal Chords. You have to *do* what you aspire to. Dreams are worthless without the effort and time and practice. In *Finding Forrester* (see it!) the two main characters are writers (Sean Connery and Rob Brown. What's not to love?) with Sean as the mentor, demanding a lot from the protégée, Rob. A LOT, especially of BIC. But his demands are effective and Rob's work takes on a maturity and fullness that is unbelievable to his teachers. That movie came to me at a time when I was not happy with my writing career, despondent, dejected, and, well, *not happy* says it all. After I saw the film, and for the next couple of weeks, I could feel things stirring inside that were like the rebirth of hope in my writing. I've joked over the years about my muse being into S&M. But that ugly, hirsute, bald muse reminds me that it's work, gritty, demanding work, not the pretty, poetic images of writing that must drive me. My muse has a whip, to remind me to, "Snap to it! Get to work!" He has boots to remind me that I have to walk the walk if I want to talk the talk, and spurs to spur me on when I want to quit. He wears a Speedo so I can see all his flaws, yet know that he (and I) can be creative. But it's all for nothing if I don't get my BIC.

2. Hero? Have I Made One?: A.) For fiction writers, both literary and genre, our plot must challenge the characters' weaknesses, which then evolve into strengths. B.)The plot must drive the weak character, then the character (changing and growing) must drive the plot. C.) Our main characters must make choices and decisions that drive the plot and their own emotional growth. Some combination of A, B, and C is what makes main characters become heroes worth remembering. Real heroes, the ones we remember long after the book or movie are forgotten, usually start off flawed, inexperienced, broken, or inadequate. When life/karma/disaster calls (or falls on) them, they rise to the occasion and develop into something far greater than they were as they solve the crisis/conflict. The flaws keep them real in the readers' eyes, make the readers want to see if and how the characters succeed despite their own inadequacies. As I write, every scene has to meet the criteria of: Am I making a hero? Does this scene make my character have to work harder to succeed? Have I shown that my character has a lot to overcome in order to succeed? Am I making it nearly impossible for him to do what I want him to do? Is there anything else I can toss at him to hurt him? And, then: Is this scene making him change? Is this awful thing that has happened making him grow? If so, then I gave Bang for my Reader's Buck.

3. Intensity and Presumption of Failure: The idea (concept) that drives a story and every scene in it must carry intensity. It has to *matter* to the reader. And it has to matter, right now, at this moment in this scene. By using flawed characters, they already start out with the presumption of failure. That's a line I like because I made it up. *The presumption of failure.* The writer and reader and the character himself have to presume he will fail, lose, even be destroyed. In a love story, it is nearly impossible for the hero and the heroine to fall in love, and then impossible for them to end up together. However, they still do. In a mystery, it is nearly impossible for the MC (main character) to solve the murder. In a thriller it is all but impossible for the MC to survive the antagonist's assault. It's my job to build that impossibility and presumption of failure, and therefore the intensity, so that the reader has a blast seeing how things work out. This has a lot to do with Immediacy which I'll cover later, but creating intensity is separate and unique. If you haven't read *Intensity* by Dean Koontz, then you have missed a writing lesson. It is spectacular in every way.

Swing Tips: Part 2

Faith Hunter

I've been breaking down my own writing for so long that I've come up with names and tags for my swing tips.

This essay covers:
Kill Off A Character. No Duh. BS (not what you are thinking).

1. Kill Off a Character: I've shared this one here before. It always gets a laugh, but I mean it utterly and seriously. It is a major swing tip for my AKA Gwen Hunter and is becoming pretty big for me in writing fantasy. Injury and/or death of someone close to us in real life is the most fearsome and awful and terrifying possibility. We hug our loved ones when we part, hoping and praying that we'll see them again. We call in the middle of the night when we've had a bad dream to make sure it all was just a dream. But when a writer has done his job and created that believability factor, and when a character (especially an important secondary character and not a minor one) dies in the middle of a story, it then becomes a part of the reader's reality. It changes the relationships between the remaining main characters. It ratchets up the intensity. So I often ask myself, "How long has it been since someone died?" If it's been a while, then my main character (MC) is getting complacent and so is my reader; things are too easy. In any novel, Rule of Thumb is "Never make things easy on a main character."

2. No Duh: Duh Moments are the result of trying to make the primary conflict easier on an MC. Making things easy is *not* my job as a writer. It might be part of a job description of a parent, a social worker, cop, whatever, but *not* of a writer. If I spot a Duh scene, moment, conversation, whatever, I rewrite and make it harder for the character to resolve the primary conflict *at this time*. Resolution is for the end of the book, not the middle. The middle of a book is for the conflict to get more difficult and dangerous and impossible. Some writer/teacher/book once said (and I'm paraphrasing, obviously) that a writer's job is to bring the main character as close to ruin—barring death—as possible. It seems counterintuitive, but the best resolutions come when things are the most difficult for the character. No Duh.

3. BS – Believable and Sympathetic: See. I told you it wasn't what you thought. My character has to be both Believable and Sympathetic (BS), yet in today's market also has to be different, unique, and well, just this side of weird in some cases. Think of Monk. In the mystery market, editors are looking for strange/ weird/odd main characters who can still be BS. The same can be said for MCs in the dark-urban and urban fantasy realms. Different, yet the reader has to care about him/her at all times. This caring part is easy to do if the character in question is a baby being held for ransom or a writer held against his will by a deranged woman. But what about the main character who is solving a crime or rescuing the princess? How do we make the character BS? I do it with a) Conflict and b) Traits.

Conflict: Conflict in the character's past, conflict so strong it affects how he does his job and lives his life during the story's timeline and pertains to the current plotline. Life-conflict that makes it harder for him to solve the main plotline conflict.

An example from one of my AKAs books, *Shadow Valley*: Mac's ex-husband was physically abusive. Her daughter is kidnapped on a photography shoot in the mountains. Mac is beaten half to death and left buried under a cairn of stones. She fights her way free of the stones but not of the ropes binding her hands. She makes her way on foot down the mountain to get help and (despite her damaged hands) joins the search and rescue. Her ex-husband, joins the scene and is part of the situation. Caleb (the main tracker) lost his son on a mountain, never found him and never recovered. In his obsessive search for the boy, Caleb lost his marriage and his job. The main characters' past conflicts affect the current conflict—to save the daughter from the man who has her. This gives the reader sympathy for the characters and helps the reader believe the way the characters work and act during the book.

Traits (we'll look at Caleb):
- Human and natural traits, AKA selfish traits. Caleb wanted to save his son, then later to find his son's body. He couldn't. He had no remorse for his suffering wife. It wasn't right and good of him, but it was part of who he was at the time. He now has a cold and unfeeling side when it comes to the people who have lost the loved ones he is searching for. They don't matter much. Only the objective matters: the lost person.
- Typical traits. Caleb has excellent eyesight, tracking skills, wood/ survival skills—the stuff you expect from trackers.
- Individual traits. He is unbearably lonely. Caleb is indefatigable. He never never never stops or gives up. He is good with horses. He pushes his searchers and himself to the brink of exhaustion.
- Moral or social traits. Caleb will give his life to save a child, even one not his own.

All this gives us a lot of BS. (Sorry. Couldn't resist.)

David B. Coe

I try to throw in some big trauma periodically as well—a death, a fight, a wound, a shocking plot twist. But—and I know that Faith is with me on this—it can't be a trauma for the sake of itself. Everything we do as writers has to further our narrative progression and/or our character's development. There has to be a point. We can't just throw s*%t at our characters because the action is flagging. It needs to be part of cohesive whole. And this is another of my personal swing tips: Keep the narrative focused.

Swing Tips: Part 3

Faith Hunter

I view every bit of my own writing with an eye to meeting certain, specific goals. I keep those goals close to my heart, like a golfer will keep his swing thoughts in mind with every swing. Without them I screw up.

This essay:
Ruthless Words. Transitions. Five Senses.

1. Ruthless Words: Words are my tool, not my captor. I use them; I don't get bound by them. That is a hard thing to keep in mind when the words are flowing and the plot is moving along. But what happens when I get lost on a tangent and can't find my way back to the original plot line? The writing is sooooo good that I can't toss it and go back to the place where I got off track. I can't! Wrong. I can, and I must be ruthless.

What happens when a scene just flows off my fingers and onto the file? When it is pure poetry, but isn't right for the novel I'm writing? That is when I use Ruthless Words. Unless I intend to self-publish (and we have agreed that there are places and people for whom self-publishing is the best method,) I need to keep in mind that a book is a one-size-fits-most product.

I'll say it in a more unsympathetic way. This manuscript? It ain't my baby. It doesn't live, it doesn't breathe. Not really. If I want to make it in the commercial market, I have to start thinking like a business person. A book is a product. It will be rewritten a dozen times according to the specifications of others. I have to be ruthless with my words. I have to be willing to cut and slash and burn when they don't work.

I have to be willing to change the flow with proper punctuation. Not punctuation the way they taught it in school. (Sorry teachers.) I have to be willing to use the skills taught there and whip them and twist them and break them into what I want, with ruthless abandon. Punctuation becomes (within limits) improper in order to meet a specific goal—the emotional impact of a scene. But I have to be ruthless even there. Too many ellipses . . . ? Cut them. Too many dangling fragments and participles and whatever? Cut them. Be ruthless. Make your prose clean and sharp as a blade. Really good prose cuts like a knife.

2. Transitions: Transitions are the most overlooked part of any book-length manuscript. I must never ignore how my character gets from point A to point B emotionally, mentally, or physically. Showing the journey *is* the plot process.

And it has to be logical!

- **Emotionally,** I have to take a character from one feeling to another in a logical manner. That seems backward, but it isn't. Most people in real life (not all, I grant you) move from emotion to emotion for reasons that—if they really want to—they can trace back to a motivational event (or series of them). A good psychologist can take years working through some tangle of emotions to his client's causative event(s). When they get there, it is a huge breakthrough. We have to be both our characters' creators and their counselors, making their emotional paths clear to the reader. Unless you are writing a character who has mental or emotional problems, the *why* (motivations), and the *changing* whys of their actions, have to be logical.

- **Mental transitions** are similar except it is easier to allow your character to make mental leaps, especially if the character is created that way in the first place, like the brilliant detective who looks at crime scene evidence in a different way, makes mental leaps, and solves the crime. But even here, it can't be magic. The character has to see or understand something in a way none of his coworkers do. It is still logical.

- **Physically,** there have to be ways and means for a character to get from place to place, and his environment has to be logical. David has talked here at Magical Words about horses and their stamina. In one of his worlds horses didn't get replaced or changed out soon enough. There was a logical disconnect. Misty's world in *Mad Kestrel* is always about water. Her boats and ships and methods of transport have to make sense in terms of water. The closed environments of her ships and boats have to be self-contained with everything she needs right there. I've had a problem writing a scene that takes place in the deep of the bayou. My character needed to set a bayou on fire. It took a lot of gasoline, so I had to find a way to get the gas where it needed to go. Logic, every-where, in every transition, is a writer's goal. And yes, even in a fantasy.

3. Five Senses: A writer's world is—or should be—fully functional in terms of its physicality. Yet the senses are often overlooked in scene setting and, when added in, can bring a scene to life. The way the light and shadows interact, the sounds that a character would hear, the way the air tastes on his tongue, the *feel* of the place in terms of temperature, humidity, etc. all impact on how a reader perceives the writer's world. The most overlooked sense is the sense of smell. The scents that are unique to a place, make me know I am there, with that character, experiencing it all. The scents draw readers in, make them one with the story. Like the memory of fresh baked cookies, the aroma warm and cozy on a winter's day. Or the milky breath of a baby or a puppy. The evergreen scent of a forest on a snowy day. The unwashed-body smell of a street person. You smell it, and it has impact. As writers we have to be aware of *all* the senses.

Misty Massey

Faith said, "This manuscript? It ain't my baby. It doesn't live, it doesn't breathe. Not really. If I want to make it in the commercial market, I have to start thinking like a business person."

When Tor first showed interest in *Mad Kestrel*, the editor wanted a huge rewrite before any offer was made. I could have refused. I could have flounced off in a huff, insisting the book was perfect as it was and Tor didn't know what it was missing. (And for a second, believe me, I wanted to!) Instead I let myself have a good, hard cry, and got to work. Because the editor's suggestions made it a much better, more saleable book. Not my baby, not the glorious reflection of my eternal soul, but a product for sale.

Faith Hunter

Misty, I think that after the changes, your book was tougher, harder, darker, with an edgy feel that it had lacked before. It was still your story in every way, but . . . distilled somehow. Clearer and cleaner. That is what a good rewrite can do when a good editor is involved in the process. Also, you proved that you were easy to work with, willing to stretch your talent.

Editors don't want a writer with an attitude and a superior mind-set. If they want to buy your book, then they want it to sell copies. The *want* to make you rich and famous, and the best way is to help you create a great book.

Swing Tips: Part 4

Faith Hunter

Immediacy: Immediacy is the way writers create suspense in the micro-scene. Sounds easy. Isn't. When you say about a book, "I couldn't put it down," it's because every scene pulled you into the next and into the next. Immediacy is the result of using power words and details to increase awareness of the conflict and pull the reader forward. The result of getting immediacy right is suspense. It is much like a dance, with words as the steps, and the writer in the lead.

Immediacy is required on every page of a novel, is needed through every scene, to keep the reader grounded in the story. Do I get it right every time? No. But it is my goal.

Immediacy happens when the writer blends the known, and is used a *lot* by fantasy and urban fantasy writers to create mood and setting. Immediacy is influenced by a few details: the Diet Coke can, the Armani suit, the Dolly Parton wig, the golden-oldie Tina Turner song on the radio.

In *Skinwalker*, I used the device extensively in the first thirty-two pages to draw the reader in. I'll break down a few paragraphs here to show what I did and why. Jane Yellowrock (vampire killer) is following a bodyguard (she has nick-named Troll) down a hallway to meet his boss. My comments are at the end of each paragraph.

I followed him down a narrow hallway that made two crooked turns toward the back of the house. We walked over old Persian carpets, past oils and watercolors done by famous and not so famous artists. The hallway was well lit with stained-glass Lalique sconces every few feet. They looked real, not like reproductions, but maybe you can fake old; I didn't know. The walls were newly painted a soft butter color that worked with the light to illuminate the paintings. Classy joint for a whorehouse. The Christian children's home schoolgirl in me was both appalled and intrigued. (*The details are rich and subdued and set the scene. Her reaction is curiosity and detail-oriented and tells us a lot about Jane. The words I worked on the most because they lead into the dance of suspense are: followed, crooked, fake, Classy joint for a whorehouse, and intrigued. They all lead us on, pulling us forward, creating immediacy. The dance image is through the active verbs, and it's similar to the opening steps of a tango when the lead and his partner take the first steps and one another's measure.*)
When Troll paused outside the red door at the hallway

end, I stumbled, catching my foot on a carpet. He caught me with one hand and I pushed off him with very little body contact. I managed to look embarrassed when he shook his head. He knocked. I braced myself and palmed the cross he had missed in his pat-down. And the tiny two-shot derringer. Both hidden against my skull on the crown of my head, and covered by my braids, which men never ever searched, as opposed to my Luchesse's which men always had to stick their fingers in. It was a partial excuse for the faux stumble and having my hands high. (*Stumbled, catching, very little body contact, managed to look embarrassed, braced myself, palmed. The rest of the para is explanation, which is necessary for the next para to work. It does slow down the pacing, but this is the first time we learn about her hidden weapons. The benefit is the reader has to wonder why she needs weapons for a job interview. More forward movement creating conflict. If we use the dance image here, it is like a tango, two characters moving together, yet at cross purposes, to create a story and set a scene.*)

He opened the door and stood aside. The room was neat and Spartan, but each of the pieces within looked Spanish. Old Spanish. Like Queen Isabella and Christopher Columbus old. The woman, wearing a teal dress and soft slippers, standing beside the desk, could have passed for twenty until you looked in her eyes. Then she might have passed for said Queen's older sister. Old, old, old eyes. Peaceful as she stepped toward me. Until she caught my scent. (*The details are slow and all of them dance around the repetitive use of the word old. "Until she caught my scent." Which pulls us into the next para, and is like a quick turn on the dance floor.*)

In a single instant her eyes bled red, pupils went wide and black, and her fangs snapped down. She leaped. I dodged her, sliding under her leap as I pulled the cross and ripped the derringer from my scalp, to the far wall where I held out the weapons. The cross was for the vamp, the gun for the Troll. She hissed at me, fangs fully extended. Her claws were bone white and two inches long. Troll pulled a gun. A big gun. Men and their pissing contests. Crap. Why can't they ever just let me be the only one with a gun. (*single instant, bled red, pupils, wide, black, fangs snapped, leaped, dodged, sliding, pulled, ripped. The action active words and punctuation give us speed and intensity. Cross, gun, hissed, fangs, claws, bone, gun, big gun, pissing contests, Crap. These pull us through the action and back into the character's head all at once. In a dance, where the lead whirls his partner into a turn and back and stops abruptly. The female dancer's dress has an instant to settle.*)

"I'm not human," I said, my voice steady. "That's what

you smell." I couldn't do anything about the tripping heart rate, which I knew would drive her further over the edge. But I'm an animal. Biological factors always kick in. So much for trying not to be nervous. *(not human, tripping heart rate, drive, further, animal, kick in, nervous. All these words are the finish of one dance movement, a micro element in the book that sets the tone, pace, relationships, conflict, and pull the reader forward into the next para and the next. We end at an impasse, the characters ready for the next movement in the dance.)*

At the end of every scene I ask myself, did I achieve immediacy? Do the readers want more? Do they want to follow me into the next dance set? Have I left them bent over my arm, stretched to the breaking/falling point, dependant on me to bring them back for more? If not, then I haven't done my job as a writer.

Swing Tips: Part 5

Faith Hunter

These two are vastly different from the other swing tips. And these two hurt. They are internal, they are part of me. They may not appear inside any of you. But for me they are the most real things in the world. My own personal dragons to slay. The nitty-gritty of what goes on inside me at the *worst* writing times.

1. No Excuses: This isn't something that I look for in every scene, but rather something that I look for, watch for, see coming, in every manuscript, and again in every rewrite. It is the time, the one single dark moment, when I want to stop. When that moment hits, it is paralyzing. It steals over me in a heavy cloud. I know that I haven't reached the goal for that day. I am at that point in the manuscript or rewrites where nothing, but nothing, seems to be going right. Every bit of dialogue is flat, the final scene is a hundred pages away, or the little things in the rewrite are done and now I have to tackle the big things and they look like a *mountain* of work and I don't see the end. Not anywhere. I am tired. Drained. Close to the edge. It is just too hard to go on. It is also when the dreaded but nonexistent Writers Block usually appears.

If I didn't have a contract and a freaking deadline I'd shove it under the bed, close the file, burn the paperwork, and quit. Find something else to write. Something that works. Something fun. Something shiny and new. God, I *hate* this manuscript, this character, this story. I Just. Want. To. Stop. Yeah. Me. I want to quit. Usually I say, "No play until I do the job." BIC, right? Usually. Well, *No Excuses* is indeed similar to BIC. But it is more. It is that thing inside a commercial writer that separates him from a happy dilettante.

I don't have any wise words for you here. I don't know why some writers push on through and finish a book or a rewrite and why some give up. I don't know. But for me it is No Excuses. It is when I keep working even when I hate it. It is what drives me back to the keyboard or the hard copy to *finish the damn book*. No. Freaking. Excuses.

2. No Fear: This, too, isn't a scene-by-scene tip I watch for. It is internal and amorphous and nebulous. It is pride. It is worry. It is the old pocketbook. It is fear that I may never write again or may never sell another book. It wakes me up in the middle of the night. It brings on depression if I am not careful—and I've struggled with depression many times in my life so I can see it coming.

But no one can help me with my fears. They are mine to do with as I please. *Mine—to do with as I please.* I can fight them, injure them, slay them, treat them with medication. But I must always remember that my fear is owned by me, not the other way around. I *can* do this! There *will* be another story. And if I have to start my career over again someday, well, practice makes perfect. I've done that before and I can do it again. Because, *by God,* I am writer.

No Fear.

Lasagna and Info-Dumps

Faith Hunter

Okay, I know you're saying, *What?!?* But hey—it's an analogy (or is that a metaphor?) that I've used in seminars for years.

There are similarities between a well-made lasagna and the way a skilled author inserts back-story into current narrative, and similarities with the way an unskilled author and unskilled chef write and cook.

There are back-story rules (rules of thumb, not actual laws on paper, with back-story police to enforce them) for every genre. And every genre is different. Can you get away with breaking the rules? Sure. But if you want to wow an agent and editor (and the discerning reader) learning how to make back-story work like a good lasagna is a very smart idea.

Bad lasagna means that the onion is in one corner, the meat is in the other corner, the cheese is in a lump. The tomatoes are sitting between the meat and the cheese, and the spices are spilled into a pile. The noodles... well they get to be stacked on the bottom like lumber and the garlic is all icky and smelly off by itself. Nothing is chopped and spread out. Every bite tastes different, is a new experience and nothing is coherent. Really bad food.

Bad info-dump is where all the info you need is squished together into one big pile and dumped on the reader, stopping the story. It reads (tastes) different from the rest of the story. It stops everything. And the next time you need to tell the reader something, you do the same thing and it tastes different from either of the other tastes.

Are you beginning to see the picture? Back-story needs to be offered in small doses, chopped into tiny bits and scattered into the book. Let's say you are writing a mystery series and you have told several things in previous books that you need to remind the reader (and explain to new readers) in order for this book to work:

A. A young woman, mother of three has been murdered.
B. There is a million-dollar insurance policy at stake.
C. The husband has an ironclad alibi because he was sleeping with the chief of police at the time.
D. No one knows the chief is gay. (C and D are the most important parts of the back-story, and have to be handled carefully.)
E. The main character is a police investigator.

There are several ways you can tell all of this:

A. Prologue scene with the chief and his lover. (Get your minds out of the gutter. Not *that* kind of scene.) This only works if you are using multiple third-person POV. If first person, then it gets more difficult.
B. Flashback and its sister, the flashback prologue. (Rule of thumb in mystery: flashbacks should only be used in second 1/3 of book, so it would be too late.)
C. Dialogue that reveals the affair and the controversy and the problem with the insurance.
D. And my personal favorite: break it up into little segments of dialogue, internal flashback (in the main character's mind), and scenes scattered throughout the book. The reader who had been with you for several books knows what's up and catches the clues and hints, and the new reader is intrigued but not overwhelmed.

You can open any way you want, as long as it fits the POV and the story line. *But!* Yeah, you knew there was going to be one of those, didn't you? Most long-time editors are pretty sick of the prologue scene and the flashback prologue. I know a couple of editors who say they'll stop reading as soon as it becomes apparent that a new (unpublished) writer has opened a book that way. So what do you do? You give the reader (in this case that editor you so want to impress) the back-story in little bits and pieces in the story-line.

I make a list of things the reader needs to know, and then I make sure the info is inserted in the first fifty pages, checking off the things as I go. No one gets bored, shocked with a new tone (taste) or pulled out of the story.

Okay, now you know about lasagna and back-story info dumps.

Happy cookin—! Uhhh . . . Happy writing!

Natalie Hatch

So do you start a story in the middle of the action and then slowly reveal the backstory through dialogue/action/reaction type things? And when is enough enough? When does a writer know they've given the reader enough to work it out for themselves?

Faith Hunter

Good question, Natalie. And I doubt you'll like my answer, because there isn't one. Of course, that never stopped me before . . .

Understanding when enough back-story is enough is the balancing act that all writers do in the creative process. I don't really just write a book, I build it, like building a house. As I write, I go back and make sure the foundation is strong enough to support the bricks and mortar of the story, and that there are windows and doors enough for the reader to see what is going on inside without dumping a *telling session* on him. It can be a tricky process. Some things need to be said twice, in fact, to drive the point home to new readers, but that is why I make a check-off list to keep track, and a constantly updated outline handy, much like a builder refers to his house plans.

The writing is there. Don't get me wrong. I *love love love* the parts that are just that wild, totally creative, can't-stop-to-take-a-breath writing, but a lot of it is more (less?) than that. It's work.

And like I said—rules-of-thumb are meant to be broken (rules, not thumbs). Catie's book, *The Queen's Bastard*, starts out with several flashback vignettes, and they worked well. But Catie didn't have one of the old-time, crusty, outspoken, NYC editors or an aged agent like I am speaking about, and also, it wasn't her first novel. Unpublished writers often have different standards to meet because they have a different vetting process. I say "often," not always, because there are *always* exceptions. It's what makes this business so tricky, fascinating, entertaining, and nail-bitingly annoying.

Conveying Background While Avoiding Info-Dumps
David B. Coe

One of the trickiest things a writer has to do in any work of fiction is provide background information, be it about a character, a pre-existing circumstance central to the plot, or a detail about worldbuilding. The last thing we want to do in telling our stories is to slow down narrative momentum with what is commonly referred to as an "info-dump." An info-dump is an extended expository section that serves no other purpose than to fill in background information. Sometimes info-dumps come in the form of narrative asides; other times they appear in highly contrived conversations. The classic instance of this is the "As you know, Bob . . ." approach, where in the guise of normal discussion a character gives an expansive description of a world's political structure, or the land's magic system, or some unique and no doubt highly creative quirk of planetary geology.

The problem we face as authors of speculative fiction is that our stories are often dependent upon arcane points of magic or worldbuilding or alternative history that our readers absolutely HAVE to know. So the question becomes, how do we convey this information without resorting to the dreaded "info-dump," without slowing our narrative, and without offering it in a manner that comes off as totally contrived?

Let's begin with a couple of basic points that I like to keep in mind as I'm writing. (As always, please remember the Magical Words Mantra: There's no single right way to do any of this.) First, as much as I would like to tell my readers everything about my worlds, my characters, my magic systems, etc. it's neither necessary nor advisable to do so. And second, just as I try to pace my action and character development, I also pace myself when it comes to giving out background information.

Put another way: I usually try to tell my readers what they absolutely NEED to know at any given moment in a book. If they need rudimentary information about, say, my magic system early on in order to keep up with the narrative, then that's what I give them. If there are more arcane points that are central to the plot, but that don't come into play until much later, then I save that information and slip it in elsewhere.

Finally, I like to keep in mind my own experience as a reader of speculative fiction. I have found myself frustrated by a lack of understanding when authors are too slow or too obscure in giving out information. But I also like to discover things about a new world as I read. That process of discovery is fun, it's one of the things I love about our genre. Give away too much too soon, and that sense of discovery is blunted somewhat, at least it is for me.

All of this is not to say that you can't give out information at all. Sometimes we have to, and just as it's important to avoid info-dumps, it's also important to remember that not every paragraph that gives background information should be considered an info-dump. Readers have to understand the world in which they find themselves. They need to know about the characters they encounter and the problems with which these characters grapple. Conversation can be a terrific way to pass on information while furthering plot. But it's important to keep your characters speaking in natural believable ways. For instance, if you were writing a conversation about our current politics you probably wouldn't do it like this:

> "So, Faith, how do you think Barack Obama, our first African American President, is doing?"
> "Well, David, as you know, he's only had 100 days in office, and has had to deal with an economic crisis, wars in Iraq and Afghanistan, a swine flue epidemic, and other crises. Also, because he is African American, and because our nation has had a troubled racial history, he's come under intense media scrutiny. So I think he's doing pretty well on the whole, all things considered."

People just don't talk that way. They don't in our world and they shouldn't in imagined worlds either. Instead, you might take a more subtle approach, give your readers a bit less detail, but still convey the important points, knowing that you can fill in information as the story develops:

> "So, Faith, how do you think Obama's doing?"
> "Not bad considering the load of crap he's had to deal with. He's had what? Three months? But with the whole race thing, people are watching so closely. I can't believe all the media hype this past week."

That's how people talk. And though the details are spare, we've still managed to convey a great deal. There are racial issues in this society, there is media scrutiny focused on this "Obama" character, times are tough, and this guy is pretty new to his office. Not a bad starting place, and we've done nothing to make the narrative or the conversation seem contrived.

Another way to convey information is through flashbacks or internal monologues as long as these, too, maintain a natural feel and don't detract from narrative flow. Here's an example from *Rules of Ascension*, the first book in my Winds of the Forelands series. The entire series revolves around racial conflict between the Eandi, who are people like us, and the Qirsi, who are sorcerers. This is the first passage in which I mention the Qirsi:

Since early morning he'd been restless and uneasy, the way he sometimes felt before a storm. Perhaps it's only that. Morna knew they needed the water. But he knew better. Something was coming, something dark.

Kara used to say that he had Qirsi blood in him, that he had the gleaning power, like the Qirsi sorcerers who traveled with Bohdan's Revel. They always laughed about it, Pytor reminding her that he was much too fat to be Qirsi. Still, they both knew that he was usually right about these things.

Two brief paragraphs, but again we've learned a fair amount. The Qirsi are sorcerers. Some or all of them can tell the future. They don't look like Pytor's people, at least in the sense that they're slimmer (actually they're frail, but that information comes later, building on this). We know that there's this Revel thing that travels the land. A fair perhaps? We know that Pytor has a woman named Kara in his life, though the way it's phrased, she might not be alive anymore (she's not). And who's this Morna person? A goddess, perhaps, from the way she's invoked here? I haven't answered all the questions, and in fact I've raised as many as I've answered, but sometimes knowing which questions to ask is a good start, and here I've at least begun the process of introducing my world and the people in it.

The fact is, I'm not always very good at this, and I could give you plenty of examples of passages that border on info-dumps (for fans of *Rules of Ascension*, check out pp. 36-37 in the hardcover or pp. 23-24 of the paperback to see how poorly I handled my discussion of the actual rules of ascension).

Again, it comes back to the points I raised early on: you don't have to tell your readers everything, and you don't have to tell them all they need to know in one passage. Give out information naturally, gradually. For those of you writing the second or third book of a series, this also pertains to the information about past books that you convey to your readers. When you reacquaint readers with characters or plot threads, you don't have to review all that's come before. Rather, hit the key points and move on with the new action. Ideally you should aim to make your book accessible to those who might not have read book I or book II, but as with other background information you don't want to sacrifice the narrative integrity of this book to familiarize readers with the previous volumes.

Faith Hunter

David, I am a big proponent of the tomato sauce method of info dispersal. Chop small, mix well, cook slow. (Or info drip! I like that too!) But in *Bloodring* my editor actually *wanted* all the world history in the first fifty pages. It blew me away!

The only way I could get it all in was to have it be the anniversary of the *day the world changed* and show it on TV. Looking back, I still don't like it. It still feels like a cheap way to do it. But hey—the editor wanted what she wanted and it was my job to make her happy. It goes back to the comment we make here so often: *there's no single right way to write a book.*

Word Choice and Pacing

Faith Hunter

The question has been asked (paraphrased here) "How does word choice and sentence structure affect the reader, and how can we do our job as writers better?"

It's a big subject and I could teach on that for days at a con. As with any topic about writing, there are the macro devices and effects and the micro devices and effects. And I think it comes back to pace. When a writer is doing a good job pacing story arcs, character-development arcs, scene anchoring, and stays in character voice, then the macro and micro parts of word choice all fall together. Pace on the macro level can be described as the speed of the conflict development, or the speed at which the story develops. Or, simpler: Macro pace is the events per page or chapter. Micro pace is the pace by line and word.

For the purpose of this essay, I'll concentrate on Macro pace and Micro pace as they relate to voice, story, and the emotional reaction of the reader.

Just a rule of thumb about sentence structure: To increase the pace, use shorter sentences and sentence fragments; to decrease the pace, use longer, more descriptive sentences. The reader *hears* the increased or decreased pace as well as *feels* it. A well-crafted scene can and will affect the breathing and heart rate of a reader. But, as with anything, it can be overdone. When a writer tosses in nothing but short sentences and fragments to speed up the pace, the reader has no time to reflect or pull it all together. Longer, more complex sentences in the midst of the shorter ones become necessary to allow the reader to regroup.

Awful sentence structure:

> His dark blue eyes and pinpoint pupils touched me where I stood, trapped and shivering in the corner, dripping wet and wrapped in my floral towel. He took a single, long step toward me and wrapped his fist into my hair as he pulled me close. I noticed the strong smell of cheap wine on his breath as he smiled.

Breakdown of what is wrong with this example:

> His dark blue eyes and pinpoint pupils *(There are two items, when the reader should focus on one)* touched me *(Just touched? Where is the menace?)* where I stood, trapped and shivering in the corner, dripping wet and wrapped in my floral *(who cares that it's floral? If I had paced the scene properly, I'd have mentioned the towels*

earlier, before the menace started.) towel. *(Are we waltzing here? I'm trying to write a scene that should grab and slap the reader emotionally. And this sentence does not do that.)* He took a single, long step toward me and wrapped his fist into my hair as he pulled me close. *(Ditto)* I noticed *(passive word choice in an action scene slows every thing down.)* the strong smell of cheap wine on his breath as he smiled.

It just didn't work. A better version:

> Pinpoint pupils in dark blue eyes speared me. Trapped, I backed into the corner. Pulled the towel closer to my dripping body. With a single step, he reached me. Twisted his hand into my wet hair. Pulled me close. The scent of cheap wine rolled over me, a wave of fear. And he smiled.

Broken down:

> Pinpoint pupils in dark blue eyes speared *(menacing word choice, and one thing the reader actually sees—eyes)* me. *(The previous sentence is not broken, but it leads into shorter structures.)* Trapped, I backed into the corner. *(Action and reaction is predator/prey response. It resonates in our primitive hindbrains.)* Pulled the towel closer to my dripping body. *(Fragments can increase tension.)* With a single step, he reached me. Twisted his hand into my wet hair. Pulled me close. The scent of cheap wine rolled over me, a wave of fear. *(Longer sentence, now, the reader gets to regroup, and active word choice, despite the fact that it's about the character's reaction.)* And he smiled.

Notice the difference in rhythms: example #1 is waltz-like and thoughtful; example #2 is more like a machine gun. The word choice is emotionally cleaner and sharper. If you want to take the bad example, or even the better one, and make it even better, go for it!

If you don't own a *really* good thesaurus, one that offers and explains the emotional nuances of individual words, then I suggest you get one. It can make all the difference in the world to your writing.

David B. Coe

You are just so good at the writing samples thing. Much better than I could ever be. This is a great way to introduce the topic. Word choice and pacing are so important to conveying mood, emotion, as well as character and narrative. You and I write differently, so my example 2 would differ from yours, but the effect would be similar I think. Wonderful stuff, Faith.

Stuart Jaffe

Sentence structure is key to pacing and your examples illustrate this admirably.

Regarding the "pinpoint pupils," in the final version they connect with the word "speared" so well. Pinpoints spearing is perfect—it's sharp, dangerous, and sets up the rest of the paragraph. Sometimes we have to go for the emotional weight of our word choices over the more practicality of the choice.

Faith Hunter

Full sentences are the product of, and stimulate, intelligence. Researchers tell us that being exposed to varied, complex language in our early years can stimulate intelligence in human young. And those young people then grow up to speak and write in full, complex sentences, a bit like the snake eating its own tail.

But under pressure, stress, fear, our minds revert to hindbrain thinking, to images instead of language, and when there is language it's broken, fractured, repetitive, and carries the rhythm of the speeding heart. (Being part of the first response team in an ER for years has given me an assurance of this.)

As a writer, I have to show the reader what is happening, what the character is feeling, without telling. Speaking to that hindbrain in us all is one way.

I once heard an agent say that he could always tell when an English major sent him a book, because the sentences were all so perfect. He was being insulting. For him, perfect sentences were lacking in voice and tone and emotional context, and I've thought about that for some time now.

Perhaps his comment had merit, in part, because perfect, complete sentences speak only to the frontal brain, not the animal brain in each of us. The hindbrain is not poetic. The hindbrain is prey and predator. We have to speak to the total person when we write, and part of us is animal.

Can it be done with full sentences, even when the character is facing great danger? Yes. Is it easy? Of course not. For a lot of us, language itself is a stumbling-block. For me, short, fractured, broken, splintered language fits with fear. For me, it works.

The Leading Edge of the Slog
David B. Coe

Let's say we've done the prep work, found our voice, and gotten to work on the opening lines and pages. At this point we've had some time to get to the meat of the project, to move beyond the opening chapter and really delve into the book. So, how's it going?

Hmmmm . . . Not the enthusiastic "It's going great!" response I was hoping for. I hear some enthusiasm, but I also hear some grumbling. So maybe this would be a good time to chat about writing the vast middle of a novel. We'll define "the middle" as everything between the end of Chapter 1 and the beginning of the climactic chapter. I did say it was a "vast middle," after all . . .

Defining the middle so broadly, it almost becomes inevitable that this will be the hardest part of the book, the place where you'll encounter the most problems. And quite often those problems begin to manifest themselves early on. The excitement of the opening is behind you; the payoff of the climax seems miles away. Now it's all about character growth and narrative flow and pacing. It's about putting the worldbuilding and background development to practical use. In short, it's about work. Welcome to the slog.

I don't mean to say that this part can't be fun. Of course it can. But make no mistake: it is difficult, long, at times exhilarating, but at times deeply discouraging. Let's look at some potential scenarios that you may encounter, and discuss possible solutions.

Scenario 1: You're forty pages into your novel. It's going a bit more slowly than you expected, in part because you've found that your plans for the book (whether in the form of a true outline, or merely the collected thoughts you keep in your head) are already falling by the wayside. The novel you envisioned and the novel you're writing bear little resemblance to one another. It's as though the characters have conspired against you—an imaginary *coup d'etat* as it were—and have taken over the book. It's not that what you've got is bad, it's just not what you thought it would be, and so you're really not sure anymore where the book is going.

Solution: Congratulations! That's great news! Seriously. Keep on doing exactly what you're doing. I outline. And my outlines rarely remain relevant for more than a few chapters. The fact that your characters are taking over means that they have come alive, that they have become something more than names on a page and collections of traits and bullet points in a history.

So what's the point of outlining or of planning a novel? For me, it gives me some guidance at the outset. It points me in the general direction and allows me to set out with some sense of purpose. But writing a book is an organic process, and sometimes that means jettisoning the outline and the plans and following your instincts. And those instincts often manifest themselves through the things your characters do and say. Where is your book headed? Right now that's a bit uncertain. But have faith in the process and in the characters you've created. They will lead you where you need to go. And chances are that when you get there it will be more similar to your envisioned ending than seems possible right now.

Scenario 2: You're a hundred pages in and everything *seemed* to be going fine, but now you've hit a wall. The story has dried up on you. You thought there was a book here, but now it seems you were wrong. There's nothing. No plot, no direction, no reason to be doing this. You were never meant to write. Why the hell didn't you listen to Mister Gerlach, your high school guidance counselor, when he said that selling insurance was a perfectly legitimate way to make a living? You've stuck to the outline for the most part, but now you see that the plot you'd outlined originally is riddled with holes, and the ending won't work.

Solution: Okay, first things first. Pour out that cup of coffee and trade it in for a glass of wine. Or brandy. Or single-malt . . . You need to relax. The story is still there; maybe not in the form you thought it would take, but in some other form that is *closer to the original than you think*. It may be that you've taken one false turn that has led you down a path to a narrative cul-de-sac. I often find that when I get stuck it's because I've done just that. I've made one narrative choice that has taken me off the path. If I can backtrack to that decision and go in a different direction I can usually solve the problem.

Sometimes though, the problem is more fundamental. Sometimes I'll plot things one way only to realize once I'm into the book that the plot points don't all line up. My impulse is to panic, but once I calm down I can usually see that the problem can be fixed. Look at your major plot points, the big events that lead you from the set-up to the conclusion. Which ones don't work? Chances are most of them still do. Your job is to find the few that don't and change them. Yes, you need to fix this, but no, it doesn't mean that your book is crap or that Mister Gerlach was right . . .

Scenario 3: Everything is going just the way you planned. You're making great progress and it's all good. No problems at all.

Solution: [Hysterical laughter] I'm sorry. I couldn't resist. Cracks me up every time. This never, ever happens. Let's move on.

Scenario 4: You're pretty much on course with your original plans, and the plotting does seem to be holding up. But the book lacks something—sparkle, punch, that breathtaking excitement you were hoping for. Whatever you call it, it's not there. What seemed like a thrilling idea seems to be turning into a somewhat pedestrian story and while you think the climax will be good, you're still far enough from it to fear that you won't hold your reader's attention long enough to get there.

Solution: Yeah, we've all experienced this one, too. Sometimes a story that looked great in planning falls flat. That doesn't mean the book is destined to fail. But it does mean that you need to shake things up. You don't want to introduce action for the sake of action—no Apple Cart scenes, as Faith would put it. You need to keep the narrative moving forward. One solution might be to introduce a new character—a love interest, a second villain, a sidekick. Someone who complicates things in such a way as to create more conflict and action. Or you can take someone away. When was the last time you killed a character? Has it been too long? Start sharpening the knives... Or you can make a small change with huge ramifications. I had this problem with the original version of the book I'm working on now. So I changed the villain's gender from male to female. Totally changed the book and the tension level, introducing a sexual dynamic to her battles with my protagonist. What can you change to shake up your book?

Of course, this is not a comprehensive list of possible scenarios. But it's a good place to start.

A.J. Hartley
For what it's worth, I find that when I run into versions of these "second act problems" it's because my character's conscious goals aren't clear enough. The story loses urgency because my characters are getting passive and I need to rethink what exactly they are supposed to be doing and why.

David B. Coe
A.J., that's great advice, and something I don't do nearly enough. We should be asking ourselves again and again, what our characters are doing and how it relates to their needs/goals/purpose. As soon as we lose sight of those things, of course the narrative will begin to languish.

Mark Wise
I am a little #1 and mostly #4. I think I know what I need to add tension and spice to the book, but I am driven to write forward rather than go back to Page 1 and make changes. I am someone who wants

to write a rough draft regardless of the quality, then go back and make the required changes.

Is that a good way to write or am I shooting myself in the foot by not stopping and fixing the problems?

David B. Coe

Mark, our usual caveat is "There is no right way to do this; different approaches work well for different people." But my answer to your question would be an emphatic NO. You are not shooting yourself in the foot. You're doing exactly what you should be doing. Get the book finished. Don't retreat into rewrites. There is nothing that can't be fixed later once you see how the entire project has turned out. I didn't always feel this way. But I do now, based on years of experience. Move forward, my friend. And then go back to fix. Make sure to jot down notes to yourself so that you remember the changes you intend to make, but then keep going.

Getting Started . . . Again
C.E Murphy

A few days ago someone asked a pretty good question on my regular blog, and I thought I'd bring it over here to answer:

"Do you find it difficult to stop writing your current work, and then pick it back up the next day? I realize that a writer writes, and must write if they want to get paid, but is picking a story "back up" the next day something you had to learn? If so, I'd love to know how."

If I'm lucky enough to find it hard to stop writing, I usually don't until I've achieved a phenomenal word-count. Most of the time that doesn't happen.

There are a bunch of tricks to picking a story back up. I know people who re-read the previous day's work, doing edits and revisions before moving on to the new day's work. I do a little of that, especially if it's been a while since I've worked on something (I'll usually re-read the whole thing then). I also know people who will stop in the middle of a sentence so they've got something they know how to finish, which gets them writing right away. (That doesn't work for me. I just forget what I was going to write!)

I do like to stop when I know exactly what the next scene needs to do. That gives me a place to pick up. I'll sometimes leave myself a note in the manuscript so I don't forget what I think needs to happen.

In an ideal situation, the book I'm writing is so compelling that I basically can't wait to start writing every day, so sitting down and getting started isn't a chore. That doesn't happen very often and it's one of the reasons I took Solitaire *off* my writing computer: it's usually much easier to start playing games than it is to start writing.

What are some other tricks to getting back to the keyboard? Anybody got other clever ideas?

David B. Coe

My grad school advisor recommended the stop-in-the-middle-of-the-sentence thing, but it doesn't really work for me, either. I tried it when I was working on my dissertation, but fiction is a different beast. I try to stop on the cusp of something I'm eager to write, that I know will come easily, like a scene I've visualized a hundred times already. Sometimes, though, I stop at a place that proves to be a better stopping point than it is a starting point the following day. In those cases, it's simply a matter of putting my butt in the chair and slogging through those first paragraphs.

And for the record, I had to take solitaire and Spider off my machine as well.

The End Game

David B. Coe

Writing a novel takes a while, and every writer works at a different pace. That's why this essay isn't called "Finishing Your Novel" or "The End" or something of that sort.

It's called "The End Game," because even if you're only a third of the way done with your book, it's never too early to start thinking about how you're going to tie off loose ends and build to that stunning climax. We give you a lot of "writing is like . . ." analogies here at Magical Words, and I'm about to give you a few more. Baseball fans: Writing is like pitching. When a major league pitcher goes through the batting order the first time, he doesn't just look for ways to get batters out. He also tries to set up the next at bat and the one after that by showing certain pitches and holding others in reserve. Chess players: When a master plays, there is more to each move than a grab for momentary strategic advantage. A great player plans her attacks three or four or five moves in advance. She lays the groundwork for a series of moves, and (she hopes) for eventual victory.

The writing end game is not so different from any of these. Even if you're a seat-of-the-pants writer, you still need to lay a foundation for your narrative progression. "But," you say, "as writers, we don't want to give away too much to our readers." And you're right. Like pitching or playing chess, the end game in writing is not just about setting up the climax, it's also about misdirection, about keeping readers somewhat off balance.

My goal for the endings of my books is for my readers to say "Oh!" and then "Of course!" In other words, I want them to be surprised, but I also want them to be able to go back over the book and see that I left clues along the way, and that the surprise ending wasn't just something I made up on the fly. Why? Because when it comes right down to it, readers love to be surprised, but they don't like to be manipulated or deceived.

Of course, it's not just about the actual ending; it's also about the build-up, that ratcheting of the tension that makes a good book so much fun to read. That's part of the end game as well, and it, too, needs to begin early in the book.

Let me give a couple of examples from my WIP, hopefully without giving away any spoilers. One of my subplots, established fairly early in the book, is actually a red herring of sorts, something that later serves to misdirect my readers as they try to figure out who my villain is and what s/he is up to. I planned it that way from the start and worked those clues into the story at intervals to keep my readers guessing. But at another point I realized midway through the book that I needed to have my hero do something dark and painful in order for him to survive a particularly difficult encounter with said villain. I hadn't realized this until the midpoint of the book. And so I had to go back through the early chapters of the book and plant the seeds for this very emotional moment. The clues I planted were subtle—early on they will seem like throwaways to my readers—but they are crucial to the impact of the plot point in question.

My point is this: you don't have to use a book outline to work on the end game of your novel. There is no reason why you can't surprise yourself when you finally figure out that perfect ending. But when revising, you might need to go back and add a few lines here and there to set it up. This is the advantage we have over the baseball pitcher and the chess player. We get to amend and adjust.

The important thing to remember about the end game is that, contrary to what many non-writers believe, writing is, in fact, an interactive art form. The interaction may come later, after the creative product is finished, but that doesn't make it any less real to our readers. They want to play along. They want to have a chance at figuring things out. Recently Misty commented on a book she was reading that disappointed her because it was too predictable. She had figured out where it was going and though she hoped she was wrong, she wasn't. There's a lesson there, obviously: you don't want your set up to be so heavy-handed that you telegraph the ending. But there's a second lesson as well: Misty was playing the game, trying to figure out the mystery. She didn't want to finish the book and say, "Yup, saw that coming." At the same time, though, I'm guessing that she also didn't want to finish it and say "He cheated! There is no way the story could end that way!"

The end game is a balancing act. Yes, a good ending surprises, but it also satisfies. Play the end game right, and you should manage to do both. You may not get it right on the first try, and this is where beta readers come in. Your first draft might give away too much; your second might be too opaque. Be patient. The end game is one of the hardest parts about writing a book. It's also the most gratifying once you get it right.

Stuart Jaffe

Another sports analogy for you—pool. A good pool player will think ahead several steps, so that when he hits the cue ball he will a) sink the shot, b) put the proper spin on the cue ball so that it will roll to the best location to make the next shot easy and c) (with a true expert) have picked the best next shot so that he can easily set up the third, fourth, and fifth shot. The end game is always on the mind of the pool player to the extent that if he cannot make a shot, he will make sure to place the cue ball in the worst position for his opponent. Of course, in writing we don't get to "punt" when things go bad—but then again, we kind of do because we can go back and fix problems so that we're not in the bad situations later.

L. Jagi Lamplighter

David, nicely put. This is my favorite part of writing. I think of it as weaving. Going back and adding this thread, another stitch of that "color" to make sure that the end is supported but not predictable.

I had something funny happen along these lines once. I accidently saw a review of my book early on that wasn't meant for my eyes. One thing it mentioned was the predictability of the end events of Book One. I looked at the book and realized that what was now the end had originally been a middle scene. I had set up expectations for what was to come at the end of that particular scene right before it happened, because it had not been a big issue.

Now, however, it was important that the end was a surprise. I had to take out the clues that revealed what was to come and weave them back in earlier chapters, where it would be present but not on the reader's mind when he reached the end scene.

I was very grateful I'd stumbled upon the heads-up for this, because it was an easy fix and one I would really have regretted not doing.

The Beginning of the End
David B. Coe

Last time I wrote about "The End Game," about the devices that we use to set up our endings, and the hints that we plant early in a manuscript. Today I'd like to build on that by focusing on the final chapters of your project, and the elements of storytelling that you ought to keep in mind as you turn your attention to the Beginning of the End.

What makes for a great ending to a book? It's more than just plot, though of course, tying up those narrative threads is part of the process. A satisfying close to your novel should tie together narrative-development in most if not all of your plot threads, character-growth among the major players in your book, and larger issues embedded in your worldbuilding or the establishment of your setting. In other words, a good ending satisfies on every level. Just as an effective novel combines character, plot, setting, and other storytelling elements into a coherent whole, so your final chapters should bring together all of those elements and have them peaking simultaneously. (Okay, forgive the aside, but I can't tell you how difficult it is to write about this stuff without descending into sophomoric jokes about a good climax satisfying in all ways simultaneously . . . But a good climax really should . . .)

[Clears throat.] Well then, let's start with plot. By the time you reach the final quarter or so of your novel, the plot points should be building toward your climactic scenes. Usually this is the point in the book where things look worst for your protagonist. Her planning has fallen apart, your antagonist has bested her again and again, her romance with what's-his-name has deteriorated, and the world you've created is on the brink of utter disaster. Now it's time for your protagonist to rally, to bring to bear her resourcefulness, her strength, and whatever other qualities you've given her along the way. It's also the time for the connections between your main plot and your subplots to become more evident.

Pacing can vary throughout a novel. At times plot points come quickly; at other times things develop at a more leisurely pace. But this is not a time for the latter. As you move into the final chapters, the pace should build rapidly. Your readers should be left breathless and desperate for more. They should be turning the pages so quickly that they risk tearing each one, and the end of each chapter should be filled with so much suspense that they have no choice but to read on, even if it's four hours past their bedtimes. At times I have spoken critically of J.K. Rowling's writing, and I'm sure I'll do so again. But I think this—plotting the ending of her novels—is something she did exceptionally well, particularly in the later volumes. Her pacing was excellent; she played *the end game* beautifully, weaving together hints and plot points she planted early on and piling one thrilling moment on top of another.

But plot is only a small part of the ending. This should also be when your character finally gets over her fears, her personal shortcomings—whatever has been holding her back. And her growth past this failing should be intimately tied to the plot points that are pushing the novel towards its denouement.

Faith and others have written a lot about character growth, and it can't be stressed enough: a story's protagonist should not remain static. She/he has to grow, change, adapt. And there should be a symbiosis between this character's development and your storyline, even if that symbiosis is subtle.

If this is the first or second book in a trilogy, then it's possible that this time the flaw will keep the protagonist from succeeding. Ultimately though, whether at the end of a stand-alone novel or in the final volume of an extended story arc, your character should face whatever has held her back, conquer it, and prevail. This is something that I believe Neil Gaiman does as well as anyone in the business right now. Read the endings of *Ananzi Boys*, or *Neverwhere*, or *American Gods*, and you will find deeply flawed characters, major protagonists and smaller players alike, overcoming their shortcomings and acting heroically, while still maintaining the essence of who and what they are. Brilliant stuff.

And then there's your "world." In my Winds of the Forelands series, the climactic battle would decide the fate of the Forelands world as my readers knew it. In my newest book, *Thieftaker* (for now that's the book's title), which I just finished last month, the future of our world is not at stake. But the future of colonial Boston might well be. In my story "The Dragon Muse" (in the anthology, *Dragon's Lure*), the only part of the world really at risk is my main character's life. But really these three examples are far more alike than they might seem. In all three cases, there is enough hanging in the balance to make my readers care. They have a stake in the ending, either because they don't want the world to end, or because they are reading a book that threatens our collective history, or because they have come to identify with the struggle of this one man.

Your ending doesn't have to be apocalyptic to be effective; in fact, you don't want to overreach. The key is to make your reader care about the same things your protagonist cares about. Most of the time, that will tie the reader to your setting as well as your character, and thus to the larger implications of your protagonist's struggles. My favorite author in this regard is Guy Gavriel Kay. Part of what I love most about his work is his facility for making setting come to life, be it an imagined world, as in *Tigana* or the Fionavar Books, or a real world setting, as in his recent masterpiece, *Ysabel*. And in doing this, he ties his characters inextricably to the worlds in which they live. We care about the people, of course, but we also see them as bit players in far larger struggles. His closing chapters bring setting and character together so powerfully that the emotional impact of his endings is increased exponentially.

Faith Hunter

Back when I wrote mysteries/thrillers, I was on a panel, and during audience Q&A, the question was asked, why murder? Why do *all* mysteries have to revolve around murder? Um . . . they don't. But when they do, the terror is heightened, the suspense is tighter, because the payoff is bigger when the hero finally succeeds. Much more bang for the reader's buck than if the bad guy steals bubble gum from the corner store.

Alan Kellogg

What do you do when you learn you don't have the beginning of the end, but a new beginning?

David B. Coe

I'm thinking that Alan was asking about creative process—what happens if, instead of your book moving toward the beginning of the end, it seems to be moving toward the beginning of a new book. Is that right, Alan? If so, I'm not quite sure what to tell you. Obviously, you follow that new inspiration, but you also need to finish the book you're working on. And so what I would try to do is figure out where the two intersect. Where does the ending of the WIP intersect with the beginning of the new idea? And, just as important, how do you create a transition between them that will give the WIP a satisfying ending while also hinting at the story to come? I'm not sure I have answers for you, but those would be the questions I would be asking myself in that situation.

The Final Words
Stuart Jaffe

Though I'm nearing the cusp of the climactic sequence in my current WIP, I'm thinking about the end, about what happens after the big battle. What I want to focus on now is the last sentences—the actual, one hundred percent no denying it, there's nothing left, *end* to your story.

In terms of getting the eye of an agent or editor, writers are often told that the first sentence is the most important. Agents and editors will only give you a few pages and if you haven't grabbed hold of them, then they aren't going to ask for more. After all, if you can't interest *them* from the beginning, they'll figure you can't interest a larger audience, either.

But the last sentences of your tale are vital as well. This is the final word you leave with your reader. This has the potential to impact the entire novel, the entire reading experience. These words won't get your work into an agent's or a publisher's hands and they won't sell a book to a browser at a bookstore. But these words do have the potential of bringing them back for more.

Think about the books that have really stayed with you. Not just the ones that you remember fondly or recall a great scene from, but the ones that when you finished, you sat there holding the book, breathing in those final words, and thinking about the entire journey you just completed. For me, John Steinbeck's *East of Eden* is such a book. (The movie starring James Dean is wonderful but only comprises a small portion of the book. The book follows the entire family through several generations and thus, the characters in the movie are mere shadows compared to the depth Steinbeck provides in the novel.)

The final sentences of the book comprise a dying man's one spoken word in Yiddish (*temshel*) and then he closes his eyes and sleeps. That's it. But the seeds for that moment, that word, are carefully planted throughout the novel, so when the reader hits that finale, the word connects all the threads of the tale. For me, it was one of those awe-inspiring moments, where I just hoped that maybe I'll be able to scratch the surface of such artistry someday—if I'm lucky. Steinbeck did what perfect final sentences should do—tie together plot, character, and theme in a way that provokes the reader to think about the experience and makes the reader want to read more by the author. The question, I imagine many of you are thinking: Great, so how do I do that?

Endings work best when they create a lasting image or comment that points the reader in a thoughtful/emotional direction. They can provide closure to the tale or open new doors for further tales or even both. Here's a film example: *Cast Away* starring Tom Hanks. The final image of the film is of Hanks standing at a crossroads in the middle of nowhere. The final scene showed him what was down one road (a woman) and he knows what is down the road he came from. Beyond that nobody knows. After the whole journey he has been on, this moment ties together the character he has changed into (from a typical Type-A American to a man who is freed from the bonds of society) with the themes of the movie (the overly-time-managed society vs. the slower world of the wild, seizing the day, getting in touch with the important things in life, etc.) and leaves us wanting to come back for more. All from a single image. In writing, we can strive for the same final impact.

Naturally there is a balance that must be found. The Tom Hanks scene works on film, but even just reading the description above shows how heavy-handed it could end up being on paper. You can overdo it and end up being didactic instead of enlightening. In effect, you can undercut or even undo all that you had accomplished up to that point. Finding that balance is a matter of trial and error. It helps to think about what the point of your tale is or who your main character has become and then see if there is a way to utilize that idea. Another approach is to look back at the opening and see if there is an image you can repeat or slightly alter to tie the piece together. Still another possibility is to think of a physical act the character can do to express the story. The list of approaches is endless. You just have to experiment.

So, tread carefully. It is not a requirement that the final sentences blow away the reader. But if you can pull it off, it is one of the most satisfying bits of "icing on the cake" a writer can ever create.

A.J. Hartley

Thanks, Stuart. I'm a big fan of final sentences. One my favorites is in William Golding's (of *Lord of the Flies*) *Pincher Martin*, in which the last sentences explain the entire book. The sheer craftsmanship required to pull something like that off boggles my mind! In my own stuff I like to leave the reader with something dense, something that packs together some of the book's core ideas, but does so—hopefully—with a light, allusive touch, so the final lines resonate but don't clang.

David B. Coe

First lines and last lines—I struggle with both far more than I do with anything that comes in between. One of my favorite endings is in Guy Gavriel Kay's *Tigana*. In a traditional sense, it's probably not a good ending at all. It raises far more questions than it answers, leaves the reader somewhat unsettled, wondering what is going to happen next. But it also reinforces that there is magic in the world Kay created, and it deepens the mystery and richness of the book. I won't say more than that; those who have read *Tigana* know exactly what I mean. Those who haven't read it yet should go get a copy.

I like books that leave me thinking, that force me to imagine what might be in store for the characters I've come to care about. And yet, I also like an ending that satisfies, that ties together the threads of the story. Talk about a fine balance . . .

On Writing Fantasy

Making Magic

Misty Massey

I love the idea of real magic. I can't help desiring a world in which something sparkling and strange could be right around the corner. When I was a kid, I used to wander in the marshes near my home getting muddy and wet, wishing the fae would come out and play with me. Now that I'm grown, I find my magic in the fantasy worlds I read and write.

Fantasy, by its nature, must feature some aspect of magic. Magic spells, supernatural creatures . . . doesn't matter as long as the fantastic elements exist in its pages. If you've decided to write about someone who can perform magic, you must know how your magic works and why. Maybe it's an alchemical exchange of energy, or maybe the Powers That Be grant the abilities when the character beseeches them to do so. The way it works is entirely up to you and your imagination. But sometimes the author is so impressed with the intricate and well-crafted magic system he has created that he feels compelled to tell the reader every single detail about it.

You've worked hard to create a fresh perspective on how magic works. You know every detail, and it thrills you to have come up with it all. You're dying to tell all of us about it. The problem is that the reader signed on for a story, not a textbook. Remember, the story comes first. The story is the reason for all this work. Don't pile a ton of information on its hardworking shoulders. If dropping explanations about your magic system begins taking up more pages than the action of the story, you'd better do some editing.

Magic systems are as individual as the writers who create them and each has a base on which it's built. Some are based on natural elements, and function best under the open sky. Others are designed in a more scientific manner, with an alchemical exchange required to achieve results. The religious magic systems depend on a deity who's paying attention and who's been properly venerated answering the calls of its faithful. Traditionally magic was considered to be overcome by the intrusion of modern technology. Much of this was due to the legends of the fae, who were weakened by the presence of worked iron. Luckily a number of writers threw that tradition aside, and have come up with gorgeous, intricate systems rooted in the steel, concrete, and fumes of the modern cities.

You can use anything you want to build your magic system, but how do you go about displaying how it works? Of course you can let your character mumble a few words and wiggle his fingers, but wouldn't it be more fun to introduce something new? A neat way to achieve that is by leaning on the old and familiar magic we all do every day. Some people call them superstitions.

Most of us have habits or rituals that we do without thinking about them.

It's our way of doing minor magic of our own. The traffic light changes to yellow just before you enter the intersection, so you kiss your palm and slap the car ceiling to keep the light from turning red before you pass under. Someone at work says, "How much worse could this day be?" and in response we knock our knuckles against the nearest wooden desktop. Two people say the same phrase at the same time, and one calls out, "Jinx!" to avoid terrible disaster. Ordinary things no one even gives a thought to in these modern times, but think about it for a second. What if they really worked? Maybe in your fantasy world, calling "Jinx" creates a wall of force around the speaker while the unfortunate slower guy is smacked sideways by a spectral hand. Or if you don't send a kiss to the traffic light, the traffic deities frown on you, changing the rhythms of the subsequent lights to make sure you stop at every one, forcing you to be late for work.

Even if you're not writing a modern fantasy, the words and motions of little superstitions can lend an air of authenticity to the magical world you hope to create. It will resonate with almost any reader, since we all have something we do for luck or safety. If nothing else, the gestures and words of simple superstitions will provide a solid starting place from which you can build something truly fantastic.

Maybe you don't care to write about human spellcasters, but you're more intrigued by the creatures of legend instead. Magical creatures appear in every culture on Earth. The familiar unicorns and dragons are common to more than one mythology, as are a number of magical monsters like vampires, werewolves and zombies. Other creatures are less commonly known—the *rakshasa*, the *penanggalan*, or the Stymphalian Birds—which makes them a bit more exotic. Thousands of years of human storytelling has resulted in more magical creatures than any one writer can use, which at first glance seems like a gold mine. You could write a dozen books and never run into the same creature twice.

In the early days of fantasy, when most of the books being written were long quests across dangerous lands of mythical beasts or retellings of fairy tales, the magical creatures tended to be the ones familiar to us through Greek, Roman and Celtic mythology. After a while, readers started pining for something new, something different, but still fantastic. Recent trends in fantasy reflect that desire, producing writers whose work leaned toward magical creatures blending into contemporary life. In the last fifteen or twenty years urban fantasy has become its own subgenre of fantasy. Unless you've spent the last decade in the Brazilian rain forest, you already know about the popularity of vampires and werewolves as romantic figures. Other writers are delving into the less well-known creatures, like skinwalkers, for example. Whether you're trying something exotic or working with the familiar, including magical creatures is definitely a plus.

So how does one go about finding these fascinating beings? As with many things, the best place to start is by reading. Read mythology. Greek, Roman and Celtic are well-known, since most Americans studied at least a little bit of those mythologies in school. There's nothing wrong with writing your own story about a familiar topic. What you have to do is make your idea fresh, so that even if it looks like something else, it isn't the same at all.

What if you want to write about some beast that no one else has tried? Despite the shrinking of the globe thanks to the internet, there are many cultures whose mythologies are still mysteries to the American reading public. Study the legends of India, for example. Take a virtual trip through the folk tales of Russia. Considering how many people think Africa is a country, you might do well to examine the many rich and diverse cultural traditions of all the countries on that continent.

David B. Coe

This is a great lesson for writers to keep in mind, not only for magic, but for worldbuilding and character details as well. Plot and character drive narrative. Explanations slow things down and distract from plot and character. Yes, the magic system based on blending pop-tart ingredients is cool (and tasty!) but only to a point. And then it comes back to the things that count. Plot and character (have I said that enough yet?).

Faith Hunter

Over-explaining is such a trap, and the magical systems are a big lure for writers. I too, went with the MC-doesn't-know-how-the-magic-works concept in both of my series, just to avoid being snared in it. Yes, I know how the systems work. No, the reader doesn't have to, or not all at once. The very questions and blank spots can create as much interest (or more) as having it all spelled out (pun intended).

Another way we writers over-explain is in the geo political, martial, or weapons systems. In the Jane Yellowrock series, my editor had me cut a lot of vamp clan stuff out of book one, and then in book two there are only four clans left instead of the original eight. Much easier for a reader to follow, and I lost nothing to work with.

Daniel R. Davis

By the by, this was always a favorite site of mine to go searching for odd monsters for my writing sessions and for something different to put into a story. Encyclopedia Mythica: http://www.pantheon.org/

Creating Magic
David B. Coe

Today's essay comes to us thanks to my good friend Stuart Jaffe who emailed me a few days ago to discuss the creation of magic systems. This is something I've done quite a bit of, and it's one of the things I enjoy most about writing fantasy. Magic is, in many ways, the defining characteristic of our genre. Yes, I know: we often say here at Magical Words that character and plot and voice are the most important elements of good storytelling. But the fact is that fantasy wouldn't be fantasy without magic. And besides, making up magic systems is really fun to do.

But contrary to what some people think, creating a magic system is not an anything-goes endeavor. It takes serious thought and careful planning, not to mention a good deal of imagination. There are, of course, a thousand different ways to use magic. I've had magic systems that are based in a psychic bond between a mage and a familiar, usually a bird of prey. The power actually flowed from that connection and was focused through a third element, a crystal. I've also had psionic (mind) magic. Power was basically as immediate as thought. I've used spell magic, blood magic, sacrificial magic. There are endless possibilities. When I'm working on magic systems, though, I like to keep three things in mind.

1. A magic system has to have limitations. You don't want unlimited magic because then your story becomes a contest between mages (wizards, sorcerers, insert your favorite word here) with near God-like powers. Magic should be taxing in some way. It should tire the people who use it, or it should have some other kind of cap that keeps it from being used all the time, for everything, without end. That said, as with everything we talk about here, there are exceptions to this "rule." You can, of course, write an effective story in which your mages have unlimited power (others have done it), but you need to make certain that you pay attention to the ramifications of this decision. If there are members of your society who don't have magic, they're going to be second-class citizens in nearly every way, unless your magic-wielders are uncommonly (and perhaps unrealistically) benign. Call me a cynic, but I believe that unfettered magical power will lead to unfettered political, social, and military domination.

2. In my opinion, magic should have a cost. For me, it's not enough that magic be limited or bounded in some way. It should also have repercussions. In the Forelands books, for instance, the Qirsi who use magic shorten their lives with every conjuring. The book I'm working on right now has a kind of cool, different system that I'm not ready to discuss in detail, but those who use magic eventually go insane. In my Thieftaker series there's no real physical cost, but there is a social one. Conjurers are outcasts. They're hated, feared, and persecuted, and so they have to be careful where and when they use their power, lest they be arrested, tortured, and put to death.

3. And finally, (this is pretty basic) a magic system has to be internally consistent. You have to establish rules and then those rules have to be as iron clad as the physical laws of our natural world. I know that sounds self-evident, but you'd be amazed by the number of writers who don't get this one, who allow their magic to work as *deus ex machina* again and again. Once you set up your system of magic, you have to write around it. As soon as you start messing with it to fit the needs of your characters or your plot, you undermine the credibility of your world. Just as you wouldn't start changing your world map in the middle of series to fit the travel needs of your characters, you shouldn't change the rules of your magic system.

As writers of fantasy, we ask our readers to suspend their disbelief every time they open one of our books. We are saying, in effect, "This couldn't really happen, but I'm going to create a world that feels so real to you that you'll come to believe that it actually could." Magic, of course, is part of the fiction we create, and it has to be every bit as "realistic" and believable as the rest of our worldbuilding. You want your maps and your histories to seem credible. Your magic should, too. It shouldn't be a perfect, boundless, painless tool; it shouldn't stretch and bend to meet the needs of your characters or your plot. That's too easy, and it will make your work less interesting. Limitations, costs, consistency: in my opinion, these are the hallmarks of a workable magic system.

David J. Fortier
One thing I notice in a lot of stories in writing workshops is characters with limitless magic. I like limitations, costs, and consistency.

Initially, I tried to stay away from assigning numeric values to the magic in my world, but I found it hard to determine who had the capability to do what. I eventually buckled in and wrote up a brief number system to help me keep track of character abilities and potential power. Unfortunately, it started to work like a gaming system, so I try to avoid looking at it unless absolutely necessary. I have heard of other authors using numeric values for their systems, particularly those who are also professors.

Any thoughts on numeric magic systems?

David B. Coe

Dave, thanks for the question. I have done very little gaming, so I come at magic from a strictly fiction-oriented perspective. Perhaps for that reason, I don't like the idea of giving numerical values. To me, that would be akin to rating my characters' looks or morals on a similar scale, which doesn't work for me either.

That said, for writers who do come at this from a gaming background, I'd imagine that a numbering system could be very helpful for keeping track of which mage is most skilled or most powerful. But I would think that it would be most valuable as a tool, rather than as something actually written into the story. I think as soon as you introduce some kind of numerical rating into your story you run the risk of having it read as a gaming story, which might hurt you with some publishers. On the other hand, as with martial arts, you may come up with a system that acknowledges the achievements of wizards by ranking them on various levels. As long as the standards are consistent and the rituals of graduating wizards from one level to the next are appropriate to your world, that could be a really cool basis for a magic system.

Mark Wise

My issue right now is that when the system is held up against your three hallmarks, I feel it is lacking #2 and #3. I have limited it by making it purely a constructive magic, it cannot do harm to most living things since it is the residual Power of Creation left over from my world's god. However, I don't have a real "cost" right now, and I haven't quite worked out the actual mechanics of it though I am thinking along a psionics/funneling of energy path.

But I guess my main sticking point would be #2, Cost. So far, there is not a cost to use it.

David B. Coe

Okay, let me start with the usual Magical Words caveat: my hallmarks are just that—mine. Just because your magic system doesn't conform to all three of them doesn't mean in any way that there is something wrong with what you've got. I like the origins of your system and the built in limitation—that's a nice backstory for the system. Very cool. It may be that you don't need a cost, although if you intend to warp this power in some way for the purposes of your story—in other words, if there is going to be some bad guy who comes along and manages to twist the power into something dark—having a cost might be handy for your story line. Or if you have been feeling on your own that there is something missing, then having a cost to the magic might fix that. But you certainly don't need a cost just because I say so. Make sure it's something that will truly add to the story and the world before you add in an element of that magnitude. Looking forward to seeing your work in print, Mark!

Wrestling the TMP

A.J. Hartley

I've been re-watching some old *Star Trek: The Next Generation* episodes on BBC America lately, remembering how much I liked the show's innovative approach to familiar sci-fi scenarios. But I'm also reminded of something that always drove me nuts: Deanna Troi's intermittent empathic sensory perception which allowed her to read people's unspoken feelings. I say *intermittent* because her ability was often crucial to the episode's story, but at other times—when it would have been really useful—it went on the blink: the emotions of the crew were running too high, or there was atmospheric turbulence of some kind, or the target being scanned was the wrong species . . . In each case, she was suddenly unable to get a clear fix on how someone was feeling.

Of course, the truth is that in most of those episodes Deanna's abilities had to be switched off or else the episode would fall apart. Without all those convenient blockages, intentions would be stripped bare, duplicity revealed, and villains unmasked. We would know by the end of the teaser all the stuff we weren't supposed to know till the last few minutes of the show. Suspense, mystery, and dramatic conflict would all go out the window because Deanna was just a bit too powerful.

I call this an example of the TMP: a plot device which has Too Much Power.

Somewhere in those early script meetings it sounded really cool to have an empath on board, someone to balance the (supposedly) emotionless logic of Data by being not just in touch with her own feelings, but clued in to everyone else's as well. But once the series was well underway the script writers constantly had to turn her emotional radar off, and the result was not just annoying: it exposed the plot as a machine which was all too easy to derail.

There are lots of these in fantasy and sci-fi: wondrous artifacts which have mystical properties, innocent looking weapons which have the effect of a nuclear strike, characters whose magical abilities allow them to summon tornadoes or turn lions into hatboxes. The TMP device often looks cool, a great way to get out of a plot difficulty or raise some interesting character issues, but at some point it turns on you and you have to start trying to explain why—sometimes— it doesn't work at all, can't be allowed to work, if all your other work on plot, character etc. is going to hold together. The TMP is a Pandora's Box or—if you prefer—a ring of power, an idea you can use to give your story something special, but which then tunnels into it and eats it from the inside (not so much fun now, is it, precious?).

I've been thinking about this a lot of late because I have a WIP which flirts with time travel, a TMP if ever there was one. Think of the dreaded Time Turner in the (otherwise excellent) 3rd Harry Potter novel: an artifact of extraordinary power that can unleash all manner of potentially fatal chaos, which has been entrusted to a school girl so she can take extra classes? Really? Okay. I can just about accept that for the purposes of the story. But then it's *not* used in future books as the body count mounts because that would somehow destabilize the universe or something? I don't want to get too literal-minded about this, but no. Sorry. Not buying it. If you commit to the TMP, you have to be prepared to use it wherever and whenever it seems reasonable to do so. Expect no mercy from your readers if you use it only when it suits you to do so.

There are two ways of handling the TMP device to your advantage. One is to do the *Next Gen* thing and hedge the device with limits and boundaries. But if you do this, those limits need to be consistent and self-evident. Deanna's occasional empathic abilities drove me mad because turning them off was so obviously a ruse: there was no clear pattern as to when they worked and when they didn't (so far as I could see), so the moment was exposed for what it was: a plot point. If you give a character a powerful ability or artifact, think about limiting it in definitive ways: it won't work under water or, for that matter, it ONLY works under water. Whatever. Just set the rule and stick to it.

The other way of foiling the TMP device before it eats your story head first is simply not to use one. Fantasy and sci-fi writers seem to find it almost impossible to resist the lure of the TMP, bent as we are on showing how the world in our stories is not the one outside our windows, but I can think of no easier way to paint yourself into a corner you can never get out of. So I say this. Beware the TMP and all its works and all its empty promises. It is one of those green-eyed monsters which mocks the meat it feeds on, and the meat—don't forget—is what was going to be your book.

David B. Coe
"Not so much fun now, is it precious?"—you crack me up!

I run into this a fair amount, dealing as I do with magic in all my books. This is one of the reasons why I believe that not just limitations but also COSTS have to be built into a magic system. When wielding magic weakens the mage or her familiar, when it requires blood or some form of sacrifice, when it destabilizes the space-time-granola continuum, you have a built-in reason NOT to use that cool spell that might have otherwise saved the day. I'm not saying this works with every narrative circumstance, but it does give the author (and the author's readers) something to chew on as they contemplate magical solutions to big problems.

My favorite TMP moment? The first Star Wars movie, when the

empire's forces have to wait for the MOON to move out of the way in order to use their weapon that destroys PLANETS.

"Um, Lord Vader, sir? Can't we just blow up the moon?"

Snap Thy Holy Fingers
Misty Massey

I love movies and books about the mystical nature of religion. *Constantine, Stigmata, The Seventh Seal, The Prophecy* . . . I just cannot resist them. The other day I watched a movie trailer for *Legion*, in which God sends his angels to exterminate the world's population. The archangel Michael (played by the wonderful Paul Bettany) is the only one standing between mankind and the apocalypse. I whispered, "Ooh, I want to see that." My teenager, sitting next to me, frowned. "If God's tired of humanity," he mused, "why go to all the trouble of sending the battling angels? Why doesn't He just snap His fingers and make the people disappear?"

He was right. If an omnipotent being is tired of his creation, why would he bother with the trouble of watching them run and scream and die? Isn't that a lot of effort for no real return? This is the problem of using an omnipotent being and trying to limit it.

Religion is an important part of worldbuilding, and you should give it at least as much thought as your magic systems. Every culture in real life has its own beliefs and rituals, some rudimentary, some highly sophisticated. It has great influence over some societies, while others treat it as just another thing to do. In your fantasy culture, it's up to you, the author, to decide how much power the religious community and the god they worship wields, and then to display that power properly in the narrative. Even if your characters aren't particularly religious, it's a good idea to weave those aspects into the story, for depth and richness. My pirates, for example, occasionally mention a god or two, but there's no real devotion shown to them. I, the author, know exactly who those gods are, what their spheres of influence include, and what they can be expected to do when their worshippers ask. It didn't come into play in the story, so the reader didn't see it. But I definitely know.

So how powerful do you want your gods to be? This depends entirely on how the story needs to play out. There's nothing wrong with using a god as a character, or for human characters to call upon and employ a god's power. But think about that whole omnipotence problem I mentioned earlier. If your god is so powerful that he can do anything and everything, it might not make a lot of sense for him to bother with sending others to do his bidding. Takes more energy that way, you know. If you do come up with a reason for an omnipotent being to take the long way around to reach his ultimate goal, be sure you make it clear in the narrative.

David B. Coe

The related issue that I deal with when creating alternate worlds is whether I want my gods and goddesses to interact with the human world, as they do in, say, Greek mythology, or in Guy Kay's Fionavar books. Or, on the other hand, whether they should be more stand-offish; more along the lines of "I/we created the world; our work here is done . . ." I love the idea of the interactive gods, but I always shy away from it because I think it would be very difficult to do well.

Stuart Jaffe

There's also the idea that there is no real god in your world. I don't mean atheism (which is certainly one way to go) but rather having people worship and believe in a god or gods, but there isn't one in the world beyond their belief. Or perhaps there are gods in the world but the ones people are praying to don't exist. I realize the non-existent god angle takes away from the "I'm writing fantasy and want my gods to play" aspect but, for example, in my WIP I have two strongly religious characters locking horns because they are convinced theirs is the real god. In the case of my tale, they both can't be right, so much conflict is created.

A.J. Hartley

Great points, Misty. You pinpoint the idea that religion as we actually experience it is usually a conglomeration of ideas and traditions which have evolved over a long time. Much of the traditions around angels clearly don't really come from a theology in which omnipotence is central. I like my fictional religions like my actual religions: each with a range of beliefs and traditions rather than an absolute position.

Faith Hunter

The problem I have with fantasy books that have an ultimate evil presented as antagonist, (you know, the evil thing that is taking over the world and killing everything) is that there is usually no ultimate good to balance it out. The writer leaves out any question of a good god to balance out the bad god. Mankind (or a man [pick your religious savior archetype]) saves the day, all alone, and I get tired of the ultimate evil, David vs. Goliath scenario. And let's face it, mankind will never fight evil because true evil is too smart to look evil. Evil (true evil) looks good, looks safe, looks appealing. Adolph Hitler looked good to his followers. They didn't think, "Let's go to the dark side today." Mass murderers we've *met* through the TV screen don't wear bones in their hair or shirts made of human skin. Pedophiles carry candy or pictures of lost puppies. They look . . . ordinary. Not the true evil they are.

Dang it, I got on my "evil" soapbox, didn't I?

Emily Leverett

I'm a Christian, and I know that is important to me . . . but I don't find it necessary to have Christ or Christianity in every book I write. Religion varies by world and reading books about fantasy religions doesn't offend me. I also have no interest in writing for the "Christian" market (for a list of reasons, the biggest being I'm sure that they wouldn't want me).

I do, however, feel obligated by my beliefs to characterize some things as good and some as evil. (i.e. ultimate selfishness at the expense of others lives, etc. is evil and the willingness to admit guilt or take responsibility is often good). Now this is, of course, my own limit. But Misty's post made me think about how my own experiences with religion affect my writing, and my writing of religion.

A.J. Hartley

Emily's second point is an interesting one and worthy of a post in itself. I feel a strong impulse to convey something of my own world view, my own ethics and morality in my books. It may not always be obvious, but it's there. I'm not sure I could stop doing this if I tried, but if I did I'd begin to wonder why I was writing.

With Worldbuilding, Every Detail Counts
David B. Coe

In many ways I consider the background work I do for my characters, and the work I do for my worlds to be very similar. I was trained as a historian—I've got the Ph.D to prove it. And I believe that if my academic background has done nothing else for me, it has at least given me an appreciation of the complexity and richness of the human past and its influence on today's world.

People—characters—are, at least in part, the product of where they come from: their family background, their upbringing, their past experiences. Nations—or kingdoms, if we're in an epic fantasy setting—are, at least in part, the product of their histories: wars they've won or lost, political movements and their aftermath, great men and women who shaped cultural trends. A person's religious background can play a role in defining her outlook on life; a nation's religious heritage can do the same for its society. Someone can be influenced by the books he reads or the music he hears or the art he loves; a society can be influenced by its artistic, literary, and musical luminaries. The similarities are unmistakable.

When I do my worldbuilding, I try to take all these elements, and others, into account. Just as I develop detailed backgrounds for my characters, I create histories and cultures for my worlds. I usually start with a map, and I spare no detail.

My historical work was in environmental history, and so I'm quite conscious not only of how human activity has impacted the earth, but also how climate and terrain shape human behavior—patterns of settlement, economic activity, even cultural expression. I then work out political histories, focusing on relations between kingdoms or nations (wars, treaties, etc.) and, at least for the most important of my countries, internal events (successions of kings, or changes in forms of government—that sort of thing). I work out economic issues—if one country is located along the coast and another is up against a mountain range and a third is in a desert, they're going to have different economic specialties and needs, right? What does this mean for trade and relative wealth? I develop religious traditions, often several. How do peoples and institutions tied to the various faiths get along with one another? Was religious tension the cause of the aforementioned wars, or did it have more to do with trade or territorial concerns?

And then there is some of the nitty-gritty detail that can make the difference between a world that seems flat and boring, and one that comes alive for the reader. What kinds of musical, artistic, literary, and dramatic cultural traditions does each nation have?

A lot of this worldbuilding happens not in those early days when I'm doing background work for the book or books, but as I'm writing, when I discover a need. For instance, in *Rules of Ascension*, the first book of my Winds of the Forelands series, I have an important character, an assassin, who sings both for his daily bread and as a way of concealing his true profession. Creating the music that he and his partner sang was tremendous fun. I believe that it also enhanced the other aspects of my worldbuilding, giving the world another dimension that readers might not have missed had it not been there, but which they appreciated nevertheless. In my first series, the LonTobyn Chronicle, I mention a literary figure from the world's past who, I think, serves a similar purpose. I've also used small historical events—things that really have no bearing on the main narrative but that add to the richness of the world—to do much the same thing.

And really, that's the point. Take a look at the books of Guy Gavriel Kay, or Frank Herbert, of J.R.R. Tolkien or J.K. Rowling. Part of what makes their worldbuilding so strong is the extensive background work they do before they begin writing their tales. But part of it is also the stray detail that gets thrown in, seemingly as an afterthought. Those details hint at a larger, richer, more complex world. They can make the difference between a world being merely the setting for a story and it being a place that readers feel they visit each time they open your book.

So when you're doing your worldbuilding, don't limit yourself to just the big events and trends. Take a little time, either beforehand or as you write, to include smaller, more subtle stuff. These details may not change the trajectory of your story; they don't have to. If they make your readers feel that your world is a living, breathing place, they will have served their purpose.

Faith Hunter
Worldbuilding has to be done in every genre, but I had no idea what it meant to do *real* worldbuilding when I was writing in the mystery field. I totally subconsciously thought (in the back of my oh-so-superior mystery/thriller writing mind) that it would be *easy*. I'd just be making stuff up, right? (Slaps own foolish head.) So not right. I'd read fantasy for years (read your first series straight through long before we ever met) and had not stopped to consider what would be involved.

And then I tried to write my first fantasy . . .

I learned fast that it was anything *except* easy, with the threads of life and society not just involved in the process (as in mystery), but changed, bent, intertwined, rewoven into a whole new cloth. Every new thing introduced in the imaginary world affected every other thing. And I was writing about *Earth*. (Okay, an alternate Earth, but still.) My mystery writing brain took a beating. I wish I'd had your post before I started. Or . . . maybe not. I may have never tried to write fantasy. And I am so glad I did!

David B. Coe

Thanks for the comment, Faith. Having read your work it certainly seems that you mastered worldbuilding pretty quickly. Your initial point, though, is well taken. Worldbuilding is more involved in our genre, but it happens in all writing to some degree. Sometimes we're bringing to life a place and time from our own world's past. Sometimes we're creating a "present". But whatever we're doing, we are always trying to evoke a sense of place. Your book, *Blackwater Secrets*, does that brilliantly. It's our world, not an alternate one. But it's a part of the country few of us know as intimately as you do (the Bayou, for those unfamiliar with the book), and you make it come alive in so many ways. Creating a setting is really just another way of saying "worldbuilding."

Daniel R. Davis

I'll mention the other side of the coin; knowing when to stop. I've read books before that I put down and never went back to because the writer didn't know when enough was enough on the detail. Sometimes a story can be lost in world info and minutiae. There are times when I don't really care about what kind of tobacco a character is smoking or where it comes from or what special time it's harvested or how it's harvested or who has to harvest it with special contraptions and why. Sometimes I just want to get back to the story.

David B. Coe

An excellent point, Daniel. There's nothing wrong with developing lots and lots of detail about our worlds or our characters. Authors need to know far more about the background of their books than they ever show their readers. But that last part is key. Just because you know everything imaginable about Herjean shipbuilding, doesn't mean your readers should be forced to read everything imaginable about it . . .

Fantasy Language
Faith Hunter

I was asked recently, by an unpublished writer, the seemingly innocent and easy question, "How do I go about creating a fantasy language?" That got me to thinking, which my hubby would say is a very dangerous thing.

When a writer starts from scratch for a language, they have to know a bit about the world they are creating. Okay, they have to have to have the world down pat. Language has to come near or at the end of the world creation. Here's why: In English, we have only a few words for frozen precipitation, and a lot of them contain the same words: sleet, freezing rain, snow, ice, hail, snowflakes, and uh . . . frozen precipitation, which is where I got started on this. The Inuit's have many more. Why? Because their survival depends on an exact wording for the different kinds of frozen precipitation. So in creating a language, I have to know about the survival requirements of my world.

If I am creating a desert world, there will different names for the different winds, the rare seasonal rains, the names of clothing for sun protection, wind protection, traveling. The names for predators and the weapons that kill them. There will be names for things that grow there, on this alien world, that may not grow here. Plants that can last in the desert heat, grow on little water.

I remember the first time I heard of breadfruit, a fruit that tastes like bread, I suppose, and I wondered why call it breadfruit? The people there have no grains . . . but the Europeans who "discovered" the land had grain, so they named the fruit what they chose, not what the native peoples called it. Bread was a survival food.

For language, I have to know about the sexual interaction between the sexes. If this is an alien world, then there may be three or four sexes. There may be a totally different manner of procreation.

I have to know the conflict of the plot line too, of course. So for me, the language would come last. And frankly, to keep readers from getting lost, I'd use English in different ways, with different syntax, rather than create a language. Remember the Jedi warrior, Yoda, the little green guy? "Lost to you, Luke Skywalker, is hope." English with different organization of phrases and words is oft-times more effective than starting from scratch.

But then, in my fantasy worlds, I always just used an alternate reality Earth, which makes it so much easier. Lazy? Probably.

Todd Massey

Introducing new language into a novel is a tricky line to walk. It can easily make or break a story. Too much and it bogs a story down by making the reader work too hard. Just the right mix and it can help transport you deeper into the world. Some invented words can crossover into the real world and end up embedded in our culture.

Of course, it isn't just fantasy that can benefit or suffer from invented words, science fiction is another realm that often has to use invented words. When an author reaches into the future you can get a few subtle words that help to transport you like "Robotics" (courtesy of Isaac Asimov). This simple word did not exist in our world before he invented it for his Robot short stories, yet it clearly conveyed its own idea and did not halt the reader or break him out of the story.

Love it or hate it *A Clockwork Orange* is one of those novels that both works and does not work because of language issues. It is so saturated with a "foreign" future language that many people are bogged down and turned off by it. But the following phrase is actually pretty clear, even though most of the important words are "foreign"— "to *tolchock* some old *veck* in an alley and *viddy* him swim in his blood." If you happen to have been fluent in Russian you might have picked up on some of the words Anthony Burgess "invented" since many of them came from Slavic speak, although slightly altered. While the book can be hard to read, he wanted to convey what actually happens to our language as time passes. Plus, these were young street thugs that speak their own language.

I think new languages/words are important for F&SF worlds to help set them apart and fully envelop the reader. It is up to the writer to masterfully and slowly drip the words into the reader's brain so that learning the new language is a natural learning progression within the confines of the story.

David B. Coe

I tried creating a new language for my first series and just sucked at it. What I came up with was totally random—based pretty much on what sounded good, as opposed to what made sense. I don't have a linguistics background and I really needed one to do what I was trying to do.

I agree with you that the best way to make the language of a book feel different—to have it reinforce the worldbuilding—without becoming something overly complicated and forced, is to find creative uses of the English language. That's how I tried to handle it in the Forelands books and now in the Southlands trilogy. The way people speak is informed by the way they live; the way they conceive of their world, the imagery they draw upon when talking or thinking about their lives comes from the realities that surround them. Climate, the imperatives of finding food and water and shelter, whether they are at war or living in peace: all of these things shape the way they communicate.

Harry Markov

I'm curious how, even if you create a language (a task I want to do for one of my worlds) it can be used. I mean since the book is written in English, how can you apply a new language?

Any ideas?

Faith Hunter

Harry, all the manuscript is in English, yes, but you can add flavor of a new language in several ways:

1. Syntax as mentioned earlier.

2. Basic words inserted in text where the reader has no doubt what they mean.

3. Basic words inserted in text with explanations following the first time you use the word and any time there has been a lot of manuscript text between usage.

4. Basic words inserted with glossary at front or back.

However, one still has to be very careful with this not to overdo and confuse the reader.

How Far Is That Again?

Misty Massey

One of our faithful readers, Daniel Davis, recently asked a very good question:

"I'm just wondering how others deal with time and distance in their stories. By that I mean, do you change the names of your time and distance from Earth standard (seconds, minutes, hours, feet, miles, etc) to something else, keep it the same, or do you even use standardized time? In a place that has no clocks or even sun dials, how does one have their characters deal with talking about time? Also, using English standard units of measure just doesn't seem right for races who have never been on Earth, but using fictitious names for them could be confusing for readers."

It's an important point. It's easy to use miles, inches, hours and such without realizing how very particular that language is to our own world. The likelihood of a race of people from another solar system using the same words to describe distance is almost nil. Time and space are necessary for a story, to keep track of the order things happen, and where. Maybe Dr Who can wrap his mind around time being a great big ball of wibbley-wobbley, timey-wimey stuff, but the rest of us require an explanation that's a bit more concrete. Our characters have to have some way of marking the passage of time, and the amount of distance. Creating a vocabulary to solve that problem seems to be the most obvious solution. Except the writer runs the risk of confusing his readers by changing all the familiar words. How far is a *frangem*? If it takes *pix hofrensesses* to reach the capital city, how long is that, really? Finding the comprehensible balance between new vocabulary and reader understanding is vital.

Most writers seem to keep the words for numbers, which is nice. Math's already hard for me . . . I don't know how everyone else feels, but if you start changing the numbers' names, you'll lose my attention. There's always a threat of overdoing the worldbuilding and ruining the experience for everyone.

Assuming that the numbers get to keep their names, we then have to look at the words for measurement. The first option, and the easiest, is to use all the words already in place. It's safe, of course, and if you do a good job of worldbuilding in all the other areas of the novel, no one will mind too much. I've seen writers use archaic words to describe distances—leagues, yonside or nigh, to name a few. It's a great place to start, since most readers won't be overly familiar with them. Read a little Shakespeare and you'll find plenty of dandy words to try. This doesn't work as well for science fiction, since the assumption is that your characters have moved beyond that somewhat vague style of measurement.

Since you're building your world from the ground up anyway, I think the best idea would be to make up your own words. Easy, right? A great place to begin would be the dictionary. Look up the words you're wanting to replace, and read about their origins, then let your imagination wander a bit. "Mile", for instance, is derived from the Latin *milia passuum*, which means "a thousand double paces." You could rename the mile in your culture as *milpache*. (This is just off the top of my head—I'm sure you can come up with a more graceful word. ☺)

If your book's people have a similarity to any of Earth's plentiful and real cultures, you can investigate the language and borrow from it as well. Be cautious and respectful, though, especially if you're borrowing from a language that's still being spoken. The last thing you want to do is misuse the language and insult anyone. So you've made up your words . . . how does the reader know what they mean?

Context. Present those new and thrilling words in context, and the reader will happily stick with you. Here are a couple of examples:

> The trip to Anferr took two *kiddles*, and Jon was exhausted by the time he arrived. He promised himself that next time he'd send someone younger, with a better back. Not everything had to be his responsibility.

OR

> "Jon! Good to see you!"
> "Finally." He rubbed his back, groaning. "I hate having to sleep on the transport for even a *kik*, but the whole *kiddle*, sitting up . . ." he straightened. "I like my bed too well. Lead me to the coffee and toast, would you?"

In the first example, a *kiddle* could have been anything—a day, a week, a six hour chunk of time. There's not much to connect to. In the second, we realize Jon was sleeping for a *kiddle*, which is much longer than a *kik*. And now he's hungry for the morning meal. The evidence suggests a *kiddle* equals a night. It's all about how you present the new and strange words. As long as you make it easy for the reader to make the intuitive leap, you're in good shape.

I used the rising and falling of the sun as the main measure of time passing in my book, since my pirates depend on the skies for navigation. They live in an archipelago, so they also determine distance by how many days it takes to get from one island to another. Fairly simple, but it's all the distance and time Kestrel needed. The Danisobans have their own methods, but she doesn't know about them, and since the book was from her point-of-view, it never came up.

I'm going to throw the question out to my esteemed colleagues and all our other faithful readers. As we at Magical Words often say, there is no single right way to do things, but there are lots of great ideas. How do y'all handle creating distance words? What books have you read that accomplished the job well?

Faith Hunter

Misty, One of my main POV characters in my WIP is an animal. She thinks of periods of time in mooncycles. There is a the *sharp-pointed moon*, and its opposite, the *pregnant moon*. There is the *hungry moon*, and the *hunter's moon*. I've had fun thinking/speaking with an animal's mind, coming up with words that might make sense to her, making it basic enough to feel primitive, yet hope I don't irritate readers with its weirdness.

Daniel R. Davis

I just thought of a possibility for determining sun span across the sky. Using a coin of the realm and holding it out so that it looks the same size as the sun and using it to estimate how many spans the sun has traveled across the sky since it rose. Kind of a simple and neat way of checking the time. Might even be able to come up with a renamed minute/hour scale that way as well. hmm.

Edmund R. Schubert

One of my pet peeves with a lot of fantasy is that frequently the language stuff is horribly overdone. Tolkien was a linguist who put a lot of thought into his Elvish; too many writers who want to follow in his footsteps think it's sufficient to make up a bunch of junk and then end up with half of their character's names having no vowels (substituting apostrophes instead); time and distance expressed in *Uveuals* and *Snarnakithims;* etc etc etc. There is a balance to be struck between giving your fantasy language distinction, and making it painful to read. Every time I come across a sentence like, "Grv'nth'k rode his horse for many *uveuals*, cover the six *snarnakithims* in half the usual time because he couldn't risk being late for his meeting with Br'th'sm'pnl," I put the book down and walk away. I want to get lost in a story and that's impossible to do if I'm constantly bombarded with gibberish.

Writing Action Scenes
A.J. Hartley

Imagine you're stopping off at the supermarket on the way home from work. It's later than you had intended and the sun is already down. You're irritated by a meeting you had earlier in the day, bits of which are replaying in your head as you start manhandling bags of groceries into the car. It's raining and one of the paper bags has started to tear at the bottom. You figure that if you're quick you can get it inside before any more damage is done, but a can of tuna falls out and rolls under the car. Cursing, you stoop to pick it up, and that's when you realize.

There's someone behind you. Someone who has moved quickly and quietly. Someone who means you harm.

You turn, rising, forming a defiant question that will mask your sudden panic, and that's when you see his fist and the blade it is wrapped around . . .

Okay. So, for most of us, writing the rest of this scene will—mercifully—be an act of imagination rather than memory, and it's a tricky thing to do. Partly, I think, the problem is with the medium itself, words on a page being—perhaps—better suited to reflection than the furious chaos of physical fighting, the danger and exhilaration of which comes across so much better in a visual medium like film. It can be done in fiction, of course, but how do you pull it off effectively?

Let me start with one of my usual calls for balance. On the one hand, we need to know what's happening so we can picture it, but on the other we want to feel what it's like to be in the fight, and those two impulses can be contradictory. Unless your protagonist is a very cool-headed martial arts expert (and I'm assuming a limited third-person narrative here), describing every move of the struggle so that your reader can act them out is going to feel stiff and dull. As with larger plot points, the important thing is to remember that the meaning of the action is finally about its effect on the reader and its consequences for the characters, so that you don't get mired in the mapping of its logistics. Real fights—even some verbal arguments, if you're angry enough—don't feel choreographed. They feel irrational, a swirl of gut-level, thoughtlessness. If your character feels like his or her life is in danger, we need to sense that, and we won't if it comes across as either a ballet or like the blow by blow account of a role-playing game.

Different writers tackle this balance in different ways, of course, and it may depend on what you want from the sequence in terms of the larger narrative, but I would caution against too much reflection during the fight. As with any action sequence, you probably want to keep the specifics tight: short, breathless sentences, setting up (and balanced by) occasional longer and more reflective beats. The reading eye leaping quickly from sentence to sentence echoes the speed of the action and (hopefully) gets the adrenaline pumping. Then you can move from the staccato to something with more detail or mood. Try this:

> The knife flashes up at your face. You block wildly, stumbling, and his other fist swings in. It lands hard on your jaw. Your head snaps back, and the night brightens. You taste blood against your teeth, and suddenly there is only panic and defiance and a wild, terrible fury. You lunge for his throat, forgetting the knife, your knee snapping up into his groin.

And so on. The first 4 sentences are short and physical, as is the last one. In the middle is something a bit longer, a bit more abstract, which provides a turn for the paragraph, a transitional moment in which the attacked becomes the attacker. The next longest sentences (the 2nd and the last) still feel short, because they're made up of three almost separate phrases which each convey an action. The longer transitional sentence is not *much* longer (though the repeated "ands" force a fractional slowing of tempo, I think, which gives weight to "panic," "defiance," and then "fury" (itself loaded with two adjectives to give even greater specificity and weight)), because action has to feel like it's happening in real time: that the number of seconds it takes to read the passage are about the same as how long the action takes to happen.

Action demands that you prioritize. What should be part of the character's or narrator's experience here? Should he/she (or "you") be aware of the color and model of the car? Probably not. Adding that kind of detail is likely to make that whole section feel like an out of body experience. There may be good reasons to include such information, but for most action sequences those things are going to feel digressive and irrelevant. When describing fighting well, the reader is most likely going to be thinking very simple things as the sequence taps into his or her own feelings of fear or exhilaration, so what will keep them reading is a focus on answering equally simple questions: will the protagonist survive and how? A secondary question might be "Who is the attacker and why is this happening?" but you barely want even that in the reader's mind during the fight itself. As the struggle goes on, you want the reader's response to be visceral, animal, rather than analytical.

The "show/don't tell" rule is especially applicable here. Each moment should feel immediate, so beware those anti-suspense phrases which telegraph how things end up before you get there: "He didn't think he had the energy, but . . ." "The first two ax blows barely made an impression on the armor, but . . ." "Only when he was down to his last bullet . . ." These are lazy phrases which effectively skip over time and ask the reader to pretend it was all gripping. Either make us experience each stroke, each shot, or leave them out.

Lastly, keep it short. If the fighting starts to lag, or otherwise loses its edge—even in the description of a big action event like a large-scale battle—it has started to subvert its own purpose and needs cutting. Dialogue and exposition can occasionally get away with being a bit boring (particularly if their pay-off is elsewhere); action can't. Action exists primarily for the thrill or horror they provide in the moment of reading. If you can't feel your pulse starting to race as you read what you've written, it probably needs attention.

Misty Massey

Sometimes I realize I've written an action scene that just won't work. One fighter needs two left hands to do what I've said he's doing, or the way I have them turn leaves them fighting each other back to back. When that happens, I call my husband and son to come into the room and block out the scene, just to make sure it makes physical sense. Once I even had my husband jump off the roof of our Blazer so I could see him land and roll. I can't begin to tell you how much it helps; I know not everyone has people willing to do this sort of thing, so I'm lucky.

I'm also lucky no one has been damaged yet. ☺

A.J. Hartley

Misty, I do the same. Walking through the steps of a fight (esp. with some deluded but helpful participant) is invaluable for visualizing exactly how things work. This goes for all physical activity in books: not just combat. While writing a scene in my last thriller where a guy was up on the ledge of a tower and trying to inch round the building, I laid out 2x4s around the walls of my house and worked my way round, pretending I was fifty feet up in the air!

Joe McBee

Great advice, A.J.! I now need to revisit the action sequences in my novel. I also love the idea of blocking the action sequences first so I can see how they would play out.

One question: In terms of spacing for an adventure novel, how often should an action sequence come up? I've read novels before that were so action packed that they were exhausting and annoying. And then I've read other novels that seemed like they could use a little more action. Is there a "rule of thumb" for how much action one should see?

A.J. Hartley

Joe, good (and tricky) question. You're right to say that different writers use different amounts of action, and that some are relentless. I'd go so far as to suggest there are genres within genres, and your best rule of thumb is probably to ask yourself what kind of book you are trying to write and then study examples of that subset. My thrillers use action rather sparingly (every fifty pages or so?) but I'm considered a bit sedate, especially next to the harder core thriller writers (esp. those set in military contexts).

Writing Action Scenes: Part 2, Battles

A.J. Hartley

After my last essay on combat, I got a couple of queries/comments which asked about larger-scale fighting, and have been considering how best to answer them. I must admit that I was surprised (pleased, certainly, but definitely surprised) when my Will Hawthorne books got positive critical attention for their battle scenes, and I offer the following with the proviso that I don't claim to be an expert on this and can only discuss what has worked for me.

1. Number

Battles, if given real attention, are inevitably big "set piece" episodes, involving lots of characters (major and minor) and pages and pages of description. As a result, they have to be used judiciously, with an eye to the larger arc of the story. It's worth remembering that though there are plenty of smaller skirmishes and action sequences in the three books of *The Lord of the Rings*, there are really only two large scale battles: Helm's Deep and Pelennor Fields. The movie versions increased this number significantly, partly to suit the visual medium and partly to add scale and drama to three separate films, but even so (and I'm speaking as a fan of the movies) they start to feel repetitive by the end, particularly if you watch all three in sequence. Battles are the *coup de grace* of dramatic action, but more is not necessarily better. For one thing they generally need to get bigger, more significant, and more dramatic if they are not to feel anticlimactic, and this alone is reason enough to use them sparingly. Opening a story with a big, exciting combat sequence certainly gets the book going with a bang, but how do you top that? Begin too big and you've nowhere to go but down.

2. Placement

Some planning—even for you pantsers—is essential. Figure out how many battles you are going to use and then where in the story you are going to put them. Tolkien's example is a good one: skirmishes at the beginning (Weathertop, Moria, and the death of Boromir), one major battle at roughly the midpoint of the story, and another even bigger one at the end. You may have more, of course, but you should think of the larger story in terms of its rhythms and stresses. I don't think they have to escalate over a series of books, necessarily, but they probably should increase in dramatic intensity in a single book, and should be placed in accord with larger patterns of plot and character. In terms of classic three act structure, the two *LOTR* battles I mentioned occur at climactic points in the middle and end of the second act. It might be argued that Pelennor is part of Act 3, but if we think of the narrative as ultimately being the story of Frodo and the ring, the third act is all Mount Doom and the return to the Shire. It is true that battles can liven up a story, but if they are simply incidental (just an opportunity to get the blood pumping), keep the scale small. Large battles shouldn't feel arbitrary.

3. Variety

If you have more than one large battle in a book you should seek ways to make each one distinctive. That might be achieved simply if the characters involved are different, but if it's the same characters each time, even the same enemy, you need other ways to make the conflict unique and memorable. There are lots of ways to do this that have nothing to do with forms of combat. Battles feel differently according to the kind of weather in which they are fought, if it's day or night, or what the terrain is. A pitched battle in open fields is very different from the assault or defense of a fortress, or the holding of a mountain pass. The nature of the troops involved, fantastic beasts, magic, or other distinctive means of fighting can all stamp a battle in ways that make it different from the others you've written. In the *LOTR* examples I'm working with, Pelennor is a classic plains conflict while Helm's Deep is a defensive siege. Factor in those battles I consider skirmishes, and you'll see what I mean: the Nazgul assault on Weathertop, the fight in the mines (which is dominated by the Balrog), and the attack of the Uruk Hai by the great river, are all radically different.

4. Combat rules/style

Just as there's lots you can learn about hand-to-hand combat, there's also research to be done on large-scale fighting. There aren't rules, exactly, but there are principles that are generally held to be true, which can be studied: why it's good to fight from high ground, for example, or where to deploy different kinds of troops. It is simplistic, perhaps, but most troop-types have strengths and weaknesses depending on who they are fighting. Cavalry, for instance, can be fast, powerful, and intimidating in a charge against infantry, but they are vulnerable to pole-arms (spears etc.). Those spearmen are, in turn, vulnerable to armored swordsmen. Archers can be lethal at range but are quickly decimated by troops who get in close. Roman legionaries had particular shield configurations designed for self-protection, while the Macedonians used phalanxes with over-sized spears, and the Carthaginians used massed war elephants to break up enemy formations. And so on. All tactics had their strengths and weaknesses, and what worked well against one opponent was disastrous against another. Break through the Macedonian phalanx and the soldiers with their long pike-like spears are powerless against short-swords. Force the elephants back on their own troops and you destroy the attacker. The basics can be learned quickly through research, and a fun way to practice the principles of battle is by playing some

RPG games (like *Warhammer*) and computer games such as *Medieval Total War II*. These aren't always accurate, but they are a good starting point. Changing the nature of the conflict in terms of troop types also helps maintain a sense of variety.

5. Size
My books tend to deal with armies of hundreds, a few thousand at most. I like this scale because I feel like my core characters can still play a significant part without disappearing, and that their experience can be written as representative. I admire the skill of authors who can handle tens of thousands without getting generalized or tedious, but I'm not sure I'm ready for that (and have been disappointed reading some old-fashioned high fantasy that doesn't do it well).

6. Perspective
Because of the kinds of books I write (the Will Hawthorne books are first person), I stay in the head of a single character throughout a battle. This creates particular challenges in terms of both maintaining interest and showing what's going on. If you can cut between different points of view you get both more variety and a fuller perspective on the action. The advantage of a single perspective (especially a first person one), is that it's easier to keep character uppermost: the account becomes less a tactical depiction and more a single participant's experience. That can be exciting and terrible in useful ways.

7. Should I stay or should I go?
Contrary to most heroic accounts of battles in film, few armies fought to the death unless they were given no choice. A twenty-five percent loss of forces was generally more than enough to precipitate a rout, which is very different from a retreat or tactical withdrawal. How long your soldiers stick around in a losing fight will depend on why they are there in the first place, and that's something you have to address when you draw up the social, cultural, and economic rules of your world. Are they professional soldiers fighting for a cause they believe in, or are they mercenaries? Are they conscripted peasants or are they trained knights ideologically invested in the code of battle even if they are only fulfilling feudal obligation? Unless you are working in the realm of absolute good and absolute evil (I'm not), you need to think hard about what factors influence how hard your troops fight and when they decide they've done more than enough to keep honor or payment intact.

David J. Fortier
A.J., wonderful macro considerations that I wish more authors would recognize. I've read my fair share of heroic fiction and it grates on my

nerves when authors don't pay attention to at least the simplest of tactical concepts or armor considerations. I'm not asking for it to be completely historical, just that the story adheres to some sense of reality.

What strikes me most in all you've written here was the last part. The fighting-unto-death heroic scenario is oft overplayed. If a unit of troops were self-sacrificing for the greater good, such as at Thermopylae, I can see them staying until the end, but otherwise it would be a rare occurrence. Most troops would fight as long as they think they can win, even if that margin of victory is slight.

I'm curious as to how you're battle scenes are done in first person. I've just written a skirmish (200 vs. 100 soldiers) and found it tough. My scene is terribly up-close and personal, but the grand scope is lost. The overall sense of what happen needs to be discovered when my character comes down from his berserker rage.

A.J. Hartley

NGD, glad you found it useful. You're right about it being hard to get a sense of the overall battle from a first person perspective. For me it helps that my character is anything but a berserker, and is therefore fairly cool-headed, if only because he's gauging when to run away. When there are lulls in the combat, of course, he can get information from others about what's going on (or what is rumored to be going on) elsewhere.

Self-Editing

The Editor Can Fix That . . .

Misty Massey

A student came in yesterday and asked me to take a look at a book he's writing. Generally speaking, I've adopted the very wise policy of many of my fellows, and stopped looking at the work of hopefuls. There are liability problems, not to mention I just don't have the time to spend fixing someone else's manuscript when mine isn't finished. But I felt a certain responsibility toward the student, so I agreed to give it a look.

He'd handwritten six pages in pencil on notebook paper. It was full of telling instead of showing, it was lacking in the kind of detail that might catch a reader's interest, and he changed verb tenses with every sentence. I could tell that he wanted to make it better, so I carefully, cautiously pointed out ways I thought he could improve his work. He seemed to accept my suggestions, until we reached the grammar. "Doesn't the editor fix that?" he asked.

Uh . . . no.

Your editor will read your work and tell you what doesn't fit. She will answer your questions, help you come up with titles, laugh with you over your crazy book trailer (or maybe that was just me!) She will send you jpegs of your cover sketches and squeal with you over them. She will remind you when your deadlines are looming, pass along the tear-sheets of good reviews and reassure you that the ugly ones don't define you and your work. But she will not write one word of your book.

One of the things expected of published people is a grasp of the fundamentals of grammar. Telling a story in the written medium requires that the writer be able to communicate clearly to all readers of the language in which he's writing. This is one of those times when you must know the rules before you can break them. One or two accidental mistakes in a manuscript are okay. We all muff things now and then. If you, the writer, can't see that you're writing a sentence in past tense, followed by one in present, and then a third in past imperfect, then back to past again . . . you're not ready for the market.

Granted I've only worked with one editor, so there could be editors out there who will do all that work for you. But I'd venture to say they are few and far between. It's still better to get it right the first time, so that your editor can busy herself with all the fun stuff I mentioned before. Wouldn't you rather keep your editor happy?

David B. Coe
My editor does many things to my manuscript (and I'm in the middle

of going through his edits on a manuscript right now) including dealing with meta-issues like plot, character, pacing, etc. He's also good at finding certain mannerisms that I'll pick up in the course of writing a book (I know that other authors have this problem at times as well)—little phrases that I'll repeat or fall back on when nothing else comes to mind. And yes, at times he'll find syntactic stuff that I miss or ignore.

That said, you're right. I try to clean up my manuscripts as much as possible before sending them in, not only because I want to keep my editor happy, but because I can find the mechanical stuff myself. What I need from my editor is insight. I need him to help me make this book as good as it can be. If he's constantly dealing with grammar and the like, he can't delve into the larger issues, and he can't help me as much as I want and need him to.

Harry Markov

I know that the writer has to have a pretty good control over grammar, but what happens, when there are mistakes infrequent or so that show that the writer has skills, but lacks in a certain field of grammar? I'm curious to know whether the writer gets totally dismissed from the business or is helped by agent and so on to prosper in that field.

Faith Hunter

I have problems with loose and lose and loss. I know a writer with problems with your and you're, and its and it's. One of those brain fart things.

An editor and/or agent is always willing to help with them, but only after one has developed a relationship with said VIP. Rule of thumb? Your first five pages have to be grammatically perfect. *Perfect!* If you have baited and hooked your VIP by the first five, then they will usually be willing to assist with detail stuff, and even much bigger stuff. Or at least that has been my experience.

Misty Massey

Harry, it's like Faith said. Once you're in, you can make a few boo-boos and the world won't end. But if you do make those mistakes, your editor will send you the pages and let you fix them.

A good critique group (or a good beta reader) can help with making those first five pages perfect.

Developing Your Internal Editor
David B. Coe

How do we edit our own work?

I often tell aspiring writers to share their work with friends or family members so that they can get feedback on their writing. Ideally, we want beta readers who we trust will tell us the truth about our books or stories, someone who will be brutally honest without being cruel. As professionals, we have editors who work through our manuscripts with us, and I've often said that you can tell when a writer gets so successful that he or she stops accepting editorial direction. His/her books become bloated, long-winded, and far less compelling. When it comes right down to it, we all need external editors, people who can look at our writing from a fresh perspective and tell us what works and what doesn't.

I would argue, though, that we writers also need to develop an internal editor. We need to learn to correct our own mistakes, to recognize when our stories are breaking down and why. Self-editing isn't an easy skill to develop. It can take years; for some writers it never fully happens. But if you can teach yourself to edit your own books and stories—if you can learn to read them with a critical eye and anticipate the problems that a professional editor might find— you give yourself a better chance of impressing an editor or agent with your work.

So how do we identify the weaknesses in our own writing? How do we overcome that proximity to our work that makes it hard to spot typos, much less significant flaws in character development or plot or voice? One easy trick is to put work away for a time. Finish a story or book and put it away for four or six or eight weeks. When you go back to read it again, you'll find that you see the story with fresh eyes, and that weaknesses you hadn't spotted before appear with discomforting clarity. The problem with this approach is that we often don't have the luxury of so much time. Either we have deadlines we have to meet (submission deadlines, assignment deadlines if you're a student) or we simply don't want to take the time out from our current writing project. *This* is what we're working on now, and we don't want to put a six week hold on our work. (I understand these concerns quite well; but I will add here that I ALWAYS put my work away for a time after finishing it, because this simple approach to self-editing works enormously well for me.)

If putting work away for a time isn't an option, I would suggest a couple of other approaches, both of which I use with some success. One is to choose a specific reader—someone whose tastes I know quite well—and try to put myself in that person's mind as I read through my work. In other words, I imagine that

I am my editor at Tor or my agent or my wife or my high school writing teacher, and I read the story as I expect they would. Sounds hokey, I know. But it works. I can hear my wife or my agent in my head reacting to passages, both ones they would like and ones they wouldn't. More to the point, this exercise imposes that much-needed distance on my reading of the story. I'm no longer looking at it as the writer; I'm actually searching for flaws, for phrases and plot points that these people I know and trust would tell me don't work. It's a role-playing game of sorts. And that, ultimately, is what self-editing has to be.

If that approach doesn't work, try this one, which involves a bit more work on your part, but will probably offer the greatest chance of success. Go back and read an older piece—a story or a novel, or even part of a novel—that you haven't looked at in some time. The distance that we are seeking with all these approaches to self-editing should be there with this work. The flaws should be fairly obvious. Keep notes as you read through it. Jot down all the mistakes you can identify: character problems, plotting issues, mannerisms in your prose that are distracting. All of it. Every ugly quirk of your writing. Then go back to the new piece that you need to edit, and read it through with the flaws of the older work fresh in your mind. Chances are you'll be pleased to see progress in your work. You'll probably notice that you've corrected many of the mistakes you made in the older piece. You're a more experienced writer now; your work is better. Chances are you'll also see many of the old problems popping up again. But armed with the insight you've gained from reading the older work, you'll find them easier to correct in the new piece.

With time and practice you can teach yourself to be your own first editor. It took me several years and several completed novels to get there. And it wasn't just the act of writing the novels that taught me. It was also going through the editorial process with my editor at Tor. Revising my work gradually taught me to recognize the flaws in my writing, and to anticipate problems so that now I can actually do some self-editing as I write. Over time you can teach yourself to do this as well. And until then, perhaps these exercises will help you develop your internal editor.

David J. Fortier

I like the idea of reading an old piece and then going back to the new one with notes in hand. I'll have to try that out.

It has been suggested to me for line edits to read the book backward starting with the last line or paragraph. This way your brain can't get into the flow of the prose. I've never tried this, but its popular idea thrown around at the OWW yahoo group.

Reading to myself aloud works to a degree, but I still find I skip over a few missing words. Recently, I've started using a text-to-speech software to read the story to me. It takes some getting used to Mr. Roboto's voice, but it's very helpful. Not only is it easy to hear missing and misspelled words, but I also notice how often unique places and names are used since they aren't recognized by the software and they're spelled out.

David B. Coe

I've tried the reading backwards thing, and it just doesn't work for me. Or maybe it's just so dreadfully boring that I can't get myself to do it with a 100,000 word manuscript. I do find that reading a piece aloud helps a lot. And I like to print out my work rather than editing on the screen. Seeing the work in a new physical format helps me with that distancing process.

Revisions: Cutting Words

Stuart Jaffe

Today I'm going to give you some specifics about an important pass I always make sure to do—cutting out useless words. Of course, this is merely one approach and, as is all writing advice, merely one opinion. Mileage may vary.

Whether we like to admit it or not, word count is an important part of writing. Too high or too low and your word count can have a severe impact on the salability of your work. Since most of my experience comes from writing short stories, the problem for me is often a case of too many words; however, everything I'm writing about today applies to novel writing as well. And the first point is that **clear** and **concise** are the key phrases to remember. More importantly (in my mind, at least) is that if I'm already well within the market's preferred word count and I can knock-off even just ten, twenty, fifty or a hundred useless words, I then have the opportunity to fill that space back up with great details, depth of character, plugging up plot holes, etc. Or I can leave those words off, fill them in with nothing else, and just have a leaner piece of writing. In other words, by getting rid of extraneous wordage, I can better shape the work into what I really wanted it to be in the first place.

Now, some specifics:

Prepositional phrases

First, not all prepositional phrases are bad and need to be replaced. In fact, a well-chosen prep-phrase can add a lot of flavor to your sentences. Also, in some instances and some genres, prep-phrases help create the proper tone—such as epic fantasy in which "the sword of the honest" may have a better ring than "the honest's sword." However, often times a sentence can be re-ordered to avoid the prep-phrase, making the sentence cleaner and gaining you a word a two of free space.

> Original: Derek pulled the ladle from the bowl with green spots and poured himself a delicious helping of chicken soup into his bowl.

> Revised: *Derek pulled the ladle from the green-spotted bowl and poured himself some delicious chicken soup.* (-7 words)

Of course, context is crucial in your decision process. I didn't feel it was important to mention the receptacle he poured the soup into—in fact, most people will assume it was a bowl unless told otherwise. But if it had been a key issue, then I would have to re-work the sentence differently. Likewise, if the green-spotted bowl is not important we could rewrite it further:

Revision 2: *Derek poured himself some delicious chicken soup.* (-15 words)

Obviously, this last revision lacks any real beauty as far as a sentence goes but it does get across the idea clearly. And frankly, does the reader need a beautiful sentence about pouring soup? If the story says YES, then this is the type of extreme cut that can make the room for more valuable writing. After all, I just gutted out fifteen words. I could now write an entire sentence that tells us something about Derek.

Revision 3: *Derek poured himself some delicious chicken soup, but he tasted little of it—he couldn't stop thinking of Sarah.* (still -2 words off the original).

Was Doing

Practically any time you come across this construction of the word *was* with a verb ending in *-ing*, you can be more direct by cutting out *was* and just using the past tense of the verb. This one can save you literally over a hundred words depending on your writing style.

Ex: The boy was running downtown.

Revised: *The boy ran downtown.* (-1 word)

Similarly, avoid having your characters "begin" to do things. Just do them.

Ex: As the night chilled, Mark began to build a fire.

Revised: *As the night chilled, Mark built a fire.* (-2 words)

Little changes like this add up over the course of an entire manuscript. You'll be blown away by how many words you can cut in order to tighten your work.

Almost

Or nearly or barely or whatever vagueness you wish to employ. There are numerous reasons to avoid this construction and word count is among those reasons.

Ex: The bullet slammed into his chest, almost ripping a hole into his heart.

Rather than tell us what almost happened but really didn't, let's cut some words and fill them back in with what did happen, creating a more exciting, more visual sentence.

Revised: *The bullet slammed into his chest, nicking his heart.* (-4 words)

Obviously, context is important here. If in the story the heart shouldn't be touched at all then forget the heart and tell us what the bullet did hit.

Revision 2: *The bullet slammed him backward, snapping a rib in two.* (-3 words)

Notice here that by being specific about the rib, I no longer needed to mention the bullet hitting the chest and could replace that prep-phrase with something offering more detail.

These are just basic examples, but this is the kind of line by line, word by word editing I will do with the purpose of tightening my prose. The benefits are enormous. Your work will be clearer, read smoother, and take up less manuscript space, thus opening great opportunities for development of the important aspects of storytelling—character, plot, description, etc. And notice that the examples provided were simple sentences. If you don't want to kill too many of your darlings, then clean up the simple sentences so there's room for all those precious words you have used elsewhere. Without any change to your concept, these revisions will improve your writing tenfold (maybe more!) and make your work that much better. Good luck!

Emily Leverett

Now I've got a question. How do you (and all the Magical Words writers if they like) deal with the past perfect tense? The "had [verbed]"? It's for events that happened before the past events . . . and so I'm not sure how it can work in narration. I've used but, I'm not certain if it is a good idea. "She had come that evening wanting a conversation, a real connection, but she found a bloody body instead." (I dunno, I just made that up as an example.) I'm just curious what you folks think about that tense.

Faith Hunter

Emily, just my thoughts, and you did ask for *our* thoughts on it . . . (grins)

Your example is a *mini* flashback.

Let's look first at a *big* flashback: rule of thumb for me—for *big* scenic flashback—is two *had*s, followed by a return to whatever tense is used in the novel.

Ex: We had been walking home from school, and the car had pulled up beside us. The passenger rolled down the window.

Then after the big, scenic FB is done, two *had*s and a return to the tense.

For *mini* flashbacks the way you did it works for me. Stuart may have other thoughts, but that's the way I do it.

Stuart Jaffe

Emily, nothing wrong with using past perfect. I find if I write in first person POV it comes up more often. The thing you have to be careful with is the whole showing vs. telling. Past perfect can easily slip you into too much telling. The only other thing I can think of off the top of my head is that you need to make sure you have the grammar of it correct. If you don't know which verbs get the "had" and which don't, look it up. Otherwise, you'll be revising yourself silly trying to fix it all so that it makes proper sense.

Writers' Crutches: Words

Faith Hunter

We all have crutches in our lives, things we do that help us get through the day. Actions, habits, favorite foods, coffee or tea for that caffeine high, harder liquids for some of us, that pill at bedtime, calls to mom or dad, and much more can be our crutches. Some are dangerous; some are more like tics, OC habits that we see no need to break. I'm addicted to tea. As long as I have my tea I can write anywhere anytime. But when we bring crutches into our writing, into the flow of the words themselves, that quickly presents a problem.

A case in point: I was reading a mass-market paperback by a well-known writer, someone new to me, a book recommended by my local bookseller. By page twenty, the writer had used the word "smirk" five times. *Five times.* By doing so, he had cheated me by taking the easy way out in describing the reactions of his characters. Cheated me by *telling* me the reactions in five letters over and over again.

"Smirk" is a word that is seldom used in daily life, so when we read it, it stands out, as opposed to: is, or, if, of, that, and, the, what, etc., which are words that we use a lot more, but disappear from the page when we read them. Some words do that; others do not (like smirk). I had to put the novel down and I'll never read another book by that writer. He was lazy. He used a crutch. He doesn't deserve my money or my time. The story was good but the execution was poor. He was telling me, not showing me, and on that very basic level, his work was amateurish. The writer didn't do his job. The editor didn't do his job. I paid the price. And yes, it really ticks me off when this happens. More so when I do it myself. Much more so.

Yes, I have writing crutches, too. In one novel long ago, I used the word "passed" over one-hundred-seventy times, or roughly one time every other page. One of my beta readers caught it; I scanned and replaced all but thirty-ish of them. I tend to use the words "smile" and "grin" a lot. And "flicked," as in, "He flicked off the light." There are other words that I scan and change before my editor sees my manuscript. Fortunately, I have an editor who takes the time to see my work on many levels, and she usually catches what I miss.

One of my writer friends admits to overuse of the word "just," which seems like a Southernism to me, and odd for her, as she isn't Southern and doesn't use it in her speech. "Really" is another word she scans for.

Other words that are overused by writers are sardonic (which is a kind of insulting smirk, right?) dark/shadowed/bloody, etc. (in dark fantasy) sexy/hot/buff/pounding, etc. (in romance novels).

Well, you get the point, (she said with a smirk).

Anyone here want to share a word crutch?

C.E. Murphy

"Actually." "Apparently." "Smiled/laughed/grinned." "Elevated eyebrows." "Gaze"—and damn but that's a hard one to work around. "Looked up." "Turned back." Oh yes, we are painfully aware—but perhaps not aware *enough*—of our shortcomings . . . ☺

Axisor

"Just" and "really" I use all the time and I've been living in MO for twenty-four out of the twenty-five years of my life. I was under the impression that it was a generation thing. (I previously had some witty statement that used those words, too.)

My other crutches: suddenly, seemed, clearly, evidently, apparently (which those last three could also be used to describe my addiction to adverbs) as well as those words like "that" and "too" and ellipses and em-dashes.

I also have a stock description per story (one: they almost all have green eyes, another black . . .) but I have always wondered why most books have eye color for every character and I barely ever notice it in people I meet in real life.

More Writers' Crutches: Style
Faith Hunter

The two most common errors in any writer's work are:

1. **Telling instead of showing, and**
2. **Passive writing.**

Sometimes, it's almost invisible to us, an insidious way of writing that creeps up and takes over and suddenly it's everywhere, in every paragraph, in every chapter. And rewriting to get rid of it is a PITA. On a good day, we'll say, "I'd never do that. I don't have to look for it." On a bad day, we reread our work and, dang if it isn't there.

Mind you, there *are* times for the passive voice and for telling. Times when nothing else will work. But when we get into patterns, then it becomes a crutch. And crutches are weak writing, amateurish writing, and they can get our work canned. So I thought I'd toss in a few examples I've seen recently and ways around them, some doing double duty for scene anchoring, character development, or some other necessary device. I'm going to give the examples, and possible rewrites, and offer some explanations of what the changes accomplished that the original didn't.

Examples:

A. She felt tears slide down her face.
1. Tears slid down her face. (Active.)
2. Tears burned a hot trail down her chapped face. (Emotional reaction used to remind reader of previous injury or previous tears.)
3. She didn't know she was crying until tears dripped onto the backs of her hands and spattered onto the table. (Character development. Less showing, but more effective use of the more passive phrasing.)

B. He spit out the blood and told him to go to hell. (This also has pronoun problems.)
1. Charles spit blood and a tooth, aiming for the sergeant. They fell short and Charles laughed, the sound breathy and defeated. "Go to hell." (Active. Characterization and/or development.)
2. Charles choked on his own blood. He coughed and spit, managing a breath. "Go to hell," he said. And his head snapped back from the force of the blow. (Active voice, characterization, followed by passive voice to

indicate a change of mental status. Yes, we could have seen that from the original, but the writer didn't make use of it. It was a lost opportunity.)

3. Charles spat his blood to the floor and whispered, "Go to hell." And braced himself for the next blow. (Ditto on voice and characterization.)

C. Rachel put up her clothes and stared into the bathroom mirror. "So who am I?" she asked. She turned off the TV, and grabbed her purse and keys. It was time for a change. (The telling and the short, choppy transition of the emotional change are jarring.)

1. Rachel dropped the stack of clothes and stared into the bathroom mirror. "So who am I?" she asked. Her eyes stared back her, so like her mother's eyes. Her mother who had died broke, but surrounded by the love of family. Unlike Betty, who was rich, but sad and alone. She sighed, knowing that she was going to regret this, and reached for her keys. (Character development and showing.)

Revising Dialogue
Stuart Jaffe

Previously I've commented that the rules of dialogue are completely different from the rules of prose. This little statement means that revision *strategies* are also necessarily different. Clear and concise will not apply, for example, to a character who is ambiguous and verbose. Cutting down on prepositional phrases might make no sense if the speech pattern, dialect, or cultural background of a particular character requires such phrases. So what's a writer to do? Well, the keys to revising dialogue are the same keys used to write dialogue in the first place—developing your ear, and understanding the character who is speaking.

Since the words in between quotes are the literal reprinting of what was said, rules like grammar and punctuation often go out the window. It all depends on the type of character you are writing. A character like Gollum would sound horrible if he had to speak formally—"Excuse me, dear Frodo, but I require the ring which you bear. It is quite precious to me." Likewise, Paul Atreides would sound equally horrible if speaking in a guttural third-person—"Mmmmm, Paul wantses the spiiiiiice." Switch the two, however, and though Gollum's grammar is horrendous and Paul's a bit stiff, they fit their characters.

So, the first and most important aspect of revising dialogue is to think about the characters once again. In fact, revising dialogue is a lot like creating a scene—think about the characters, what they want, how they plan to accomplish it, what stands in their way, etc. Then look closely at the words they use. Do the quotes fit with their goals? Do the quotes fit with their characters? Do the quotes fit the characters' voices?

At its best, this is all the advice one needs. Of course, none of us are ever the best, most perfect writers we would like to be. So, here are some practical basics to think about that will both clean up the flow of your dialogue as well as cut wasted words:

Tag lines: You've heard it before, now hear it again. 99.99999% of the time the only tag line you need is "s/he said." Anything else is wasted words. Also, learn your pronoun rules so that you A) know when you need to bother with tags at all, and B) don't confuse your reader by mixing pronouns.

Utterances: Though a lot of real life speech is filled with *um, well, so, y'see, y'know,* etc., it does little for smooth-flowing, effective dialogue—unless such utterances are a specific character trait (and even then, it should be used sparingly or else you risk annoying the reader). For most characters, however, these things tend to slow the pacing. Think of utterances like cayenne pepper—a little bit goes a long way.

The Point: As in, get to it! This is another one of those situations where written dialogue does not mimic real speech. In a real conversation, we may talk for several minutes before we get to anything of substance. In a story, that's a sure way to lose your audience. Look at the best writers and almost all their dialogue enters and exits at the key parts of the conversation. The rest of it is told (not shown).

Ex: On the date, Bob and Jane talked for hours about their jobs, their pets, and their family. Then Bob leaned in and said, "You ever kill a man?"

The first sentence tells about the unimportant gabbing they did. The quote tells us that something interesting is about to be discussed and we don't want to miss any of it.

Names: Most people know their name and don't need to be reminded of it. If you find your characters addressing each other by name over and over, you've found a place to do some cutting.

Pauses: This is one I worked hard to stop in my own writing. A typical dramatic quote of mine from the past would read "I . . . won't . . . let you . . . do that." I got in this habit, I think, from my theater days. I could hear the actor in my head and wanted to recreate the speech pattern on the page. The problem is this—it doesn't work. Readers tend to ignore all those ellipses and just read the sentence straight. Those that do have the ear for the pauses suffer through every . . . single . . . pause . . . thus . . . slowing . . . down . . . the . . . story. Nowadays, I write these things straight—"I won't let you do that." I still use the ellipses for pauses, but only in rare instances and usually to show somebody out of breath, injured, incoherent, or such.

So, these are a few thoughts to get you started. Unfortunately, the ability to write good dialogue is mostly developed over time. You get an ear for it. The better your ear, the easier it is to revise dialogue. Hopefully, these little suggestions will help you on that journey.

David B. Coe
"This," he said, "is a terrific post." Really. Wonderful stuff. One of the things I do too much is have my characters use the names of those they address. Particularly my villains. I love the way it sounds, but I think I overdo it, particularly in early drafts. This is why revisions are so important. But that's another post.

Having an ear for dialogue is something that writers can develop through simple observation and, I hate to say it, eavesdropping. That said, Stuart is spot on: we want to be authentic in our writing, but not too authentic. Characters in a book need to be more directed in what they say and more articulate in how they say it.

Stuart Jaffe

David, I find all authors have at least one bad dialogue habit. I almost wrote "crutch," but they really don't help us as much as muck up the works. As long as you recognize what your habit is, then it's just a matter of revisions.

Faith Hunter

Stuart, I needed this post fifteen years ago, (where were you then???) and will keep it bookmarked to share with other writers. *Excellent* advice!

I totally overused ellipses in my earlier books. When they come back into print as backlist it gives me a chance to take out about 70% of them. And it makes me cringe to see the numbers. Why didn't some editor, somewhere, tell me to *stop with the dots, sweetie!?* Arrg.

I love to eavesdrop. For a writer it seems as important as people watching. And a lot more fun. Not too long ago, Misty and I were having tea at Starbucks and we realized that someone was listening to us. Really hard! Wonder if she was a writer? (grins)

Stuart Jaffe

Faith, fifteen years ago I was drowning in my own sea of ellipses! ☺ It's only now, after enough rejections, that I've figured this stuff out. Of course, fifteen years from now I'll be pounding my head against the stupidity of whatever I'm currently doing wrong in my writing. I don't think it ever ends.

Revisions: A How-To Guide

C.E. Murphy

A reader emailed me a writing question a few days ago, and gave me the all-clear to use its answer as a blog post, so I'm going to give it a shot. The question (and its surrounding commentary, which I thought was relevant) follows:

> "I know that some authors find rewriting easier (in some ways) than the initial creative process. Me, I can whip something out of nothing without breaking a sweat. But whenever I try to approach the highly necessary rewrite, I almost immediately get overwhelmed by the minutiae of things that need tending to. I am pulled this way and that, trying to keep track of the myriad of details that need to hover simultaneously in my forebrain—and I end up just fiddling with the niggling little grammar nits, polishing word choice, questioning whether that adverb is really necessary, and reassuring myself that all the independent clauses are safely sequestered within their parenthetical commas.
>
> "Consequently, the real work—that is, deleting scenes and rewriting the whole cloth of large sections—goes undone because of these distractions of questionable value. Sometimes, I think I might be better off deleting the damned thing and starting over from scratch.
>
> "So, my question: In your subsequent drafts, how do you keep the story from getting in the way of your rewriting?"

I know writers who do, in fact, just start their second draft from scratch. I don't personally, but sometimes I can see the appeal. I also am not one of those writers who finds the revision process vastly more rewarding than the initial writing process, although I do like the end result of all that work. But the actual revisions are exhausting, because I'm trying to hold three different versions of the story in my head at once: the story as it was, the story as it is *in process of being revised*, and the story as it needs to be.

From the lead-in to the question, it sounds like it's the second stage where it's falling apart for the writer. This makes sense to me, because it's the second part *I* find to be really headache-inducing. Knowing what you have to do, knowing what the story should look like on the other end, is a lot easier than figuring out how to do it. And I hate to say it, but on one level it's just a matter of practice. It's also a lot easier if a third party (like an editor) has said, "This is a part that doesn't work. Make it work," or, "I need to see some motivation for this action," or "I need more sense of setting here," because that gives me something to work off of.

Okay. *Rubs brain* This is hard to think about, actually, or at least hard to explain, because so much of it for me is just grim determination to get it done. But one thing I do is start with a hard copy. I *have* to start with a hard-copy. If I just try to work on screen my brain dribbles out my ear and I lose all will to live. More importantly, my brain is extremely consistent: if I start doing revisions on screen, I think, "Oh! This is a place to insert a clever line!" and I revise to insert it, then discover that a page and a half later, I already had that clever line in place. Hard-copy prevents me from doing that, and believe me, after doing it for the fifteenth time, I'm very happy to have read the bloody book all the way through and make myself aware of where my brain is likely to come up with clever lines that it has already come up with. ☺

Having a hard-copy also means I can physically strike sections out, even if all I leave myself with is a note saying "MAKE THIS MORE BETTER" (which, yes, is usually exactly what I write). It is, one way or another, a visual cue that this part needs *work*.

I usually start at the beginning of the story, but I don't think there's any compelling reason to do it that way. Another advantage of hard-copy for me is that when I'm further into the book and I've found something that needs setup earlier on, I can go back and leave myself a note on the paper that says "Joanne's facing Wile E. Coyote on page 235, there needs to be some kind of foreshadowing *here*, in this scene where I can stuff in a Looney Toons reference without it being too gratuitous." Then when I get to that in the on-screen revisions I can go "oh yeah" and take care of it immediately instead of having to flip back and forth.

Trust yourself—and when I say "trust yourself," I mostly mean "forbid yourself to nitpick"—on the sentence-structure level. There will, yes, be times and places where the sentences need work, but put that into a different mental space. That's copy-editing, not revising. It comes *after* revisions.

I frequently cut-and-paste the sections that need work out of the manuscript. So if I need to strike seven pages out of chapter three and just rewrite them wholesale, I'll take a version of chapter three, save it into the Second Draft folder, and then delete everything that needs to go in one big chunk. It's completely psychological for me: somehow it's less awful to gut chapter three by itself than it is to take it out of the manuscript and watch the whole page count of the manuscript collapse by eight pages. It also gives me a place (or usually more than one) where the original version of the chapter or scene is saved, so if I need to go back and rescue a sentence, I can snag it out of the original.

I use a lot of white space when I'm working on screen. If I'm working on a specific part of a scene and I know there's still lots to do further down, I just hit carriage return until I can't see the later material. Again, it's pure psychology. It's a matter of being able to *face* one page at a time; having new text that needs work continually scrolling up to face me is just disheartening.

Focus on one major problem/storyline/thread/whatever at a time. This year an editor asked me to do a major revision on a book. M.A.J.O.R. revision. What ended up happening was I rewrote the first half of the book heavily and the second half less so, and then in the second round of revisions, ended up rewriting the second half of the book heavily. I *knew*, when I submitted it the second time, that there were still problems facing the manuscript, but I had just run out of steam. I needed someone else's feedback to say "these are the things that can be punched up." Basically what I did was face one set of problems the first time through, and an almost completely different set the second time around (they had been touched on in the first revision, but it was sort of an emotional storyline revision vs. an action storyline revision, and I didn't have the mental capacity to manage both at once to the degree they both needed it).

David B. Coe

I like to revise on hard-copy, too, but I don't always do it. When I revise on screen, I employ some of the tricks Catie describes here. I'll copy a chapter into a different file and then revise, or I'll make a copy of the book and only fiddle with the new version, leaving the old one intact, in case I screw things up beyond repair. And I'll create that white space Catie mentioned, too. And yes, it's all psychological— creating a computer-based work space where I can feel free to tear stuff down and rebuild. Ultimately, that's the point for me. When I have trouble moving past the little stuff, it's usually because I'm afraid to make that first huge change. It gets easier for me after I've started the process.

You Know What I Mean?
Misty Massey

This morning I was watching the news and saw a story about a small-town mayor who was insisting that the police engage in no more foot chases after suspects. The cost of their injuries was driving the city's insurance rates sky-high, so she'd sent a memo to the department, saying "no foot chases, under any circumstances whatsoever." A reporter asked her what she expected the police to do if they witnessed a crime a short distance away and could easily overtake the suspect. Shouldn't they run over and intervene? But if they did, weren't they breaking the rule she wanted to lay down? She waved a hand and said, "They know what I mean."

Many writers do exactly the same thing. The world is so clear in their heads that they forget to tell the reader what they see, what they hear, and what precisely is going on. They assume the reader will just know what they mean. That's a dangerous thing to do. It's a little like traveling to another country and being certain you'll be able to find someone who speaks your language. Suddenly you're wandering the streets unable to even ask for directions. You're lost.

Readers can get lost easily. When they do, they stop reading. It's up to the writer to provide signposts and clues so the reader stays involved. The writer has to be certain he's saying exactly what he means on the page. Never assume the reader will get it. I've been guilty of it myself—reading out loud at critique groups, only to discover that the brilliant prose wasn't making any sense because I was writing so fast I forgot to let the reader keep up with my thoughts. Be brilliant, be thrilling, but be clear. Your reader will thank you.

Speaking of that, know the words you're using before you type them. Vocabulary is a joyful treasure, but only when you're using it correctly. If you're not sure what a word means, use the dictionary to look it up before you type it. And don't trust the SpellCheck. It can be a handy tool, granted, but it can lead you astray when it suggests other words for you to use instead of the one you misspelled. Once upon a time, a woman in my writing group was describing a murderer's living room. She mentioned the color of the walls, the soft carpet, the way the sunlight warmed the room, and then she wrote about the Nubian laid across the back of the sofa. I burst into giggles, and nearly choked on my soda. The writer stared at me as if I'd lost my mind. "It's just another word for a blanket. What's so funny about that?" she asked. She'd used the SpellCheck, which indicated that she could choose a different word than the one she initially typed, "afghan."

Trouble was, an afghan is a blanket. A Nubian is a person.

Daniel R. Davis

Yeah, I have dictionary.com bookmarked. It has thesaurus.com as part of it. Both handy tools when you're trying to keep from repeating a word too often or when you're trying to figure out whether a word means what you really think it does.

http://dictionary.reference.com/

One of the things I asked my proofers for are any places that I need to expand or any places that didn't make sense or lost them.

David B. Coe

This is another issue I've encountered recently working with a student. As you say, the story and setting and magic system are all quite clear in this person's head, but the explanations are too rushed and too vague to convey much to the reader. The end result is that none of the cool stuff this person is writing about reaches its intended audience. All the character development and worldbuilding in the world can't make up for unclear prose.

C.E. Murphy

laughs out loud Oh dear. The poor woman. ☺

I look up words even when I'm sure I know what they mean. I'm almost always right, but occasionally I do not look up words when I'm sure I know what they mean, and that way, surprisingly often, lies disaster. Or it'll be a word that I'm sure I know what it means, and it turns out I've got one letter wrong, and it makes it into a whole different word. Dictionaries are our friends.

BIC and Rewrite Tips

Faith Hunter

I have always believed that *everyone* is driven to tell stories, and that the need to do so is hardwired into our genetic structure. Early tribal survival depended on keeping the knowledge gained through pain and suffering available to future generations. Hence, humans stored knowledge in stories, which were easy to remember and offered wisdom, information, tactics, and strategy on many levels at once. Therefore, when someone tells me that he *wants to, needs to, must* write a book, I totally believe him. I completely understand that natural, deeply driven desire.

My usual reply to the quest for writing a book is this: The only way to learn to write a book is to write a book. That said, there are things a published writer can share that can make a difference. First, very basic stuff . . .

1. BIC. Those of you who have been here a while know that BIC stands for "Butt in Chair." If you don't keep the old keister in a chair in front of the keyboard (pad and pen work, too), you will *never, never, never* write. It doesn't matter what comes out of your fingertips at first. And trust me, you will look back at the early stuff and cringe, maybe weep.

2. Study everything you can find on writing. Read books about writing so that you will have an understanding of POV, narrative voice, character voice, dialogue, and all the other stuff you have to know, intellectually, in order to be a commercially-published writer. And read your favorite authors. Buy the books, don't borrow them, because you should read with multicolor highlighters, and highlight things that work and things that don't. This teaches your brain to recognize and be able to reproduce the techniques.

3. Go to conferences. Yeah, it's pricy. But if you can swing it, conferences give you a chance to do the one-on-one thing with editors and agents.

4. Stop agonizing over the editing. Write that *first* book all the way through. Push through the barriers. Just *do it!*

5. And, um . . . BIC.

Now for the less basic stuff that you need to have when you actually finish that first book. It's called rewrites. There are several things that writers (old hands and newbies) have to do in a rewrite. BTW, I have used sticky notes, colored pencils, and highlighters to track things on hardcopy. Track what? Let's start with the Macro Rewrites:

1. Track the plot arcs. Make sure you keep on track with the primary conflict story-line. Plot-lines need to be the foundation of every scene, every character interaction. When you find *anything* that is not part of one of the storylines, cut it and put it in a different file. That way you can pull it back out if you need it later. If you are thinking about future books in a series, be careful to not loose sight of the current conflict-line in *this* book. David B. Coe and C.E. Murphy (waves to David and Catie) are great at this! I haven't read Misty Massey's second series book (waves to Misty) so I don't *know* but I am sure she will nail it because she did so well at leaving hints and clues in *Mad Kestrel.*

2. Track every single character. Make sure no one disappears, never to be seen again.

3. Track your own voice. Find a hilarious scene in the middle of the book? You love it? But it's a drama and the scene doesn't fit? Cut it.

Then come Micro Rewrites:

1. Do my character's emotional arcs flow? Which brings us to transitions . . .

2. Transitions . . . also called "arcs," but I like transitions better. Everything in your book has to follow a logical ebb and flow. If you have two characters in a shower-room in a gym after a workout, arguing, we need to follow not only the argument, but the shower stuff. Is the floor wet under their feet? Is the scent of the place moldy or full of chlorine? Are the characters too mad to dry their hair (great for chick lit)? Do they drop their towels? Do other people come in and out? A lot of this is scene setting, but it contributes to the immediacy of the character interactions, too. Then: how does the argument contribute to the overall progression of the book?

3. Do I use powerful action words with strong emotional overtones? I just had the privilege of reading the first page of David B. Coe's new novel. OMG! Every word was filled with action and emotion. Very gripping! (Thank you David for letting me see it. I am honored.)

4. Do I spell well and punctuate properly? Do I make emotionally gripping paragraph changes? Don't laugh. *Where* a writer breaks a paragraph can strongly impact a scene.

I admit that I don't always do this stuff consciously anymore. I seldom pull out the pens and pencils, but I have used sticky-notes to mark and track plot changes in the last few books. I've got a lot of books under my belt and that makes rewrites easier, but I do still run through a book three times when I rewrite, and I pretty much do it by the Macro, then Micro method.

David B. Coe

I find that my macro-editing often takes place while I'm writing. I'll do something with a scene or character in, say, chapter 15, and realize that I need to go back and fill in earlier occurrences of that place or character to make the development consistent. For this reason I always write with what a house contractor might call a punch-list next to me. When I think of these things I jot them down on my list—AND THEN I KEEP WRITING. I do not stall the momentum of the book to retreat into rewrites (as one of the few good writing teachers I ever had put it). But at the end of the book, I have a list of macro issues to address, which provides me with at least a starting point for revisions.

On the micro stuff, I read through the manuscript out loud to catch transition issues, syntax problems, dialogue issues, etc. Reading out loud, as if for a conference reading, makes me conscious of how stuff sounds—and that, for me, is the best way of determining if it reads well.

I'd also add here that it's taken me a long time to learn to edit myself. I feel comfortable doing that now, but I'd written three or four books before I reached this point. This is why having a friend or partner you trust to read your stuff can be so valuable. And when I speak of trust, it's not always a matter of trusting them to spare your feelings by offering criticism gently. Sometimes, it's trusting them to be honest with you, to be willing to risk bruising your feelings in order to make your book as good as it can be.

Faith Hunter

Thanks, David. I agree totally about the punch-list and I keep one going, with and without sticky-notes, in the *after-the-book-is-sorta-kinda-finished* stage. I tend to keep a running outline going (as a computer file) and add the changes to be made into that—in bright color, usually red, which I change to teal when I have made the changes.

My pal Kim Harrison used to have sticky notes all over her desk with her punch list. It looked like she was decorating for the holidays!

There is no right way to do anything in writing.

Turns Out, Length Really Does Matter . . .
David B. Coe

Writing a novel is difficult enough; how am I supposed to write my book to a specific length? How do I know before I start writing whether my book is going to be 90,000 words long or 175,000 words long?

These are important questions, particularly in today's market, where book length has once again become an important issue for new authors and experienced ones alike.

Let me begin with an anecdote from early in my career. I was fortunate enough to contract my first novel on the basis of five completed chapters and an outline. When the contract arrived I read through it and laughed at the clause stipulating that upon completion the book would contain "approximately 100,000 words." I passed 100,000 words in chapter ten of a book that was more than twenty chapters long. I barely paused to wave at 100,000 words as I cruised past on my way to 200,000+.

When I finally sent my editor the completed first draft of the novel, it was 206,000 words long—well over 800 manuscript pages. He contacted me immediately to say that he had started reading it and it seemed pretty good, but that I should expect to have to cut the thing by approximately one third. Now, it turned out that the first draft had some serious flaws and I had to do extensive rewrites, but all of them had the effect of lengthening the book, not shortening it. Later in the process, when I asked my editor about the cuts he mentioned, he said that he hadn't seen anywhere to make significant cuts and we'd go to press at its current length. The finished book came in at just under 211,000 words.

That was only a dozen or so years ago, but in terms of the evolution of the market, it might as well have been a century. Unless your name is George R. R. Martin, you probably aren't going to be publishing many 200,000+ word novels, particularly if you're a first-time author. Brick-and-mortar bookstores want shorter novels for a number of reasons: limited shelf space, a desire for lower price points, and concerns about shipping costs, to name a few. Standard lengths for epic fantasy are now closer to 120,000 words. For urban fantasy the number is closer to 100,000. The third book in my Blood of the Southlands series came in at 140,000. The book I just wrote for my new project, which is not quite epic fantasy, but not quite urban either, came in at 107,000.

So, if you want to get published for the first time, those are probably the numbers you want to shoot for. As the example of my first book shows, editors will be flexible if they feel that a book works at a greater length, but those instances are the exceptions, and if you try to pitch a manuscript that's 225,000 words, you're going to have a hard time getting someone to read it.

Okay, so how do you write a novel to a certain length? (And please, let's keep in mind that all these numbers are approximate—you should aim to get within five to ten thousand words of these numbers. You don't have to hit them dead on.) There are two answers to this. The first is, "You don't." After thirteen novels, I've gotten to the point where I can write to a certain length and pretty much get there as planned. But I couldn't do it early in my career, and really there was no need for me to. The easiest way to get your novel to a desired length is to write the novel as it needs to be written first. Don't worry about length. Just write your book. Get it finished, *then* edit for length.

Let's work with some hypothetical numbers. Let's say your epic fantasy comes in at 180,000 words. Ouch. That's about 60,000 words longer than you want it to be, or half again too long. So you need to cut your book by one third. Looked at another way, if your book has, say, twenty-five chapters (this is another way in which dividing your book into chapters helps), you need to cut 2,400 words from each chapter. At 250 words per double-spaced manuscript page, that's about nine pages per chapter that you need to cut. Daunting, yes, but not impossible. Okay, maybe impossible. But let's say you do your best and you manage to cut five pages or 1,200 words per chapter. That's certainly manageable, and you'll get your word count down to 150,000 words. Not ideal, but certainly better than 180K. At least now you're far closer to the target length than you are to 200,000 words. More to the point, you'll probably improve your manuscript in the process. Cutting your word-count can force you to find more concise ways to say what you want to say. Or . . . Cutting your word count can force you to be more concise. See? I just saved eight words.

Going back to that question again—"How do you write a novel to a certain length?"—the second answer is, "You don't." Okay, I'm getting annoying, I know. But what you do is you write your chapters to a certain length, and you plan out your novel so that you have the right number of chapters. It's much easier to write a shorter piece to a certain length. If someone tells you to write something that's 120,000 words long, you'll laugh in his face; if someone asks you to write something that's 5,000 words—well, that's easy, right? Twenty-four chapters at 5,000 words comes to 120,000 words. You prefer shorter chapters? Fine, write 3,500 word chapters—about thirty-five of them. And if in writing your novel you find that you need one or two extra chapters (or one or two fewer) you'll be all right—if your 120,000 word novel comes in at 127,000 or even 132,000 no one is going to mind.

"But I'm a seat-of-the-pants writer!" you say. "I can't plan out my thirty-five chapters or my twenty-five chapters or even my next chapter!" Well, at the beginning of your career, as you're trying to get that first novel published, you need to try. I started out as a dedicated outliner; now I'm morphing into something of a "pantser." You can change, and if you're finding yourself writing novels that are forty or fifty thousand words too long, you might want to consider a new approach.

Even as I've come to rely less on outlines, I continue to use the chapter by chapter approach to estimating book lengths. I said from the outset that I wanted my Blood of the Southlands books to come in at around 140,000 words each, and I got there by planning each book at about twenty-five chapters. My chapters were coming out between twenty and twenty-five pages long. So if you do the math, twenty-five chapters times an average of twenty-two to twenty-three pages, times 250 words per page, equals about 140,000 words.

This isn't a very romantic notion, I suppose. We like to think that books just flow from a writer's imagination, word counts and chapter numbers be damned. But the fact is that we are not only artists, we are also business people. Our art is subject to the limits and trends of the market. I love to write and I want to continue selling books. So I do what I can to make my books as marketable as possible, including writing my books to specific (approximate) lengths.

The first five books I published were all over 200,000 words long. The next book I sell to a publisher will be slightly over half that length. And it is probably the best thing I've ever written. If I can learn to write shorter, more marketable books, so can you.

Mark Wise

I worry about coming in under limit, rather than overshooting. Is there a problem if a fantasy comes in at 80K instead of 120K? Would an editor come back and say, "This needs to be longer. Add more."

David B. Coe

Mark, it is possible that an editor of epic fantasy would look at an 80,000 word manuscript and think it was a bit thin. You might want to see if there is another thread you can add to the plot to make the book a bit fuller. On the other hand, it's your first book, and the market is looking for leaner and tighter, so 80,000 might be just what some editor out there is looking for. Also, is it adult or YA? If it's YA, 80,000 is perfect.

Slotted Spoons and the ABC(D)s of Beta Readers

A.J. Hartley

I was serving peas with dinner the other night, using a slotted spoon to get them out of the pan, and I had one of those moments of wonder at the sheer useful-ness of the utensil in my hand. I mean: it's a spoon—and therefore excellent for collecting things—but it has holes, so all the unwanted water doesn't wind up on your plate. Brilliant! Simple but effective, requiring no skills or training to use. And who invented the slotted spoon? We know not. If we did, we'd put up some kind of spoon-shaped monument. With holes in it.

My point. Some things are so fantastically useful that you just stand in awe. Today I offer one of those things. First off, let me say that this is not my idea and you may have come across it before. I heard it at a conference and, though I can't for the life of me remember who said it, I feel sure that she wouldn't mind my reiterating it here. So here it is, a slotted spoon for writers.

Specifically it's for dealing with beta readers. Most people to whom you give your manuscript, give you advice which, though well-intentioned, is muddy, self-contradictory, or platitudinous. Worse, some beta readers really want to be alpha writers, so their advice is colored by The Way They Would Have Done It. So. The slotted-spoon idea is designed to take much of the waffling out of the process, making it as easy as possible for your readers to clearly convey their experience with your manuscript.

You ask them to read the manuscript (hard copy or electronic: doesn't matter) and ask them to periodically mark any passage that strikes them with one of the first 4 letters of the alphabet. This is not a ranking system, and you might prefer to leave the A out entirely. What it stands for is this:

A = Awesome. Something about this just blew me away. Excellent.
B = Bored now. Ten pages on minor character's lineage? I'm sure it's
    really clever and all but . . . I've got QVC to watch.
C = Confused. He said what? The people of Anth believed in what?
    He can get out of the rabbit burrow because . . . ? Huh?
D = Don't believe it. His horse just happens to be exactly where he
    needs it? He's never picked a lock before but he manages it in 30
    seconds? No way. Sorry. Not buying it.

Exactly how you spell them out doesn't really matter, beyond the key word (bored, confused, don't believe). Use this and you'll discover two secrets of the beta-reader universe:

1. Giving readers nothing but one of four letters makes them more honest. They don't have to explain or be polite because they know you don't expect them to.

2. The Slotted Spoon works for both you *and* your reader. The reader doesn't have to worry about how to phrase (or remember) their thoughts (esp. their critical thoughts) and they don't have to keep extensive notes. You get clear, precise feedback which—whether you agree with it or not—will help you address potential audience response to your book.

Without other clutter to think about, your readers get better. They can go with the flow of the narrative without getting bogged down—pausing only to scribble a letter periodically—so what you get is much closer to actual reader response rather than Attentive, Thoughtful Beta Reader who Must-Think-of-Something-Smart-To-Say-If-Only-To-Prove-I-Really-Read-It response. Put a few of these marked-up narratives together and see if patterns begin to emerge. If reader #1 gives an A to what reader #2 gives a B or D, chances are it's a wash and you need someone else to break the tie. But if reader #1 and 2 both say it's a C, you know you still have work to do. In the end, it will come down to your instincts anyway. But where patterns do emerge, you can concentrate on figuring out what's wrong and how to fix it.

One final note. If you find yourself disagreeing with the patterns that emerge, you have one of two problems. The first, and easiest to deal with, is that some or all of your beta readers are wrong for this book and don't reflect your target audience. If so, fire them politely. You don't have time to be polite with readers who wish your dark urban fantasy was Jane Austen (the original, not the one with zombies). Find the right readers for your genre and move on.

The second problem is more serious. There's no point having readers of any kind if you don't listen to them. If you can't find readers whose input you value, and you persist in giving your own writing A's where your readers give it B's, C's and D's, you need to seriously re-evaluate your work and your goals. It's fine to write for yourself, but if you want to be published and read by others, you have to pay attention to what people think of your work. If you have to explain to practically everybody why your book (or chapter or sentence) is actually good, it probably isn't.

And that's it. This will be my shortest post ever on Magical Words, because if you over analyze a slotted spoon, the thing loses its mystery, and no one wants that.

Revisions: When is Enough Enough?

Stuart Jaffe

I had planned to write something else, but I've come across several discussions (including a few here at Magical Words) concerning when to *stop* revising. Revisions are a necessary aspect of the creative process, but how do you know when you've gone too far? Where is the point when you're doing more harm than good?

Of course, there's no easy answer to this. There never is. It's mostly (but not entirely) subjective. And yet, we authors have to get a feel for this mystical demarcation point or else end up ruining our manuscripts with infinite revisions.

Well, just as the writing process is unique to each writer, so too is the revision process. There are those who are methodical and meticulous, just as there are those who play it fast and loose. However, if you're just starting out (and thus don't have a process firmly in place) or if you're looking for a new tactic, here's my suggestion: Make a battle plan. With this technique you'll address everything in a manner that will leave you feeling you've left no stone unturned, yet you won't feel the need to keep going over the same territory again and again. Here's how it works:

Decide which key elements you want to revise in each pass through the manuscript. Perhaps you want to focus on a particular character. Perhaps the plot doesn't feel strong enough. Perhaps you want to make sure your dialogue is tight or your metaphors and similes are the best they can be. Perhaps you simply want to make sure all the core elements are working effectively. Whatever you feel is important, list it on a piece of paper. It's okay if it's a long list—it probably will be.

Now, combine some of the ideas that go well together. Metaphors and similes will go well with tightening all description. Dialogue may fit well with pacing issues. Try to keep it down to about two ideas for each pass. At this point, your list may consist of about five to ten passes. If you're thinking ten rounds of revision sounds insane, I agree. Don't worry. You'll probably do a lot less. If your thinking ten isn't enough, you have my sympathies.

When you start revisions, keep focused on whatever your list denotes. It's okay to fix other problems you notice along the way (if they're small), but try to stay focused. For larger issues that don't apply to your current focus, jot down a note so you'll be sure to tackle it at the appropriate time. This simple approach has numerous benefits:

- You'll know you've handled the issues you intended to handle and have done so to the best of your ability.

- You'll have cleaned up many little things (typos, misspellings, grammar, etc.) that will make subsequent passes easier.

- In the course of re-reading your manuscript, even though your focus was on one or two main aspects, you'll have started picking up on other problems. By the time you get to the third pass, you'll already have solutions for many items on your list (and probably several not on the list).

- You'll gain a deeper knowledge of your manuscript and how the pieces fit together, making each revision more productive.

- With practice, you'll be able to juggle more tasks in each revision.

In the end, you'll find a number of revisions that works for you which addresses everything in a solid, systematic fashion. For me, I find around three in-depth revisions, each handling about three main points, are more than enough. Lately, I've been trying to do more revising as I write the initial draft (I'll talk about that in another post), so perhaps I'll be down to two passes. Anything more than five sans editor/agent/reader feedback sounds like overkill to me, but each writer is unique, so I make no judgments. Just remember that by approaching revisions in a focused, clear-cut manner, you can rest assured you've done your best. You don't need to keep going back. You do need to send it out, cross your fingers, and get started on the next piece.

David B. Coe

I do a lot of polishing as I write—that's just my approach. But I make notes to myself as I go about issues that need to be dealt with, be they big meta-plot problems or tiny things like inconsistencies in spelling or capitalization. Then I fix things, look for my various crutches. Finally, I do a slow read through in which I try to see how the book flows and what, if anything, still needs work. This is where I am now with the WIP. When I'm done with this, of course, I send it off to my editor and agent for their comments. I do another set of revisions with them, then copy edits, then proofs. By the time I'm done, I've read the book through 4 or 5 times. But I find that I need distance between each reading. If I read through and revise, then immediately do another pass, I start to glaze over and miss stuff. Just me.

Faith Hunter

Stuart, I enjoy seeing how other writers revise. And I adore the term "battle plan" as it applies to revisions. Cutting, slicing, splicing, pasting, dumping . . .

I like it! I'm stealing it!

And I particularly agree with this: "Just try to keep it down to about two ideas for each pass." When I started out, that was all I could manage, and I did maybe five passes for each book, all in hard copy. Oy . . .

But lately, I've been able to cut it down to two passes, one to revise and one to make sure I actually did what I wanted to do. I revise all in one pass with my wonderful multicolored sticky-notes on hardcopy.

The Business

Artistic Choices and the Market

David B. Coe

Two common themes come together in this essay. First, I've written and spoken before about how often my characters surprise me in some way, be it through the assertion of a trait I hadn't seen in them previously, or through the unexpected twisting of a plot thread. My favorite example of this is the time one of my Winds of the Forelands characters told me that she was pregnant literally as I was typing the words. Now fortunately this character was a woman, so it didn't make things TOO difficult for me. Still, I've informed my characters that in the future I could use a bit more notice on such things. Not that they listen to me. . . .

The second thread is one that comes out of a question readers ask me quite often: "Does your publisher or your editor ever impose changes on you—force you to change things for marketing or 'political' reasons?" The answer to this is: "Less often than you might think, but occasionally." (Examples forthcoming.)

So today, I'd like to talk about changes that we as authors sometimes have to impose upon our characters and our plot. It would be great if we were able to listen to our characters always, to follow them wherever they take us regardless of what doing so might do to our plot outline. After all, life is like that, right? We are at the mercy of circumstance; any one decision can ramify through the rest of our existence.

To which I say, "Yes, but . . ." Writers are artists. Every story is an act of creation. And while spontaneity is certainly a crucial component of the creative process, so is control. My brother is a brilliant painter, and as he describes his art, it's clear that much of what he does with color and brushstroke happens in the moment, "unplanned" as it were. But he still has to impose his will on the work; there are matters of composition and balance that have to be maintained, or else the painting falls apart, becomes merely a collection of shapes and tones rather than a visual tale. The same is true of writing. We can't cede control of our work to our characters. Have you ever taken a child on a hike? She wants to explore, to stray from the path, and occasionally it's fine to let her. But you are responsible for seeing her safely home, for keeping her out of the poison ivy and away from the cliff ledges. Well, so it is with your characters. They may be adults in the story, but they're as self-centered and irrational as children, and they must be controlled.

But even more, there are times when we have to make decisions regarding plot or character or book structure that have less to do with the creative process than with more pragmatic considerations. Back when I was in the middle of Winds of the Forelands, which was originally planned as a four book series, my editor asked me if there was a way I could split the fourth book of the series in half. Booksellers were becoming concerned with book length and price point (the price of a book printed on the jacket), particularly with respect to hardcovers, and wanted to see smaller books. There was no way for me to split that final volume in half without destroying the narrative integrity of the book. But the third book wasn't out yet, and I found a fairly natural stopping point earlier in book three that enabled me to divide books three and four into three complete books, thus making it a five book series. This was not an artistic decision; it was a marketing decision. But it helped sales for the second half of the series in a way that did little or nothing to compromise the narrative structure of the overall project, and so it made sense.

I have, on a few occasions, had my editor ask me to tone down some language or make a scene slightly less graphic than it had been when I wrote it. I've had it suggested to me that I change a character's name or the name of something on one of my maps because the name might offend or put off or confuse readers.

Right now with my WIP I'm seriously considering changing the gender of a lead character because there is some gender imbalance in the dramatis personae as it currently stands. What difference does that make? Plenty, actually. To some degree people enjoy reading about characters like themselves. Well, currently my books are getting a lot of attention from *Romantic Times*. The Southlands books are garnering very good reviews from *RT*, and my female readership is on the rise. This is something I want to nurture—a majority of all readers are women, and I want them to continue to read my books. And right now my book has too many boys and not enough girls. Does this make me crassly commercial? Maybe. But as I've started thinking about this change, I've started seeing exciting possibilities for sexual tension between the character I'm considering changing and my lead character.

Yes, I'm an artist, but I'm also a businessman. Part of my job is to be true to my characters and my story, but part of it is to sell books. I say this not to rationalize or justify. Well, okay, maybe a little bit to rationalize and justify. But also because this is the reality of what I do. To some degree I write for myself, and I have been known to fight long and hard to preserve an artistic decision with which my editor does not agree. I also write for my audience, however, and part of my goal is to maximize that audience. The key for me is finding balance between the artistic and the commercial. If I thought that changing the gender of a lead character would compromise the integrity of my story, I wouldn't do it, no matter the commercial benefit. As it happens, I see artistic potential in a choice that might also help me commercially. I'd be a fool not to consider it.

If I can be so bold as to offer advice: you should always strive to be true to your creative vision, but you shouldn't ever be embarrassed to think about the commercial ramifications of your artistic choices. There may be virtue in sticking to your artistic principles no matter the cost, but if nobody reads your book, who's going to know how virtuous you were . . . ?

Misty Massey

David said, "There may be virtue in sticking to your artistic principles no matter the cost, but if nobody reads your book, who's going to know how virtuous you were . . . ?"

wild applause

I had to rewrite *Mad Kestrel* twice for my editor before Tor bought it, and I became so tired of hearing people tell me I had sold out for doing what my editor asked of me.

If the changes he wanted had been out of whack with the final story, I'd have argued. But they weren't. His suggestions were solid and improved the story, and I ended up published. I think it all comes back to knowing what we want out of writing. ☺

L. Jagi Lamplighter

Nice article, David. My husband, John, actually had an editor request a change for political reasons once. John wrote his first novel in the 90s, but it came out soon after 9/11. In the book, he had a bunch of bad guys who were soldiers in the U.S. Army. After 9/11, his editor did not feel this was appropriate any more.

John sympathized with his editor's point of view. He added a scene that made it clear that these particular soldiers were bad guys who had been recruited by the enemy for this purpose and not average soldiers. The scene both met the editor's criteria and improved the story (it added additional dimension to some of the lesser villains.)

David B. Coe

Thanks for the comments, Jagi and Misty. Seems to me that the lesson here is clear: editors will ask for changes on any manuscript. Some of them will be purely aesthetic in nature; some will stem from marketing concerns. We as authors have to decide what we want to do with those suggestions. No one would say that you need to accept them without first examining them critically; but neither should you reject them out of hand. You want your book to be as good as it can be. You want it to reflect YOUR creative vision. And you want it to sell. Your goal in evaluating editorial comments and artistic decisions should be to find the best balance among those three things.

A Conversation With My Editor
C.E. Murphy

A couple weeks ago my Del Rey editor called me up to talk about revisions for *Truthseeker*, the little paranormal romance I'd written for her. Now, my agent had mentioned a few days earlier that she'd talked with my editor, and that my editor had some concerns about the level of romance in the novel. I wasn't, personally, absolutely certain that the romantic elements in the first several chapters really meshed with the rest of the book, so I was okay with that.

This is what my editor actually said, though: "I'm afraid the book might fall too perfectly between romance and fantasy, and therefore satisfy neither. Would you consider rewriting it to remove the hero's point of view and strengthen the heroine's?"

I said, "Er." And then, "Er, my agent didn't mention striking the hero's point of view . . ."

My editor, somewhat wryly, said, "She was probably afraid to."

Now, my editor made it very clear that this was a request to be considered, not an order from on high. She was even willing to give the book to one of the house's romance editors, to see if they thought it might do better *as* a romance, which I thought was pretty cool of her. (Although it gets into a whole different set of complications, because I'd probably want to publish it under a different name, then, and . . . yeah, all sorts of things. Anyway.)

Obviously this is a bit of a shock, for a writer. The book is about 86,000 words, and the hero's point of view is about 20K of that. My first thought (after "buh, uh, uh, um, uh, buh") was, "Well, I can almost certainly *reduce* his point of view . . ." I told my editor that I'd have to re-read the book and see what I thought, but I'd certainly take the idea of cutting him entirely into consideration. She thanked me, and added that although she'd read the book twice, she still didn't, in the end, really feel like she *knew* the heroine very well.

Augh! The book *definitely* needs revision, in that case. I sort of reeled and said, "Okay, that's a really good thing to know, that's important," and went to think and re-read and try to deal with that problem.

Clearly, reducing the hero's point of view so I can get further into my heroine's head and let the reading audience know her better is one way to deal with it. It's not going to change the *story*, just the delivery of it. Right now, though, boy howdy, does it feel stiff and awkward and unwieldy. I'm trying to remind myself that I really need more than two chapters of revisions to be able to say whether this will or won't work.

The truth is, it probably will. Here's a secret about editors: they're usually right. Not always, but usually. And this kind of thing is part of the job. Most of the time you're not asked to rewrite a third of the book, but sometimes it happens.

It behooves you not to throw a hissy fit. Even if in the end you decide your editor is wrong—and that *is* an option; if for some reason it turns out this really is *not* working, I will be able to go back to my editor and say, "Look, I tried, it turned into a cludgy mess, how else can we approach this?"—you're going to get a lot further with an attitude of, "Aagh, okay, holy crap, let me step back and think about this," than you are on "OH MY GOD YOU WANT ME TO EVISCERATE MY BOOK⁉!"

Ultimately, we're *all* trying to get the most sell-able book on the shelves as possible. My editor didn't ask for these changes because she's mean, or because she hates me, or because she hates my book, or because she wants me to flounder in obscurity. She asked for them because, in fact, she's trying to make sure the book hits solidly in the ranks of what people want, and so my sales numbers stay strong, and so I get to keep writing and publishing more.

We can't know if it'll work. We can do our best, and one thing that's part of *my* job as a writer is to understand that my editor has, y'know, a pretty good idea of what works within my genre and what doesn't. (So does my agent, who liked the book as-is—but my agent also represents romance, whereas my editor is more like me (and many sf/f readers) in that she doesn't read romance at *all*, and so the romantic elements of the book as it originally stands weren't so much to her taste. If they weren't to her taste, she figures there's a big segment of the sf/f audience for whom they won't be tasty, either.)

This is a bizarre job, guys. It's hugely creative, but it's also hugely commercial. Do I feel like I'm selling out, or selling short, by seeing if I can change the presentation of the book to make it more palatable to sf/f readers? Absolutely not. It's my *job* to give people what they want, and if that means I have to take my ego off the plate (which to some degree, with this book, I do, because I was *proud* that I'd managed the romantic elements as well as I had!) and go back to the keyboard, then that's what I'm going to do.

Which isn't a very romantic, frothy, happy-bunnies way to look at it, I admit. But the business side of this is just as important to me as the creative side, so it's a-revising I go.

Faith Hunter
No happy-bunnies, no. And OMG what an awful rewrite. But what a wonderful editor to show you a way to make it work. Of course, you may find another way while you are writing, Catie. You are just that good!

On a panel at ConCarolinas, I mentioned that a favorite writer of mine posted a note to his fans (in the front his latest book) bragging that his editor said he was such a good writer that he no longer needed editing. The editor lied like a dog. It was awful. It *needed* editing in the worst way. (grins) I'll never read another of his books.

Writers all need editing. You have an amazing attitude. I'd have cried and wailed for a couple days before diving in. Good for you!

The Presentation of Your Submissions
David B. Coe

My fellow writers and I often say on this site that there is no right way to do something when it comes to writing. You have to listen to your own muse and allow your characters to do the things they're telling you they need to do. And ninety-nine point nine per cent of the time that "no-right-way-to-do-this" rule works. But there are exceptions, and one of the most important involves submissions.

Let me backtrack a moment and begin with this: many writers who are just starting out assume that agents and/or editors are always searching for that next new star, and to a certain degree this is true. But these same writers extrapolate from this a second assumption: that agents and/or editors will look through manuscripts submitted to them with an eye toward finding that star, and will therefore be looking for reasons to love their manuscript. And that, my friends, isn't the case at all. (A note here: much of what I'm about to say is equally true of editors of anthologies or magazines looking for short stories.)

Editors and agents get stuff from aspiring writers *all the time*. They have gobs and gobs of stuff to read *all the time*. When they are looking through these piles of submissions (or, more accurately, when their assistants are looking through them) they are not looking for reasons to love your manuscript; they are looking for reasons to reject it. Let me repeat that. Those who read through submissions are not looking for reasons to buy a book or a story, they are looking for reasons *not* to.

"What?" you say. "But . . . but that's awful!"

Actually, no it's not. It makes perfect sense. They have a pile of manuscripts and only so many hours in a day to read through them. The faster they can find a reason to reject the one they're reading, the sooner they can move on to the next, and get one submission closer to being done. This is why the hook is so important.

But at a more basic level, editors are looking at *presentation*. Does your manuscript look professional? Is it printed in a simple, readable font? Is it double-spaced, does it have proper margins? This sounds like foolish stuff, right? It's not. These folks are dealing with serious eye-strain. (That's only partially a joke.) More to the point, every publisher, every literary agency, every journal or magazine or e-zine that might want your work has submission guidelines that will tell you exactly how your manuscript should look. These guidelines (GLs in professional parlance) can be found online or can be requested by snailmail with a self-addressed, stamped envelope (SASE). They will tell you how your manuscript should look, where your name and address should appear on the first page, what other info should be on that first page (some magazines want a word count for short story submissions, some don't), what font size and spacing format you should use, whether you should send the whole piece or only a certain number of chapters, what other materials to include (cover letter, bio) etc. Get these guidelines for each place to which you submit work; don't assume that the GLs for one publishing house or agency will work for all the others.

If you submit to a place and don't follow their GLs, chances are your manuscript will be rejected without having been read at all. Professionals follow GLs. Don't follow them and you make yourself look like a wannabe, and a foolish one at that. And that's what the readers will assume. "This person doesn't care enough to follow the GLs? Then I don't care enough to read the manuscript. Next!"

Moreover, your manuscript should contain no typos. None. Okay, if they ask for three full chapters and you have a typo on page 42 in the third chapter, it probably won't doom you. Frankly, if they've gotten that far in reading it, you're doing pretty well. But a typo—any single typo—in the first five pages will probably lead to a rejection. You're aspiring to be a professional; take pride in your work and make it look and read perfectly. Professionals edit and proof their work; they find silly mistakes before they send out their work. That's what you should do, too.

Other miscellanea: don't use different colored fonts or "cute, interesting" fonts. Don't bind your submission or give it a fancy cover or put acetate over it. Just give them the manuscript and let it speak for itself; your work should sell itself. Professionals don't mess with bells and whistles; neither should you.

Presenting your work professionally will not guarantee you a sale, not by any means. But it will guarantee that your manuscript will get a fair reading. Look at it this way: those tired, overworked editors (or editorial assistants) are looking for excuses to throw your work to the side and move on to the next submission. By presenting your work professionally, you're denying them that excuse. You're forcing them to judge the submission on your terms not theirs. If they don't like the premise, or your hook doesn't work for them, so be it. But don't shoot yourself in the foot with your presentation.

A few other points: I always send short stories in a 9×12 envelope with a second, self-addressed 9×12 envelope folded inside with proper postage already affixed. I like to get my stories back, just in case the editor has made any margin notes (usually they don't). It's been a while since I submitted a book manuscript on my own (as opposed to having my agent send it), but I believe the assumption is that your manuscript will not be returned, so skip the SASE.

The key to all of this, though, is professionalism in your presentation. Again, make them read the submission on your terms, rather than allowing them to reject it on theirs. At least then you give yourself a fighting chance.

Faith Hunter
David, that "reason not to read" translates to other forms of judgment as well. I was a judge of the Mary Higgins Clark award in . . . '04, I think. I had specific criteria to follow and had 90-ish books to read. I would open that day's reading and if I saw an F-word or an onscreen sex scene I'd close the book because it didn't meet the criteria. The book might be *great!* but if it didn't meet the criteria, I didn't have to read it. Same with an agent or editor. Reasons not to read are important to them. Don't give them one.

Bait and Hook

Faith Hunter

Let's say you don't have mega-luck on your side. What can you do to improve your chances of a first-book-sale?

The answer is—a lot! It's a writing (and advertising) device called Bait and Hook. Not Bait and Switch, which a lot of writers try, but Bait and Hook.

I love to tell the story of the way one of my agents does business. He's a one man agency, and he gets an average of thirty-five submissions a day, seven days a week, holidays and vacations included. Some are email queries which he handles with a quick yes/no form letter. He has three:

- Yes, send three chapters and a synopsis.
- Yes, send the whole manuscript, and I want an exclusive. (Not used often.)
- No, thank you.

That will leave ten to fifteen full-manuscript and three-chapter submissions to read. *Every dang day!* So, he has a rule of thumb, phrased as a question: How little do I have to read to stop reading today? That is where you, UnPub come in with Bait and Hook.

If the first sentence is not a grabber he sends a rejection. If the second sentence is bad, ditto. If the first paragraph is okay, he'll set it aside to read further. When he has weeded out all but five, he'll read the first five pages of each. If nothing grabs him, it gets a no. If something grabs him, he'll send it to his daughter. She will read the first five pages, and send it back with a graded reply:

- You should take a look at this one.
- This one is fantastic!
- This one stinks. (Lots of those.)

His daughter is sixteen-years old. She has been his reader for four years, weeding out the non-acceptables. Yeah, a twelve-year-old was rejecting writers' manuscripts, and doing a great job at it. How sad is it that even a twelve-year-old girl can see when a book stinks? Does that mean that your book stank? No. That may have been the day he was on vacation and sent out blanket rejection letters. I know—*Ouch*. But every agency has days like that, which is why, if you don't have a personal entrée to an agent or editor, it becomes a numbers game.

Every agent I know has a system (criteria is the polite word) to answer the most important question of his day: How much (or little) crap do I have to read until I know I can stop reading today? So, UnPub's job is to blow the agent away. Bait and Hook.

At this point in a seminar I usually stop and talk about conflict, which makes the attendees feel like I missed something. No, I didn't skip over the Bait and Hook part. Bait and Hook is *all* about conflict and marketing. Every writer needs to be able to blurb his book in twenty seconds or less and then give the conflict blurb in twenty seconds or less. These blurbs are to be used in verbal meetings and pitches with agents and editors and in queries and proposals. Then that info has to appear in some form in the first paragraph(s) of the manuscript. Let me say that again:

That info has to appear in some form in the first paragraph(s) of the manuscript.

Examples? Sure. I'll use one of my own.

Marketing Blurb:

Early Anita Blake meets Jack Palance, when a kickass Cherokee skinwalker/ vampire hunter is hired to hunt down a rogue vampire killing off cops and tourists in New Orleans.

Conflict Blurb:

Jane Yellowrock has never met another skinwalker, or a sane vampire. When she is hired by the vampire council of New Orleans to track and kill a rogue-vamp who is killing and eating cops and tourists, she is placed in danger of being hunted down and killed herself. And her preconceptions about vamps and their blood-servants are challenged, along with her view of herself.

First two paragraphs:

> I wheeled my bike down Decatur Street and eased deeper into the French Quarter, the bike's engine puttering. My shotgun was slung over my back, a Benelli M4 Super 90, loaded for vamp with hand-packed silver-flechette rounds. I carried a selection of silver crosses in my belt, hidden under my leather jacket, and stakes were secured in loops at my jeans-clad thighs. The saddle bags on my bike were filled with my meager travel belongings—clothes in one side, tools of the trade in the other. As a vamp killer for hire, I travel light.
>
> I'd need to put the vamp hunting tools out of sight for my interview. My hostess might be offended. Not a good thing when said hostess held my next paycheck in her hands and possessed a set of fangs of her own.

BAIT and HOOK:

Consists of an introduction and development of a central character and/or his conflict. This device is a mixture of several other devices, used the first time you introduce a character, or open the story. When it works best, it is almost always a *mixture* of character and conflict together. It is best seen in the opening of a story.

In BAIT, you are also introducing the TYPE of story you are writing and trying to hook or interest the reader into reading. BAIT may offer both emotional tone and setting, character and action, or any combination of story. But its purpose is to introduce, modify, show evidence of change!

- In an idea story, you present the idea of the central conflict.
- In a character story, you present the main character
- In an action story, you start with action crucial to the central conflict
- In atmosphere story, you open with the setting (though this type of story is seldom published. An example would be "The Fall of The House of Usher").

Think about the beginning of your own novel or story and see if you did the job of BAITING your reader with the opening words—like tossing fish-food pellets to koi in a pond. Do it correctly and the agents and editors will gather just as quickly around your offerings.

Christina

Say you meet an agent and have a good face-to-face, give the agent your manuscript, and then six months go by with no response? What do you do? How do you get them to read what you've sent?

This is the second time I've had a six-month or more wait on a response. Is that normal?

Even if I have any talent, the great barrier for me seems to be getting anyone to even take a look at my stuff at all.

Faith Hunter

Christina, re: the six month wait. Arrrg! That is sooo frustrating!

When I send a *full* manuscript in, I include a card/note offering the agent a one month exclusive. After one week, I send a polite email thanking him/her for agreeing to look at manuscript and asking if he got it.

After one month, I send a polite email thanking them for the one-month exclusive, not mentioning that the month is up. After three months, I send a polite email asking if they have any thoughts about the manuscript. If you don't get a reply, screw 'em and move on to the next agent. If you get a reply, play it by ear.

If they asked for a partial, same three notes, but with out the exclusive comment.

IMHO

One Step Shy

C.E. Murphy

A friend of mine, whom we shall call Robin for the purposes of this essay, is sending out her first novel to agents. She emailed me recently because she'd gotten a confusing response from an agent, and was looking for advice on how to react.

The initial response was incredibly positive; the later response seemed to backtrack and asked some questions. The question that threw both Robin and myself was "Where do you see this novel being marketed?" which seemed like a real step backward from the initial enthusiasm. It also, to me, threw up a warning flag: an agent who has to ask that may not be the right one for your book. Ideally, your agent will be someone who has a very clear idea of where your book *should* be marketed. I asked who the agent was, and what agency he was with. As it turned out, this was not a new agent working for a flash-in-the-pan agency, which was my expectation. In fact, it was an established agent working with a major agency, which reassured me in terms of quality if not necessarily in terms of being certain this would be the right agent for Robin.

Robin emailed with her ideas about where the book might be marketed, and in turn asked where the agent thought it might be marketed. As it turned out, the agent was asking because he felt her book wasn't quite enough of any one thing to fit into the obvious markets, and he was essentially testing the waters to see if Robin was absolutely strictly wedded to the book as it was. He suggested a couple of books which he believed it could be marketed similarly to, under the right circumstances. And ultimately, he decided to turn it down—but provided a detailed revision letter, and said he would be very interested in seeing the book again if Robin did the rewrites.

I read the rejection letter, and in case Robin wasn't absolutely clear on it, told her it was an *incredibly* positive letter—which came as a relief to her. She'd *thought* it was, but then also felt that maybe he was just playing the role of fourth grade teacher and saying, "Tsk, tsk, Robin, you're not living up to your potential."

That is absolutely not what he was doing or saying. This, guys, is what one-step-shy-of-publication frequently looks like: an agent or an editor taking the time to tell you you're doing well and where you've gone wrong. It's not a failure to live up to potential: every single one of us as professional writers get at least one revision letter per book, sometimes more. Professional editors and agents are a step outside our books; they see things we miss, and usually they're things that make us go "Argh, why didn't I think of that?!?!" So as an unpublished writer, if you get that kind of response, for pity's sake, for my sake, for *your* sake . . . listen to it.

It's possible the requested revisions will take the book somewhere you as a writer don't want it to go. If that's the case, it's fine; it is, after all, your book. But it's incredibly important to remember that the person responding is a professional who believes you've got enough raw talent to spend several hours of his own, unpaid time suggesting ways to make your book better. If you get a response from an agent like this, *please* believe me: they're not jerking your chain. They're not being nice. They're not doing this out of the goodness of their heart. They think they can potentially make money off you, or they wouldn't have spent this much time reading and responding to your work and your emails.

They're also looking to see if you're capable of responding well to critique, because if you throw up a wall or disappear or argue or never respond, hey, you're not worth the time. I've read Robin's revision letter. It's a good one. It addresses important points, some of which are very easy to fix, others of which are going to require much deeper and more complex rewriting—and Robin is bouncing off the walls with new ideas on how to address these points.

This is a case, I'm extremely happy to say, where the new author is doing everything right. She had the wisdom to come to another writer—somebody who speaks fluent Agent, as she said to me—when she got conflicting messages, rather than flying off the handle and either panicking or responding to the agent in a hostile manner. She had the sense to pursue the question of marketing and get clarification on why the agent had asked. She's picking up the books he thought it might be marketed similarly to, so that she can develop some sense of what he might be looking for, and whether or not she'll be able or want to revise to something of that ilk. She has responded gracefully to the rejection letter, and in fact asked for a couple more points of clarification if they have time to provide them. She's handling this beautifully.

So take a page from Robin's book. You cannot do better than she's done with this interaction. If you get as far as she has, remember that this honestly *is* one step shy of publication. It may not pan out this time, but it means you're very, very close to that brass ring. Be professional, calm and courteous with the agent. (You can freak out on your friends. That's what they're there for.) Do not be discouraged by a rejection at this level: if you get this kind of response, you are *doing something right.* Don't blow it now.

Faith Hunter
One of the benefits of MagicalWords.net is the opportunity for as-yet-unpublished writers to read info like this. Agents and editors don't have time to reply to every query/partial/whole manuscript in depth. Getting something like Robin got, from a reputable agent, is like a gift of gold. Foolish is the writer who wants to wait until after a book is sold to make any changes. And I've met some like that.

Networking
Stuart Jaffe

Networking is, quite simply, the act of building business relationships. That's it. It's talking and laughing and sometimes even drinking. It's lunches and dinners and talk in the hallways and elevators. It's intriguing conversation and boring dialogue.

Networking is getting to know people in the industry so that at some point down the road—not right then and there—you could get a little pay off. That might sound cold and calculating, but remember, this is a business relationship, not a friendship. Sometimes friendships develop, but initially, you're networking is business oriented.

So, here are some practical guidelines for those initial conversations:

1. Relax.
Easier said than done, I know. But the truth is that you're not in disguise, secretly infiltrating anyone's ultra-guarded, hidden lair, so you don't need to worry while talking to Faith that she'll point her finger at you and say, "Aha! Imposter! You don't belong here! You are not worthy to speak to me!" Not going to happen. With extremely few exceptions, all the authors I've ever met love to talk with other writers. Those who have been published know and understand how hard it is to achieve publication. They also know somebody who has helped them along. They want to return the favor. And the first step is talking. But . . .

2. Don't be NEEDY.
You can't go up to people wanting/needing things from them. It oozes off of you and turns them away. Just try to talk like a normal human being and not an aspiring writer who *really, really, really, really* wants to get published. Forget about asking for your manuscript to be read. Instead, find something worth talking about that's not about you. If you saw the author in a panel, come up with a point regarding something she said. If you like his writing, tell him so (authors love positive reinforcement). The point here is, don't go into the conversation trying to get something from the author. If the author offers, great. If not, that's fine, too. Have your pitch ready just in case, but don't go in expecting to pitch. First time around, you simply want to make a good impression, or at least, not a bad one.

3. Slow down.
Networking is a long-term process. You build relationships by being a friendly,

reliable, trustworthy person. You need to show that a) you're not going to be annoying, b) you might be interesting, and c) you understand and appreciate the professional nature of networking. The things you're craving to have these people see—your ability to write, for example—will be discovered later, often while you're not even looking.

4. We're all in the same boat.

All that time you spent fretting about approaching Misty to tell her you liked *Mad Kestrel*, all that time you wasted sweating over how best to say hello to David or A.J.—well, the truth is, they're going through it, too (just not over you). David probably had to swallow a hard lump of nervousness before approaching George R. R. Martin. And I guarantee you that we all would be sweating if we had the chance to meet Stephen King or Neil Gaiman. See, networking never ends. Meeting those that share the same level of success as you does make it easier (it certainly gives you common ground to talk about), but there is always somebody higher up that you want to network with and it's always hard. Luckily, authors, agents, and editors are usually nice, approachable, and happy to chat for a short time—which is all you want, initially.

5. Have something to offer.

This is my best advice. It's the opposite of being needy. When I first started networking, I was writing book reviews for several venues. After a simple, undemanding conversation, I could always end by offering to review the author's book. I was doing something for them—not the other way around. The end result was a good networking contact. The author knows I'm not just self-serving, but I'm willing to do things for him. So, figure out if you have something worthwhile to give. The rewards can be immense.

Please note that these "rules" (really just guidelines) are not intended for the fan who just wants an autograph and a little gush time. This is about the business side of things. Some authors you'll meet will break these business rules quite successfully; some expect you to follow them rigidly. You have to gauge each situation as it comes. Also, this essay is about the first few times you meet with a professional. After that relationship is established, it will define itself, including what is acceptable and what is over-the-line.

Ultimately, networking is about your people skills. The better you are at dealing with others, the more success you will have in this endeavor. Be patient. It takes time and mistakes to learn how to do it.

Sarah Goslee
Very nice. I think it all boils down to: be polite, be professional. Very

few pros are amateur-eating monsters, but *everyone* is turned off by inappropriate and unprofessional behavior.

Not fiction-related, but the same kind of networking happens at other professional conferences. I attended one earlier this year, and the very coolest thing happened. BiggestNameInTheField spent the entire opening reception wandering around the room with a beer, walking up to random groups of people. "Hi, I'm X" (as if we didn't know!). "Are you a grad student", or if that seemed unlikely "Where do you work?"

It was awesome. I never expect to be BigName, but I hope that if I'm ever in a similar situation I'll remember his behavior.

Con Tips

Misty Massey

I was recently a guest at Balticon, the Maryland Regional Science Fiction and Fantasy Convention. While I was there, I met a number of con-goers who hope to be published one day, and who'd come to meet authors and editors and get a little help in that direction. The vast majority of these hopefuls were great people, full of interesting questions and just as pleasant as they could be, and they were definitely in the right place. Publishing professionals attend cons because we want to share, and we love meeting not-yet-published writers with their goals firmly envisioned. But every now and then someone pops up that makes a con guest want to run screaming to the safety of her room. One very nice young lady asked me how she'd know if she was being overbearing or obnoxious, and I told her that if she was concerned enough to ask, she was probably neither one. So how do you know if you're being fabulous or freakazoid?

1. Ask questions and listen to the answers.

I sat in on a few panels and served on others, and I noticed that people would occasionally ask questions, then start chatting with a neighbor during the ensuing answer. Maybe there's only one author on the panel whose opinion you are initially interested in hearing, but that doesn't mean the other three or four authors don't have something to say that you ought to hear. As we say often here on Magical Words, there is no one right way to do anything. One of those authors might have just the answer you need.

2. Pay attention to what others ask, and listen to the answers.

Nothing gets under my skin like audience members who ask the same question someone else just asked and received the answer to. It means that he was so busy composing his question in his head he wasn't really listening to the panel. If all he wanted to achieve was ten seconds of speaking directly to the authors, he might as well have waited until the signings. Participate fully in what the whole audience is doing, so the short time isn't wasted.

3. Remember that you're not the only person in the audience.

This happens at least once at every con I've ever attended. Someone in the audience decides she's having a personal conversation with the panelists, and chimes in every few minutes with some lengthy comment or other. The panelists know that sometimes audience members may have more knowledge than they do about a subject, and appreciate hearing the occasional comment. But when one audience member acts as if she is a secondary panelist, it irritates the rest of the audience who came to hear the panelists speak. Not to mention adding work for the poor moderator, who has enough trouble wrangling the panelists. Share if it's important, but don't monopolize the hour.

4. Don't dis anyone.

Maybe it's because I was raised by a strict Southern mother who insisted that I say nothing at all if I had nothing nice to say, but I don't think it's right to trash other authors during panels. Even if they're multimillionaires who probably don't care what a few folks on a panel think, don't go there. But it's not just authors you should spare. Don't dis agents or editors either. I'm aware of an incident in which a writer was trying to convince an editor to ask for her manuscript. In the course of conversation, the writer said some unkind things about an agent who'd offered her representation. The writer didn't realize the agent was a good friend of the editor. Oops.

5. Easy on the alcohol, and remember that people are watching what you do.

In the evenings, the parties start. Publishers host parties to promote their authors, authors host parties to celebrate book launches, fan groups host parties to attract more members . . . there is never a dearth of partying at a con. Go, dance, sing, drink and have a wonderful time, but know your limits. If two glasses of wine are enough to start you dancing on tables, control yourself and drink only one. Publishing is a tightly-knit business; everyone knows everyone else and people remember if you act outrageously. Blaming it on the alcohol is just an excuse. The wine didn't force itself down your throat.

And a codicil to this . . . sometimes folks go to cons in the hope of a little freaky-deaky. Be aware that if you stagger down a hallway trading sloppy kisses with your chosen hook up, people notice. If you don't want to face those knowing snickers in the con suite the next morning (or an angry spouse), for God's sake be discreet.

6. Embrace personal hygiene.

Antiperspirant. Toothpaste. Shampoo and soap. I hate that this needs to be said, but I always run into at least one or two people who don't take the time to properly prepare themselves. Maybe you live in a naturalist commune in which everyone bathes with water only and appreciates the odors of the body, but when you're coming to a con, don't ever assume the other con-goers think that way. If you habitually wear perfume or cologne, tone it way, way down. Some people are allergic, and you don't want to be responsible for their misery.

Cons are a marvelous place to meet like-minded souls as well as your favorite authors, and we sure do want to see you! Just remember these tips so that all of us will enjoy ourselves!

Moira Young

Oh, yes. A list like this should be mandatory reading for every convention and conference. #3 especially.

I attend Penny Arcade Expo, a video game convention in Seattle, and they make a big deal about all of these points. Of course, they also have their resident deity, Secretary of Geek Affairs Wil Wheaton, and his number-one catch phrase is now law: "Don't be a dick."

David B. Coe

The one I would add to this is: Respect people's personal space. Many people at cons are openly affectionate. They give hugs to one another, place their hands on each other's backs and shoulders in casual conversation. That's fine. If you know the person, and you know for certain that he or she doesn't mind, grope to your heart's content. But there are also people at cons who do not like to have their physical space violated, and unfortunately some of the former give nary a thought to the feelings of the latter. Keep your hands, hugs, caresses and kisses to yourself.

A.J. Hartley

Another one to add: Don't pitch your story unless asked to, and when you do, do it briefly with a few well-chosen phrases. I was passing a stall at a con once when a young guy who had self-pubbed a novel asked if I liked edgy fantasy. Trying to be supportive, I said yes. He launched into a point by point plot summary of his book without pausing for breath. I stood there for a couple of minutes feeling embarrassed and irritated, then apologized and walked away. When people offer an inch (out of the kindness of their hearts) don't take a mile.

So There I Was, In the Elevator, And Who Walked In?

Misty Massey

Blurb

(blûrb):

1. a brief advertisement or announcement, esp. a laudatory one
2. to advertise or praise

I'm sure you're familiar with blurbs on book covers, lines of praise that are used to help sell the book. Blurbs are also excellent tools for the author approaching an agent or editor. I don't know how many of you have been to any writing conferences or met many agents. Sometimes these events are so crowded that your chance at a one-on-one may come in an elevator, or while waiting in line for the lunch buffet. Trust me . . . if you luck onto two minutes of an agent's undivided attention, you'd better be prepared. There are a thousand people ready to jump in when the agent turns his head in another direction, and you want him to remember you.

Say I've written the gripping saga of Lisette, a lady's maid in *fin de siecle* Portugal, who discovers her own latent magical ability to throw fire from her eyes when she accidentally sets the family home on fire while the lord of the manor is molesting her, and must learn to control her strength while she's on the run from the Inquisitor and his vicious knifemen who hope to catch her and cut out her heart, which will transfer her power to the Inquisitor if he consumes it. Oh, and she falls in love with one of the knifemen when he meets her in her disguise as a stable lad, did I mention that?

Yeah, that's long. And unwieldy. If the elevator is an express, we probably reached the agent's floor before I got to the part about the knifemen. Since I would never dream of following the agent to his hotel room (and I'm sure you all know the bathroom is even MORE off limits!), I've blown my great chance. So what should I have done?

The seven second blurb is the one you've prepped for just this sort of occasion. It's the general idea in a few carefully chosen and delivered words. You're not trying to tell the agent everything. You're just trying to make his eyes light up. Instead of the lengthy paragraph, I could say, "Lisette's magic will set Portugal ablaze, unless she discovers a way to control her passions." It's quick, it's full of strong words, and it tells the agent enough to know whether he wants to hear more. If the agent is interested on the basis of the seven-second blurb, that's when I can take a little longer and spill my thirty-second blurb. Something like, "Lisette never knew she could create fire with her thoughts until the day she nearly killed her family. Now she's in hiding from the Inquisitor who hopes to cut out her heart and take her power for himself. Only when she learns to control her power will she defeat the Inquisitor and find true happiness." See? Still short and to the point, and probably enough to make an interested agent ask for three chapters and a synopsis.

David B. Coe

I have to say that in dealing with an agent, I prefer the blurb that shows I've thought about how to market my book. For instance, my blurb for *Sorcerers' Plague*: "It's a medical thriller set in a medieval fantasy." It gives a sense of who it might appeal to, how one might sell it to a publisher, and it even has a hint of alliteration to make it easier for the agent to remember.

Charles E. Dunkley

I have a one sentence blurb about my WIP, but reading the one David B. Coe just posted puts a whole new angle on pitching a book in a single sentence.

Here's my one second blurb, which I jotted down in my LJ back in August:

What if the only way to save your family's throne was to betray it?

But looking again at David's that will take some thinking.

David B. Coe

Once again I offer the "there's no right way to do this" caveat. As I said, that's what I prefer, because I think that agents think in terms of marketing. But I like that blurb CE, and I really think it would be great as the teaser line at the top of the back cover of your book.

The Ideal Editor

Faith Hunter

I've written previously about the importance of a good, professionally trained, experienced, NYC publishing house, acquisitions editor. There were a lot of comments and questions, including this one:

"What qualifies an editor to be an editor? Where do editors gain and/or hone their talent for improving a writer's work? Is it just practice via critiquing?"

First, off, there is a major difference between an edit and a critique.

A thorough edit addresses pacing, plot progression, character development, plot and story arcs, the very structure and heart and soul of a novel or story. It breaks down a story into its component parts and rebuilds it with more flesh, bigger muscle, and a tightness to the composition that is often staggering. This doesn't count the copy edit, line edit, etc. which are usually done by others, not a book's actual editor.

Second, I know of *very* few NYC editors who write. Okay, let's be honest. I know of none. Not one. There was one some years back who left the biz to become a writer, then later stopped writing. But I know of no editors who have the time or energy to work 60+ hours a week and then write, too.

Third, there is a lot more to a good editor than talent. A LOT! I've had quite a few of them since I sold my first book in 1989. For the purposes of this essay I will use the universal "he," though most NYC editors are female and in their mid to late twenties.

1. Most NYC editors have a degree in literary arts, often a masters.

2. My ideal editor has at least five years working under a senior editor in my genre. If I am a bestseller, then I want the senior editor, but I'm not, so I'm not pushing it.

3. He practically knows (by heart) the *Chicago Manual of Style*.

4. He has studied his particular genre back and forth and can quote sales numbers, genre trends, new promo methods, and give me the latest NYC gossip because he is plugged into the scene.

5. His best friend is the buyer for my genre at B&N, and he dates the buyer for my genre at BAM, and his mother is the buyer for Borders, and he gets along famously with all of them. (None of #5 is likely, but I can hope.)

6. He knows agents and editors in his field and in other fields. They like him enough to buy him drinks at cons, and to steer clients his way when they discover a gem-of-an-author who is not right for their house. Yes, I've known that to happen.

7. He returns my emails within 24 hours (except weekends and when he is out of town.)

8. He returns my phone calls within 24 hours (except weekends and when he is out of town.)

9. He has no fear when it comes to fighting for good slots (this is a place for my books in the publishing lineup for the coming year), good promo money, and the very best PR person in the company's PR department.

10. He likes me. And if he doesn't like me (because we simply don't connect in that special way), he still works with me as if he is my pal.

11. He likes my work. Really, this should be number one. An editor who likes my work is a gift from heaven. *That* is the editor who will fight for promo money and for a better slot in pub dates (see #9). In addition, he will fight for expanded attention from the buyers of the chains, and will coo about my work to other editors from other houses, thus expanding my name recognition in the business, and my likelihood of being asked to do more work.

I am sure there are more. Feel free to add thoughts about the job and value of a good editor.

A good editor is worth his weight in gold. They make writers better writers.

A.J. Hartley

Just to expand on item #4, that being "plugged in" as far as the genre is concerned is key. A good editor has seen it all. He knows what has been done to death and what's considered the next wave even before readers do. I can't overestimate the importance of this because there is nothing worse than an editor saying "this is a great book, but such and such a body at such and such a press has just beaten you to it and your work looks stale by comparison." When an editor knows what you are working on, they can spot this kind of problem down the road and get you to redirect. Or they can say, "since you're writing X, you should read Y to see how to do it and what to avoid." Apart from everything an editor does to help you craft a better book, he or she can be crucial in retooling the book as something you can sell. Much of this is true of a good agent, too.

David B. Coe

I'd add "Turns manuscripts around, with extensive revision notes, in a timely way." But I have an editor who meets nearly all of your criteria and NOT that one I just listed, and I'm very happy with him. So I guess it's not the most important thing. The slow pace can be frustrating, though. And I can think of another editor who was at a major genre house—a terrific editor by all accounts—who was canned and turned to writing and is now enjoying a very successful writing career. But as you indicated, these folks are the exceptions.

The Ideal Writer
David B. Coe

Being a writer is about more than simply putting words down on a page (or up on a screen). There are ways in which we comport ourselves through the writing and publication process that might well make our books more successful, and that will certainly make editors and agents more inclined to work with us. The things I've included in this list are things that I have tried myself (with varying degrees of success), and as you work on your books and look to break into the publishing process, you should think about doing them yourself. You'll notice that the attributes listed below don't have anything to do with style, or even with process. We all work differently; we all write what we love and what we feel. We deal with "How Do We Write" issues quite a bit at Magical Words. This essay is a little different. (And like Faith, I'll use the universal "he." No offense intended.)

1. The Ideal Writer hits his deadlines. Yes, I'm starting at the end here. I'm assuming that the other stuff—the stuff that gets you to the end of the book—has been or will be covered by other essays in this book. But at root, a writer's job is to write, and finish, a story or book. Deadlines are fluid things in publishing. Manuscripts and production run late all the time, but to the extent that a writer can make his deadlines, he puts himself in good standing with his editors, agent, and publisher. And that's good.

2. He also turns in a clean manuscript. What does "clean" mean? Let's start with what it doesn't mean. It doesn't mean "perfect." But it does mean that he takes the time to proofread his work, eliminating typos and other mistakes that shouldn't need an editor's attention. Yes, a manuscript will be copyedited and proofed further along in the process. But every mistake the Ideal Writer finds on his own simplifies the production process down the road, and allows the editor and copyeditor to focus on more important matters.

3. He accepts criticism without ego, without defensiveness, and with an open mind. He understands that the comments he receives from his editor and from his beta readers are not meant as assaults on his creative vision, but rather as attempts by allies and friends to help him make his book as good as it can possibly be. He is not so wedded to any phrase or element of his story that he can't at least consider changing it to improve the piece.

4. A corollary to #3, he views the revision stage of writing a book (and yes, he absolutely goes through this stage with every story) as an opportunity to rethink portions of his first draft that might not have worked. In other words, he approaches revisions the way he approaches the first draft: as a creative endeavor rather than simply a corrective one.

5. He goes out of his way to show his appreciation for the work of the "support staff" of his publishing house(s). I mean the people in the publicity, art, and production departments. These are people who work very hard to make certain that his book looks great and reaches as many readers as possible. They can make or break a book, and they deserve to be treated with respect and courtesy. They are also people who he *should want to like him*. Ticking them off would be stupid, and yet you'd be amazed by the number of writers who treat them poorly, or ignore them entirely. Don't be that guy. Along the same lines, he treats his agent and editor as equal partners in his work. He always—ALWAYS— finishes his conversations with his agent and editor the same way: with a "Thank you."

6. Again, a corollary of sorts to #5. He goes out of his way to be polite to fans, to reply (when he possibly can) to emails and letters from fans. These are the people who buy his books; why would he want to give them the impression that he's a jerk?

7. He works hard to publicize his work, understanding that publicists at publishing houses can only do so much for any one author. Book signings, guest blogging, web site maintenance, con appearances—all of these things can build up readership, and since an author's future writing success is often directly linked to his most recent sales performance, self-promotion is a must.

8. In helping to market his books, the Ideal Writer makes an effort to get to know workers in his local bookstores. He befriends them, he treats them with respect and courtesy (of course), he tells them about his books, and he offers to sign stock. In short, he forges strong connections with those who are most responsible for hand-selling his books.

9. He does not take too much satisfaction in good reviews, nor does he waste energy in responding to bad reviews. No book can please everyone; and even the worst books get some good reviews. The Ideal Writer writes the best book he can and lets the reviewers do their job.

10. He gives thanks every day for being able to create characters and worlds and stories, and get paid for it. He remembers that for every writer who is as lucky as he is, there are ten or fifty or a hundred or a thousand others who are just as

talented, just as passionate about writing, just as committed to the craft, but who haven't yet gotten that lucky break.

Kim Harrison
#11 Understand that the writing arena is just as political as a regular office situation and watch what you do/say around your peers. New York is a very small place, and everyone knows everyone else, so resist the temptation to enjoy yourself too much at a convention.

Stuart Jaffe
I'd like to second Kim's #11 and add that watching what you say/do at a con is also important to fans. I've seen some downright horrible behavior from some well-known authors at conventions. They seem to have the attitude that their numbers are so good they can do what they want. To some extent that might be true, but only in the short run. See, I had intended to buy a book by this one author—and if I liked it, I'd probably have gone on to buy several more. To date, this author has made ZERO sales to me. That author's behavior cost several sales to just me alone. How many other potential sales were lost at that con? In the long run, that author's numbers might go south because of this type of thing.

A.J. Hartley
David, I wonder if you might offer any thoughts on how writers deal with adversity, be that the struggle to get published or the kinds of difficulties that can arise later in your professional career? This last has been a hard year for a lot of people in the business and it can get very depressing. I spoke to David Morrell (famed author of *First Blood* (among other things) and all-round nice guy) when I was having some problems and his advice (very much from experience) was simple: out-last the nay-sayers. That's not a direct quote, but it's in the ball park. I guess that's what I'd add to your list: persevere. 85% (or something) of success is showing up. So don't quit, ever. Not if you really want it.

David B. Coe
Yes, yes, yes, and yes! All great additions to the list.

Kim, absolutely; this is crucial. It's not just a matter of being polite, although that can be hugely helpful. One also has to be discreet. Once, early in my career, I had a con moment that could have destroyed me. Fortunately, the big-name writer I insulted was generous and understanding, and I managed to grovel my way back into his good graces. But that was a lesson I took to heart.

Stuart, I've witnessed some truly boorish behavior from writers whose work I love, and yes, it soured me on their books. It is remarkable that professionals should need to be told, "Don't be a lout; it might hurt your sales," but it seems that common sense doesn't always get people there.

A.J., I probably should have put as my number one, "The Ideal Writer puts his butt in the chair every day and writes, even if its just a page or two, regardless of whatever else is happening professionally." Perseverance, refusing to fail, stubborn faith in oneself . . . however you want to phrase it, that is an essential ingredient for success. I think I was so focused on the professional relationships and comportment, that I ignored one of the fundamentals of writing professionally.

Business Realities for the Beginning Writer

David B. Coe

I thought I'd jump in and give you some sense of the economic realities of being a beginning writer, so brace yourselves for a dose of reality. It's not going to be pretty.

Let's start with a little quiz: What do you think is (approximately) the average advance given to a first-time writer of genre fiction? a) $5,000; b) $7,500; c) $10,000; d) $12,500; e) $15,000. Think about it for a while. The answer is coming later.

So, you've won over an agent and together you and she have managed to interest an editor in your book (and we'll assume that this book is completed). Good for you. Let's say you get a call from your agent in December and she says, "Congrats! Editor X from Fantasy-Books-R-Us has agreed to publish your book! We'll have a contract for you soon. Editor X has some changes he wants you to make, but your book is going to be published!"

You pop open the bubbly, you take your spouse or whoever out to dinner. And you wait. And wait. And wait. Let's be generous and say that the contracts finally arrive in March, and let's use the middle figure in our quiz and say that the publisher is offering you a $10,000 advance. You eagerly sign the contract, send it back, and wait for your advance check. Which comes in May (again, we may be a bit generous with this). But your advance check isn't for $10,000. No, chances are that your advance has been divided into three parts: you get part one upon signing the contract, part two upon delivery and acceptance (D&A) of the manuscript, and part three when the book is finally published. Sometimes advances are divided in half (part on signing, part on D&A), but division into thirds is more typical. So your check is for $3,333.33, right? Well, no. Your agent gets her 15%, so your check is actually for $2,833.33.

But wait, you say. My book was finished when I sold it, so don't I also get my D&A advance? And when my laughter subsides, I'll gently tell you that, no, the key words are "*and Acceptance*," and as your agent mentioned, Editor X has some changes he wants made to the manuscript. It takes a couple of months, but you eventually get X's comments and spend several weeks on rewrites. You hand in your manuscript and a month later you get your second check. It's now September, and believe it or not you're doing really, really well. You've made $5,666.66 this year. Before taxes. (And again, my timeline has been pretty generous.)

So you've handed in your completed manuscript. Congratulations! The book now has to go through copyedits, proofs, and various production processes. And as a beginning writer, you have to expect that you'll be placed pretty far down the line in the publishing schedule. My first book came out two years after it was first turned in (before I did revisions with my editor), but we'll continue with the generous timeline and say that your book is published in August of the following year, a bit less than a year after you receive your D&A check. So that year you get your last advance check of $2,833.34.

Okay, so it's been about a year and eight months since your agent gave you the good news about your book sale, and you have been paid a total of $8,500.00. But wait! you say again. Now I'll start earning royalties, right?

Excuse me. I was laughing again. A few things about royalties. First, that advance you got is more properly referred to as an "advance against royalties", which means that the $10,000 you were paid (of which you received 85%) is money you now need to earn through book sales. How long will it take to earn back $10,000? Well, it certainly won't happen overnight. Let's say your book first comes out in hardcover (which is a very good thing to have happen) and its cover price is $25.00. For every copy that sells, you'll probably get a royalty of about $2.50. So if they print 4,000 hardcovers (that could be a bit high) and you sell every one of them (highly unlikely) your book will earn out before it even goes to paperback. Let's say you sell 3,000 copies. That would be a good sell through (the ratio of books sold to books printed) of 75% and would leave you only $2,500 short of earning out your advance. Now the book goes to paperback. It sells for $8.00 and you get $0.64 per copy (that's 8%—pretty standard, although 6% also is common). So when you sell your 3,907th copy of the paperback, you'll finally have earned out.

So what kind of timetable are we talking about? Well, generally the paperback comes out about a year after the hardcover, so that paperback comes out in August 2011, and if sales go well, you could sell that 3,907th copy within a month. Let's say that by the end of September 2011, you've sold 5,000 copies. The publisher now owes you $700 (minus your agent's cut that comes to $595.00). When do you get that? Well, assuming that the publisher is no longer holding back reserves against returns, you could see this money as early as April or May 2012. Yes, that's right. Most publishers report royalties in 6 month periods: Jan. 1-Jun. 30; Jul. 1-Dec. 31. For the first period you get a royalty report (and hopefully a check) in October or early November; for the second, you get your statement and check the following spring, April or May. So now it's been three years and five months since you sold your book, and you've finally earned additional royalties, pushing your total earnings on this book to $9,095, or an average of $3,031.66 per year.

A couple of notes: reserve against returns is an evil, evil phrase that I could spend several paragraphs trying to explain. Basically, the publisher bases "sales" numbers on bookstore orders, rather than actual sales. But since bookstores often return any books that don't sell in a fairly narrow time window, they have to protect themselves against paying out royalties on unsold books. And so they subtract a reserve from the amount owed. In the first royalty reporting period for any given book, that reserve can be as high as 2/3 of all moneys owed. It decreases gradually with each subsequent six-month statement, but it can be hiked up again with each new edition that's published (so if a paperback version of the book comes out, the reserve can be increased again).

Second, the answer to our quiz was b) $7,500.00. That's the average first advance for a new writer. $7,500.00. Minus 15%, for a total of $6,375.00, divided into three payments of $2,125.00 each. So all those earnings we just assumed were actually higher than they ought to have been, though the good news is that your book might earn out faster than we assumed.

And third, all my assumptions in this essay have been fairly generous. The sell-through, the timeline, even the contract terms (royalty percentages for example). Very generous. There's a good chance that the average beginning writer won't do as well.

I write because I love it. I write because I have characters and stories in my head that are constantly clamoring to be given voice. I make a good deal more money now than I did as a beginner, but I still only barely make what any normal person would call "a living." If you are writing because you have to, because the very idea of NOT writing makes you want to cry, because you love it so much that it's all you can imagine yourself doing, then by all means write. But don't give up your day job. Not yet. And if you aspire to be a writer because you think it might be an easy or quick way to make a buck . . . well, I feel another fit of laughter coming on . . .

J. T. Glover

One question: would you ever consider returning any of your advance to aid in promotion of the book? I've read that James Ellroy's big break came when he offered to return half of the $30,000 advance he got for *The Black Dahlia* if the publisher would match him dollar-for-dollar in increased promotion. They would, he did, and the book was a smash hit. I know that's a different genre, and Ellroy was not at the very start of his career when this happened, but I'm wondering about the general principle.

David B. Coe

To answer your question, no, I would never consider such a thing, for several reasons. First off, I do a great deal of self-promotion on my own dime, and part of a publisher's responsibility is to do promotion on its end. There's a reason why royalties only amount to a small percentage of each book's sale price—that other money is supposed to pay for production, editing, and, yes, publicity. I shouldn't have to pay more for something that the publisher is supposed to be doing and paying for anyway. No author should, in my opinion. In a way, the amount of an advance is a way the publisher indicates its commitment to the book in question. If I get a $5,000 advance on a book, the publisher is making a statement about how hard it intends to push the book, in order to make back that money. By the same token, a $30,000 advance also demonstrates a level of commitment. I would be undermining that by giving back some of that money. I'd be saying in essence, I don't believe that the faith you've shown in me with this advance is justified. I just don't think it's a good idea.

Daniel R Davis

So has anyone posted the differences between getting published traditionally and self-publishing? A friend of mine thinks that self-publishing is a cop-out and doesn't make you an author, just a hack, which I don't agree with.

David B. Coe

Thanks for the question, Daniel. As with so many things in publishing, the answer to your question depends largely on what you want to get out of writing. If you're a hobbyist and would love to see your book in print and don't really envision writing as a career choice, self-publishing can be a great way to go. On the other hand, if you want to be a professional writer and hope someday to be published by one of the big NY publishing houses, self-publishing can actually hurt you more than it helps. Fair or not, there is still a stigma attached to self-pub, and many houses won't touch a book that has previously been self-pubbed. Some won't even touch an author who's gone that route with a previous book. There are a few authors who have self-pubbed and gone on to have successful careers with big publishers, but they are few in number and very much the exceptions to the rule.

Royalties
C.E. Murphy

. . . also known as Why It's Hard To Make A Living As A Writer.

Let's look at royalties.

I'm lucky. I'm making money—pretty decent money—on my books, above and beyond what my publishers gave me as an advance. That money is still considered royalty money. Basically, the publisher gives you, say, $10K for a book up front, and then you don't see any more money on that book until they've gotten back their $10K that they've paid you. Only after that do you start getting paid what we generically refer to as "royalties" as opposed to "advance money".

If I weren't earning royalties above and beyond my initial advance checks, you could take away . . . pauses to count . . . um . . . two-thirds of what I've made in the last twelve months. That would leave me with around $13K, which would rather violently remove me from the "living wage" scenario I'm currently managing to stay within.

Realistically, what's keeping me in that "living wage" arena is that I have, in my nascent career, sold four series (*The Walker Papers, Negotiator Trilogy, Inheritors' Cycle, and The Strongbox Chronicles*). Between advance checks and royalty checks, I'm making a living as a writer. But I've published ten (soon to be eleven) books in the last three years to do it.

Most people aren't going to have two concurrent series at the beginning of their careers, much less four. (I say most people. I suspect a number of you know some of the same people I do—Charles Stross or Elizabeth Bear leap to mind, and they, like me, rather blow the lid off the idea that nobody does this. But *most people* don't.) So if you strip away the three series I sold after the *Walker Papers*, what I'm left with as income for the last twelve months is the $19 or so K from royalties.

It's a living wage, but just barely—and you've also got to take out 15% for the agent, and if you're in the States, withhold 25% (33% if you're nervous, which I typically am) for federal taxes and social security. As a writer, you get double-stung: you have to pay both employee and employer social security, so between those things, you're looking pretty safely at cutting forty or forty-five percent of your income out before you can even start thinking about spending it. (And I haven't even touched the topic of health insurance.)

By this time you're thinking, "Yeah, but ALL THAT MONEY! ALL AT ONCE! I CAN GO NUTS!" and believe you me, that's what a person starts to think when she gets a several-thousand-dollar-check deposited in the bank.

And then she thinks, "I have no freaking clue when I'm going to get paid again," and all of a sudden that big lump of money doesn't look tempting, it looks cruel. Because if you're trying to live on a writer's income, you flat-out can't afford to go batshit crazy when you get a big check.

This is just not an easy business to make a living in. I've been insanely fortunate, and have been making one, but it's not just a matter of selling as many books as I have. It's being able to control the money once you get it, and keeping in mind that yeah, in fact, *$big chunk o' change* is great, but it's very possibly the only payment you'll see for six months. It takes nerves of steel to live with it. Hell, it takes nerves of steel to be married or partnered to somebody who gets paid this way, even if the partner has a steady job. I *regularly* think about finding some kind of day job, simply because it would be so very much less stressful all around if I were pulling in any kind of regular paycheck. Even if it's *tiny*, the regularity would be a huge relief. So yeah, when people ask writers, "When are you going to quit your day job?" most times the answer is going to be, realistically, "Never."

David B. Coe
Making a living from royalties and advances is incredibly tough. Foreign sales help. For those who don't know, when a book is translated into a foreign language that usually means that the author (or the publisher) has sold what are called foreign language subsidiary rights to a publisher in a particular country. The translations are done in-house by the publisher, so for the author this is found money. We don't have to do any extra work for it. The amounts can range from tiny ($800 in some smaller countries) to several thousand dollars per volume for a series.

Foreign sales make up a good chunk of my yearly income, so that at this point I earn enough to feel that I'm contributing to the family finances. But if my wife didn't have a good job with benefits (retirement, health care) I couldn't afford to write full-time.

Wow, That Must Have Cost A Lot!

Misty Massey

Becoming a published writer isn't complicated. The writer writes a brilliant manuscript. He sends it to a literary agent he has researched carefully, following all the guidelines that agent requires. The agent loves the manuscript, and starts shopping it to all the editors she knows. One of those editors sees the brilliance in the manuscript and makes an offer. See? Published!

Okay, settle down all of you. I didn't say it was easy—I said it wasn't complicated. There's a difference. Most of the time publishers and agents make their guidelines easy to find and simple to follow. The difficulty comes when writers decide the rules just do not apply to them. Susie handwrites her manuscript on pink scented paper, even though it clearly says "typed, double-spaced on white paper." Jarod sends his 980 page novel to an editor who prefers lengths of 110K to 120K words. Maria mails a paper copy to an agent who only takes emailed submissions. Hubert sends the entire manuscript when the agent only asked for three chapters. I attended a writing conference years ago, during which an agent was meeting with each writer individually for a manuscript critique. We'd been instructed to send the first thirty pages of our manuscript ahead of time. The first evening, a woman was railing to the group about the epidemic of agents stealing people's work by doing these critiques. She, however, had worked out a way to foil the agent. She'd sent in thirty random, nonconsecutive pages from her book.

If you're sure I have no idea what I'm talking about, and that the rules truly do NOT apply to you, great. There are people who're just dying to make money off of your dreams and desires. They dress themselves up as publishers, create websites that assure you your writing is fantastic and it's just that good-old-boy mentality in New York that's keeping you down, and for only $1,295, they will make sure your book sees the light of day. Pink paper? Handwritten manuscript? It's all good. They'll accept whatever you send as long as a check is attached.

Money should always flow TOWARD the writer, never away. Paying someone to print your book is merely that: printing. It's not publishing. The worst part is so many people have gone this route that it's almost expected. I can't tell you how many times I've been at a signing or speaking engagement and heard someone exclaim, "Gosh, you must have paid a lot to get this done!" There's nothing wrong with paying someone to print your book, if that's all you want. Say you've written a family memoir that only forty or fifty of your relatives will want. Pay the company and receive a nice product. But if you've written a fantasy blockbuster that you hope will put you in the same company with George R.R. Martin or Stephen King, paying someone to print it won't get you far. Distributors don't usually carry those books, and bookstores don't want to stock books they can't return. You'll be stuck selling your books from your garage. Not to mention the stigma such books acquire. They're almost never properly edited. The covers are usually created with Photoshop, so they look amateurish. They're priced ridiculously high because the print run is low and the company doesn't expect to sell many copies (except to you.)

What's that? You say Christopher Paolini did it? Well, not exactly. What he did accomplish took an extraordinary amount of hard work combined with a stroke of pure luck, not to mention a lot of his parents' money.

If you want to base your book's success on luck, I wish you well. If you want to pay for a book so you can put it on your shelf and show it off to visitors, knock yourself out. Write the check and enjoy your shiny book. But if you want to tell stories to lots of people, sell books from coast to coast and maybe build a career, then do it right. Write a brilliant story. Rewrite it. Make it the best you can make it, and accept criticism when it comes your way. Follow the rules. And don't pay money for it.

It's not complicated.

Faith Hunter

Oh Misty, I want to copy this and hand-carry it to conferences. Pass it out. Make people read it. Not that they will think it applies to them.

One of the worst *do it my way* things I ever heard was the writer who sent out cards to everyone in NYC publishing. Once every week they all got this card that said something like *It's coming . . . THE DARK. In Six Weeks.* Then the next week, something similar . . . *In five Weeks.* Then *In four Weeks.* And you know what? They were all curious. It actually started them all talking. They wondered, *Could this be a well-written book? The next block buster?* There was actually a buzz.

Until week one came and . . . no THE DARK.

A week later they all got a round of cards that said, "Sorry. A Small Delay. THE DARK has hit a small snag. It will be ready in a few weeks."

That writer shot himself in the foot. If THE DARK (or whatever the title was) ever came out, I never heard about it. Had it been a wonderfully written, professional manuscript, with great characters and an easy to follow storyline, he would have found an agent and publisher. Just because of his moxie.

For most of us, becoming a commercially published writer is just plain old hard work. Time. Sweat. Tears. Learning the market. Learning how to write. Hearing the word "No." A lot.

P.S. No, don't try this stunt yourself. It entered the realm of urban publishing fact, and it wouldn't work now. Not at all.

Who Pays Whom: Part 1, Agents and Editors

C.E. Murphy

This essay comes thanks to one of our readers, who had questions after my last essay. I may get a little strident here, so I want you all to know I'm not yelling at anybody, I'm just yelling because this is *incredibly* important. ☺

The essence of the question is this: "For the benefit of newbies, who pays whom?"

Frankly, if I never write about anything else, this alone would be worth the time. It's that important.

Money flows toward the author.

It is not "usually" ill-advised to pay an agent up front. It is *always* ill-advised to pay an agent up front. The agent works for you. The agent does not get paid until you get paid.

The editor is paid by the publishing house. The editor is the one paying *you.* There is no legitimate publishing scheme in which you give the editor or the agent any money. Ever. Period. End of sentence, end of discussion.

Okay. I'm going to start with agents, then work my way to editors. I'll talk about print-on-demand and vanity press later.

So: agents.

It is my *personal* belief that getting an agent is a vital career move. I got my agent after getting an offer from a publishing house that accepted unsolicited submissions. I could almost certainly have continued to sell books without an agent (mostly by making personal contacts), but I felt, and still feel, that having an agent, someone between myself and the editor, is really important. Also, your agent will get you more money. Mine got me nearly twice what the publishing house initially offered—which more than covers her 15%. Fifteen percent is the industry standard for literary agents.

Typically this is how they (and you) get paid:

Publishing House buys your book. Agent hammers out the advance, the contract details, you read it all and sign it and send it back. Publishing House sends a check to the agency. The agency sends you a check for the amount of the advance, minus their 15%.

That's it. That's how they get paid. That's how you get paid. There are no other hoops to jump through, although occasionally there may be photocopying or printout fees (which technically my agency is allowed to take out of my advance, and never has).

There is no scenario *what-so-ever* in which you pay your editor. They're employed by a giant conglomerate publishing house and they write *you* the check. (I know I said that before. I may say it another six times. ☺)

Now: an editorial *service* is something else.

An editorial service is someone you *do* pay to go over your work. It's like a first reader or a beta reader hopped up on speed. Ideally it's someone who has either worked as an editor or agent or who is a successful novelist themselves. I personally know two authors running editorial services whose services I would recommend: Laura Anne Gilman, a former editor at Berkley, Dutton, and New American Library, who is now a full-time author of fantasy and romance novels, and Judith Tarr, a fantasy novelist who is frankly one of the most amazing writers I've ever read, who offers mentoring services which can include editorial-level critique.

Neither of these women, nor **any other editorial service**, will get you published.

What they will give you is a professional-level critique, which may be extremely useful. It may also be emotionally devastating (because, well, critiques usually are, even when they're handed out as nicely as possible). It is *not* the secret password, though. There's no such thing. All they—and others like them—are offering is a *service,* an attempt to help you make your book better. They're not publishers themselves. I'm willing to mention these two because I know and trust them, but as a general statement I would urge new writers to be inherently suspicious of editorial services.

If you have the *slightest* doubt—in fact, even if you *don't*—please, please, please go to Preditors & Editors, which is the internet's #1 resource for scam agents, editors, publishing houses, editorial services, and pretty much anything else you might need to know to make sure you're signing with someone legitimate, whether it's an agent, a publishing house, or an editorial service.

Misty Massey
wild applause I spoke to a high school group recently, and this question came up. One young woman wanted to know how much it had cost me to publish *Mad Kestrel,* because she had been trying to convince her mother to spend $4,000 to get her book "published," but her mother thought she could find someone cheaper. Eek! ☺

Who Pays Whom: Part 2, Vanity Presses

C.E. Murphy

Last time I talked about editors, agents, and editorial services. This time I'm going to talk about the evil side of vanity publishing, and I'm going to use Chris Branch's comments as a springboard. Chris wrote to me, saying:

> "Regarding paying to publish your own book, I guess it's clear that no writer wants to do this, but maybe the thinking goes like this (DISCLAIMER: I know this is wrong—or at least idealistic—I'm just justifying for argument's sake why it might be easy to think this way):
>
> As a writer, I have a product to sell, and I have to sell it in order for the money to "flow toward the author." So, who is my customer? The tendency is to say: the reader. But wait, all I have is a manuscript and a handful of rejection letters. I can't sell that to the reader; what I need is a book. The responsibility for turning my manuscript into a book lies with the publisher. If they would just do their part, then the money could start flowing. This might lead me to conclude that turning my manuscript into a book is a step I can do myself and cut out the middleman. Sure, I might have to pay for it, but hey, sometimes you've got to spend money to make money. The self-published book might not sell as many copies as a traditionally published one, but it can't be worse than the zero copies that are being sold when all I have is a manuscript."

Chris' thought process sounds quite logical. Now let me explain why it's wrong. ☺

The most basic wrongness about this belief is the idea that ultimately your books are going to end up somewhere that people will be able to buy them.

They won't.

Occasionally a local bookstore can be harangued into carrying a copy or two of your vanity press book, but mostly they won't touch them. They will not be available on Amazon (although you could set yourself up as a seller, I suppose). The only people who will buy them are your family, except your family largely expects you to *give* them the book. You could go the door-to-door route, but really, that's not what you're imagining, is it? When you say, "My book has been published!" you want people to be able to go to the bookstore and buy it, not for you to be hoofing around the neighborhood trying to sell it like it's a vacuum cleaner.

What this means, in essence, is that you will have spent a thousand, or five thousand, or ten thousand dollars on books that will fill up your garage. I suspect most people can see the flaw in this plan right away. And I'm sorry, but that's the reality of vanity press publishing.

Worst of all, if you go to the trouble to get a table at a local convention or conference and spend the whole weekend hard-selling your vanity-press book in an attempt to drum up some sales, what you will end up with at the end of the weekend is a conference full of people who are trying very, very hard not to meet your eye, and who will go away from the con wincing and muttering, "Did you get stuck talking to that guy, too?"

This is not really the image you want to leave behind. Overall, I cannot emphasize enough what a bad idea vanity press is. I truly do believe that if you write a good book, you will in time find a traditional publisher for it. The vicious truth is that if you *can't* find a publisher, there are one of two things working against you. The first of the two things is actually positive:

> You've written something that's genuinely too hard to categorize and publishers just don't know what to do with it. If this is the case, chances are very good you'll be getting rejection letters that say, "This is actually quite good and we can't figure out how to sell it." Having an agent will go a long way toward helping to alleviate this particular difficulty. So will writing another book and trying to sell it instead. If you're getting rejections that say, "Sorry, we don't know what to do with it," you have talent and will sell. Just try something else.

The second of the two things is somewhat less positive:

> You've written something unpublishable. Not because it's genre-defying, but because it's bad.

The vast majority of vanity-published pieces fall into the second category.

Now, there *are* times and places for vanity press publishing. The collected family recipes, for example, so everybody can have a copy, is a good reason to do vanity press or Print On Demand. Generally people aren't under the impression that the whole world would like to buy a copy of the family recipes, so yeah, that's a good use of the system. But if you're trying to create and sell the great American novel and you want to become rich and famous (or at least moderately well-known and paid), you don't want to go the vanity route.

Faith Hunter
Catie, on the whole I agree with you. I know several people who went

the vanity pub rout and went broke doing it. One guy even spent his son's college fund (nearly $40,000) and ended up selling less than a hundred books. On the other hand, there are the *very* few success stories like Kathy Wall, who self-published her first mystery novel, lives in a touristy small town spot that is featured in her novels, is so well liked that all the businesses in the town recommend her books, busted her butt for three years proving that she could sell, and got picked up by St. Martins. She is still with them, still busting her butt, still selling books.

Will many other people make money doing this? Do other writers have parents who will dedicate their entire lives to selling their books? Do they have money to push their books and a venue that will carry them? Probably not.

Avoid the vanity press idea. Even POD vanity press is not worth it. Bookstores hate them.

David B. Coe

I feel that I need to add here for those looking at Faith's comment and Catie's essay that in essence the two of them are saying the same thing, even if they appear to disagree. Catie is absolutely right: vanity press is a bad way to go. It's almost impossible to make money, and rightly or wrongly, most professionals, including not only writers, but also agents and editors, will look at your self-published book and assume it wasn't good enough to be published any other way. The fact that Faith can point to a few exceptions (and yes, there are others) only serves to reinforce the point. The stories of people actually breaking through via vanity publishing are so rare that they have become the stuff of legend. Thinking that your self-pubbed book will make you the next Christopher Paolini is just as realistic as thinking that the book you're trying to publish traditionally will make you the next J.K. Rowling. Could it happen? Yeah, sure. But basing a career plan on that hope is a little like basing your household budget on that Lotto ticket you just bought.

Who Pays Whom: Part 3, Print on Demand (POD)

C.E. Murphy

This time I want to tackle POD, or Print On Demand.

First off, to steal a phrase from Laura Anne Gilman, "POD is a process, not a publishing style." This means that the book you're ordering isn't created in the physical world *until* you've ordered it.

Once upon a time I would have categorized POD as solely a vanity press thing, something which was largely there to bilk writers out of hard-earned money by promising they would print your book *just as soon as someone ordered it!* Of course, with no publicity, no books on the shelves, no word of mouth, it wasn't very likely your book was going to get ordered, even if you've already paid to get it "ready."

I think the Internet Age has changed that significantly. I still believe that POD can be part of a vanity-press scheme, but at this juncture I'm going to trust that our readers understand what's bad about a vanity press, and instead I'm going to talk about what's good about POD.

1. It can make otherwise out-of-print books available to readers.

One writer I know got critical acclaim for her first novel, great reviews for her third, but the second didn't do as well. The publisher made the decision not to reprint the second in large numbers, but did make it available through POD, so if a completionist wants to pick it up, they're going to be able to find a copy.

There are also downsides to it—if you're a professional, you want to make sure there's some kind of caveat in your contract regarding how many POD sales over what period of time constitutes in or out of print, because otherwise your rights may never revert back to you—but it can potentially be a helpful scenario. This use for POD is seen with some regularity by university presses and small presses.

2. It can help a small business reach an audience it would otherwise be unable to afford to.

Evil Hat Productions, a small press RPG company run by friends of mine, is a great example of this. Evil Hat has taken advantage of the POD technology to create independent role-playing games and gaming guides that they don't have to warehouse, thus saving an enormous overhead cost. They're not making vast amounts of money, but they are making enough to continue forward, which is quite an achievement.

3. It can make self-publishing, with no press at all, a viable possibility.

I say this with some caution because by and large I believe right down to my toes that if you've written something good enough, you will find a traditional publisher for it. I'm reluctant to press the idea of self-publishing.

That said, Magical Words has readers who've spoken up about their own self-publishing decisions, among them a poet, a self-proclaimed hobbyist, and one who has decided to become his own publisher after receiving encouraging rejections from traditional publishers.

For any of them, POD could be a viable choice. The poet had books made up as gifts, but could use (for example) lulu.com's marketing tools to potentially reach an audience beyond the friends and family he initially made the books for. (I have to admit, with no prejudice meant against the poet, that may be the most viable publication scheme available for poetry. It's not exactly a profitable market . . .)

The self-publisher and hobbyist could potentially use the same process to reach an audience without the outlay of costs that a vanity press generally demands. There *is* room for this kind of publication—but it requires a lot of marketing and forethought to make money.

For total disclosure, let me confess to having a print-on-demand product myself: a 2010 Ireland calendar. For further total disclosure, let me also mention that I've sold exactly one copy. To a friend. And that's with advertising on all my various sites. ☺

Lulu and other POD systems like Zazzle (which is what I'm using for the calendar) *do* take a percentage out of sales, because they have to make money somewhere for this to be a viable scheme. But they take their percentage out of *sales*, not from up-front costs; there's no way I'd have tried the calendar thing if I had to put money up to do it. (That would be vanity press in its evil form. We shall consider POD to be vanity press in its good form. At least in theory.)

So in a nutshell, I think POD can be pretty damned cool. There are probably about a million applications I haven't touched on here, but I hope I've covered the ones most relevant to people considering a career in publishing.

Faith Hunter
Catie, I am so glad you addressed this. My AKA has several backlist novels out in POD format with a small press. (I/she got the rights back and resold.) I still sell a goodly number a month and get a pleasant royalty check two times a year.

Because so many traditional presses are going to POD with their backlists, having a good agent keeps the rights revertible. In my current contract, if a backlist sells less than 300 copies a year, I get rights back, which was negotiated by my agent. Another good reason for a good agent! When I get them back, I'll POD them through the small press.

David B. Coe

I'm having out-of-print issues with my first trilogy—the first book is still in print, but not books #2 or #3. Crazy I know, but that's how this business works sometimes. We're trying to get them back in print on a POD basis, but are wary, of course, of the reversion issues you bring up here. This is the wave of the future: Warehousing is becoming more and more expensive and POD is becoming easier and easier. I expect to see more of this in coming years, along with smaller print runs. And as a result, reversion rights clauses are going to become more contentious issues in contract negotiations.

Axisor

What do cover-art rights do when the book rights revert and an author takes the book to POD?

C.E. Murphy

The cover art belongs to the publisher, not to you, so it goes back to the publisher when the novel rights revert to you.

Creating A Web Presence
C.E. Murphy

Here's the thing. Me, personally, I've had a website since (holy jeez) 1994. I've had a blog since before that was a word, since about 1998 in the loosest sense, and fairly regularly since about 2001. I have a personal site (mizkit.com) and a professional site (cemurphy.net), which basically only has career-relevant news on it, and which is meant to provide information to people who really don't care what I had for breakfast. Still, there's content there—short stories, teasers, book covers, even a book I wrote a decade ago—so hopefully it's enough to keep people interested and coming back. But there was nothing there to draw new readers in until I had books on the shelves and people had an external reason to come looking for me.

There are people whose blogs have helped them launch a successful fiction writing career; John Scalzi's Whatever leaps to mind as a primary example, as does Cory Doctorow's BoingBoing, or Wil Wheaton's WWdN. The thing is, though, that they all had something to say or do that was of interest to people outside of their writing ambitions. BoingBoing is a repository of Cool Stuff; WWdN is, among other things, the story of a guy we all grew up watching on TV struggling to put together a life that encompassed both that kid we watched on screen with the self-defined "just a geek" he grew up to be. Whatever's tag line is "Taunting the Tauntable," which is certainly a theme that appeals to a lot of people. Critically, all of these sites are done well enough that people not only come back for more when they discover them, but they're inclined to point other people *at* them.

A moment of truth: I didn't know at all whether Magical Words would have an audience. There are a lot of writer blogs out there, both group-based and individually run. I thought it was distinctly possible that we could throw a blog and nobody would come. I'm exceedingly pleased that people *have* come, and that we've gotten ourselves a community here, but I honestly didn't know if it would work. What *makes* it work, I imagine, is that we are authors who pretty much know what we're talking about with regards to the publishing industry and writing. If we were unpublished writers with stars in our eyes, people might come to watch our journey, but for all the published writers out there who are trying to impart kernels of knowledge, there are a whole lot more unpublished people whose journeys can be watched—or not.

I think to try to get an audience you have to at least start with the "If you build it, they will come," attitude, but you've also really got to provide, some-how, something that people want. You have to post regularly so that there's continuous new content to keep people coming back. You have to say to your blogger friends, "Hey, can you mention I've started a blog," and hope they do it. You put meta tags into your page layout, and hope there are people out there looking for what you're doing.

Actually, the whole thing is a lot like selling a book, now that I think about it. "All you have to do is write a really good book." "All you have to do is provide something people want." Great. No problem. We'll get right on that, shall we?

David B. Coe

To be honest, I didn't know if Magical Words would work either. That it *has* pleases me no end, but I had my doubts.

I think that the key, as you say, is similar to that of writing. You have to want to do this stuff anyway. You have to want to blog and have a website, and to hell with the world if they don't look. It's like looking for a date: if you stink of desperation, if everything you do has "Look at me!" written all over it, you probably won't attract people. If you're confident and you remain true to yourself and your interests and just do it, you'll be successful. Because success will be the act of creating the blog or website, rather than the hit count you get . . .

Faith Hunter

Catie, this is a very detailed and info filled essay. I can add only one thing, directed only at the newly published writer. Network with like-minded people and with people who are just different enough from you to add spice. And, if possible, with people who are a little further along in their writing careers.

Working with people is so very helpful, as at this site, working with Catie, Misty and David, means that I don't have to come up with something interesting to say every day. (Okay, some people say I am interesting only once a month or so, but I try to ignore them.) I can even take off a week or two if needed for personal or writing purposes, and the site still draws readers.

Getting the networking here off to a good start wasn't hard to do. Misty and I knew one another already. I met David at a con and we clicked, and I liked both of their writing. We three wanted to do *something* online, but had no clear idea what—though the nebulous idea of appealing to writers and readers of fantasy (as well as other genres) was there at the start.

Terms and Definitions Every Writer Should Know

Edmund R. Schubert

While I was at NASFIC 2010 in Raleigh, N.C., I attended a panel where an established writer started talking about cover letters. However, it quickly became clear from context that this writer was actually referring to query letters, not cover letters. The distinction between the two is not insignificant. So I thought I would take this opportunity to share a list that I frequently hand out at workshops: it contains a variety of terms and definitions that every writer should know, and know properly. It covers basic terms, terms specific to non-fiction, and terms likely to come up regarding contracts.

GENERAL

BYLINE Indicates who the author is. May sometimes include promotional material on the author. Example: *Edmund R. Schubert is a freelance writer and editor. Information about his novel,* Dreaming Creek, *can be found at his website: www.edmundrschubert.com.*

COOL DOWN Setting aside your writing for anywhere from a few hours to a few months (for book projects) to allow you to return to it with a fresh eye for polishing and revision.

COVER LETTER A cover letter is a brief letter of introduction that accompanies any submitted work. In many cases these are optional; in all cases they should be brief.

CRITIQUE GROUP A group to read, edit, and offer advice and evaluation of your work. VERY IMPORTANT for writers to have people they can trust to offer honest feedback on their work. Can be an organized group that meets at a regular time, or a loose group of friends who read each others' works as needed.

ESSAY An essay represents the personal view/opinion of the writer.

FREELANCE WRITER / EDITOR A freelancer works on various projects by contract, and is not the employee of any single magazine or publisher. However, freelancers often do maintain long-term relationships with editors and/or publishers.

IDEA FILE A folder where you collect articles, columns, essays, phrases, words, reports, or anything else that catches your eye. When you're searching for ideas on what to write about, go to your Idea Folder for inspiration. A must have for writers.

GENRE The category a story, article, or script falls into. Examples: thriller, horror, science-fiction, romance. Non-fiction genres for magazine articles include self-help, how-to, opinion pieces, essays, inspirational, question and answer, interview, fillers, etc.

HOOK The opening of your article or story is usually referred to as your hook; it is how you grab a reader's attention. In a short story it is usually your first paragraph or two; in a magazine article it can be as little as your first sentence or even your title. In a novel it can be as much as your entire first chapter.

MARKET GUIDE Includes submittal information on how to query magazines, editors, and publishers. *Writer's Market* by Writer's Digest books is probably the best known market guide.

MULTIPLE SUBMISSIONS Sending more than one piece of work at a time, i.e., mailing an editor three different query ideas all at once. USUALLY NOT A GOOD IDEA.

NICHE Defining a specialty area to write for. For example, parenting, cooking, technology, etc.

OUTLINE / SYNOPSIS A detailed description of a book (fiction or non-fiction) that you have written/are proposing to write. These can vary in length from one page to fifty pages, depending on the requirements of the publisher.

PIECE Casual/industry term used almost interchangeably with "story" or "article." Refers to a "piece" of work you're submitting. (See "Work" under CONTRACTS.)

QUERY / QUERY LETTER In fiction, a query letter can either be a letter checking on the status of a previously submitted piece, or an inquiry as to a publisher's interest in seeing a particular piece. In the case of the latter (gauging interest), this is done almost exclusively with novels, not with short fiction.

RESPONSE TIME Term usually found in writer's guideline indicating how long an author should expect to wait before hearing a response from the editor/publisher who is assessing their work. Do not query the editor/publisher until after this time has elapsed.

SASE Self Addressed Stamped Envelope (needs to accompany all snail-mail submissions).

SELF-PUBLISHED This means exactly what it sounds like: you published it yourself. On the one hand, it means that you incurred all the costs and risks associated with publishing a work (usually a book). On the other hand it also means that you did all the work and are entitled to 100% of the profits. Opinions vary on the pros and cons of self-publishing.

SIMULTANEOUS SUBMISSION Piece (query letter, article, short story, or novel) sent to more than one market at a time. VERY GOOD IDEA to simultaneously submit if allowed; VERY BAD IDEA if not. Check writer's guidelines (usually posted on the publisher's website) to see if allowed.

SMALL-PRESS PUBLISHER This term generally applies to any of the smaller publishers working outside of New York City. They can vary considerably in their size and their ability to distribute/promote your work.

SUBMISSIONS GUIDELINES A set of guidelines or rules the publisher wants all writers to follow concerning when, where, and how to submit work for publication. It covers everything from subject matter to font size and margins. Guidelines are readily available on the publisher's website and should be strictly adhered to.

WRITER'S BLOCK Times when you feel uninspired or unable to write. Some writers believe writer's block to be a real obstacle while others consider it little more than an excuse to be lazy.

VANITY PRESS Term used to describe any of the companies that you can pay to publish your book. Similar to self-publishing, but usually of a lower quality. This is generally considered to be the bottom-rung of the publishing food chain.

VOICE The distinctive manner in which you choose and arrange words, phrases, ideas, and sentences on the page. Your writer's "voice" reflects your personal take on a subject. Well-developed writer's voices are often immediately recognizable on the page.

WRITER'S GUIDELINES Specific details set out by a magazine on what type articles they're seeking, length of articles, how to submit, who to contact, etc.

CONTRACT TERMS

ADVANCE / ADVANCE AGAINST ROYALTIES This is money paid to you by the publisher for a book (fiction or non-fiction) before the book is published. You will not be paid any more money until the book sells enough copies to earn this amount back for the publisher. Some publishers (usually smaller ones) do not pay an advance; they simply start paying royalties right away.

AGENT / LITERARY AGENT This is essentially a professional negotiator who will represent your book when it is time to get/sign a contract. A good agent will protect the interests of you, their client, and only get paid when you get a contract from a publisher. *If anyone claiming to be a literary agent offers you representation but asks you for money up front (anything from a signing fee to administrative fees), they are probably a scam artist.*

ALL RIGHTS Avoid this clause. This means you are selling *every* right you have to your work and so, in effect, it is no longer yours. You forfeit the right to ever use the work again and you are not entitled to additional payment if the magazine goes on to use your article again in any way.

ELECTRONIC RIGHTS Becoming more common. Some print magazines will offer an extra fee to publish your work on their website (as they should!), though most will state in their contract that they're buying unlimited electronic rights. You usually have to fight on this one if you don't want to give it away.

FIRST RIGHTS These are the rights that the writer offers a magazine/web site to publish an article for the FIRST time, i.e., the work cannot have appeared anywhere else (including blogs) before appearing in the magazine you've offered first rights to.

FIRST NORTH AMERICAN SERIAL RIGHTS (FNASR) (occasionally FNSR) The magazine/publisher has the right to be the first one in North America to publish the piece. FNASR and All Rights are the two most-commonly found rights asked for in contracts.

KILL FEE Usually 20-30% of the agreed upon fee, this is the amount you'll be paid if the magazine accepts your piece but then decides not to use it.

NON-EXCLUSIVE RIGHTS You retain the right to resell the piece.

ONE-TIME RIGHTS Gives the magazine the right to publish the piece once, but not necessarily first.

PAYS ON ACCEPTANCE / PAYS ON PUBLICATION This clause of a contract determines when the writer will be paid for their work, and is primarily used for short stories and magazine articles, not for books. Payment on Acceptance means the writer will be paid when the magazine accepts the story for publication. Payment on Publication means the writer will be paid when the story is published (ranging anywhere from six weeks to nine month or more after acceptance). It should come as no surprise that Payment on Publication is the *much* more commonly used clause.

REPRINT RIGHTS / NON-EXCLUSIVE REPRINT RIGHTS Reprint rights tell the publication the piece has been published prior. Usually reprint rights are approximately 35% of the agreed upon fee for First Rights. Non-exclusive reprint rights mean you retain the right to re-sell the work yet again, maybe even simultaneously.

RIGHTS Publishers are contracting for the right to use/publish your work and they should pay you to do so. (Some smaller magazines only have the resources to pay you in copies of the magazine in which your work appears, but hey, you've got to start somewhere) There are a lot of different kinds of rights; the more the publisher asks for, the more they ought to pay you. In the absence of a formal contract, it's usually assumed that the magazine gets FNASR.

ROYALTIES This is the percentage of the profits that will be paid to you for sales of your book. If you've received an advance, you do not receive any royalties until the book earns out its advance. Royalties are commonly between 10% and 15% of the book's profits (though some publishers pay a percentage of the books net profits, and some pay a percentage of the gross profits). This only applies to books; magazines do not pay royalties.

ROYALTY PERIOD This is how often your publisher will pay you royalties. It is usually twice per year, but some contracts call for either annual or quarterly royalty periods.

WORK Formal industry term used in contracts, interchangeable with "piece" or "article." Refers to the "piece" of "work" you are signing the contract for.

WORK FOR HIRE Pretty much the same as giving away all rights for a set fee. All work you do becomes the property of the employer to use as they like.

A Writer's Life

The Gregorovich-Feister Idea Farm and Fresh Market

Misty Massey

"Where DO you wacky writers get those crazy ideas?"

I don't know if fantasy writers get this question more often than mystery or romance authors, but we get it quite a bit. And I have decided, in the interest of fair play and brotherhood, to share the Secret. Yes, you guessed it—there IS a place we all go to get these nutty ideas: the Gregorovich-Feister Idea Farm and Fresh Market. It's a coop tucked into the high grass along Interstate 26 between Columbia and Charleston. Take exit 132.5 (it's a dirt road, so be sure and slow down on the curve, else you're liable to go flying!) and drive at exactly forty-two miles per hour for exactly seventeen minutes. Stop at the seventeen minute mark, close your eyes, and whisper, "I just can't think of what to write," and the gate will appear on the left. Drive in quick, since it only stays open about thirty seconds.

Once you're inside, you can pick up a bushel basket and hit the fields yourself. The urban fantasy trees are over on the west side of the farm, under those dark clouds. Keep one eye open for the random questing parties in the epic fantasy orchard, and whatever you do, don't pluck the golden rutabagas in the mythic fields—the demi-gods are terribly sensitive about that.

If you don't feel like doing your own work, you can go straight to the fresh market and buy the ideas Viktor Gregorovich picked first thing that morning. Viktor's a darling, and if you can't find what you want, he'll waddle out to the fields to find it for you. (Don't ask him where Feister is, though—it's still a sore subject, ever since Hurricane Hugo came through.) They only take golden dollars and dull pennies in payment, so stock up before you get there.

Okay, you're not buying the story. The truth is that when I answer that question honestly, people never seem quite satisfied with the truth. The wacky ideas are all in my head, just as they are in yours. My first novel was born on a trip to the Olympic Rain Forest in Washington State, when my husband started telling me about a news story he'd read about lost trees at the bottom of Lake Superior. The second novel I began came from my love of Renaissance faires, and the third, *Mad Kestrel* . . . well, heck, I was missing the beach and the ocean, and pirates could take me there fastest. I get ideas from flipping through the latest issues of *Newsweek, Scientific American* and *Skeptic*. I half-listen to news stories on the radio, and let my mind run wildly with the portion I did catch. I hear songs that send my mind fluttering in another direction than the poor songwriter meant for me. I read histories and wonder what secret ambitions drove this general or that dictator to do the things he did. The trick is to think "What if?" instead of assuming what you heard or read is all there is to the story.

Faith Hunter

Misty, I *loved* this! But I do have one comment—I don't think all people have zany ideas. I don't think all minds are created to be creative in storytelling. I used to think they were, but now . . . not so much. I now think some people have brains wired to think in numbers and quotas and linear concepts. Others to think in color or musical notes. Others for other ways of cognition. Not writing or storytelling. In fact, they think we are totally nuts.

David B. Coe

A story from when I was first working out the plotting and world-building for my very first book: I had just finished my Ph.D, and was actually out in California to hand in and defend my doctoral disser-tation. While I was there, I stayed with my closest friend from my history program and told him about my book idea and how I was con-sidering giving up on academia to pursue a career as a fantasy author. I was still struggling with the decision in a big way. So he and I went for a long walk through the campus of our grad school and I told him all about the world I was creating and the magic system, which was rooted in a psychic bond mages form with birds of prey. And just as I was telling him about this, I looked up into the tree we were walking past. And there were three baby Great-horned Owls looking down on us. A Sign? A gift from the writing gods? Call it what you will. But I'll never forget it.

Christina Stiles

David, I'd like to hear more about your decision to turn away from academia. I take it you didn't already have something published at that point? I'm always fascinated by how writers got the point they're at now.

And those of you who are working full-time, workaday jobs, how do you balance the two? For instance, do you just do the job to get by, or do you find yourself trying to achieve promotions and such at work? Or, is all your extra energy expended on making sure you excel at the writing?

David B. Coe

I'd had doubts about academia for some time, Christina. A few years. But I'd started the graduate program in history and invested much time and energy into getting my degree, so I saw it through to the end and finished my dissertation.

I'd wanted to be a writer for years, since high school, and had only gotten away from it because it didn't seem to be a practical career path. (Had that right! ☺) Anyway, I finished my dissertation in May 1993, and really couldn't start to apply for academic jobs until September or October. So my wife said, basically, "Since the day I met you you've been talking about writing a book. You have a few months now. Why don't you try writing and see if you like it?"

So I began work on what would become my first book (my first published piece of fiction of any length), *Children of Amarid.* And that fall I applied for several academic positions. Long story short: I was offered a job teaching U.S. Environmental History at Colorado State on a Thursday in mid-March. The next day I got a call from an editor at Tor Books telling me that he was interested in buying my book. So I took the weekend to decide. Actually it was no decision at all. The Colorado job was my history dream job if ever there was one. And the thought of taking it made me sick to my stomach. Writing had been my dream for years and finally I had the opportunity to do it professionally. I turned down the job offer, signed a contract with Tor a couple of months later, and never looked back.

Misty Massey

Christina, my job is a paycheck, honestly. I love working with the students and the books, and I have the most amazing principal to work for, so it's a relatively pleasant place to be. I put forth my best effort every minute I'm at school, so it's not as if I'm just lazing around. My principal badgers me on a fairly regular basis about going back to school to earn my Masters in Library Science and my certification. It makes me feel good, of course, to know she values me so highly, but I know how much time and work and money would have to go toward a graduate degree, and subsequently how the writing would suffer.

Things I Did Wrong

A.J. Hartley

A few weeks ago I was speaking to a Sisters in Crime meeting and I realized that my mini-autobiography had morphed into a series of bullets that might be titled *Don't Do This: A Writer's Guide to Decades of Failure*. As some of you will know, mine was a long road to getting published, and the gap between writing my first complete novel and getting one published was eight complete novels and a little over twenty years. It didn't have to be that way, and I'd like to steer you through some of the mistakes I made in the hope that your road to publication will be shorter and faster. The result, I trust, will balance confessional blather about myself with stuff you can really use. I confess that some of what I will say here will be blindingly obvious to anyone who isn't me, circa 1985.

Writing in a Vacuum.

No, I don't mean drifting in the vastness of space (though it can feel like that). I mean writing by myself. I would start working on a project, hammer it out over a few months or so, polish it, and then send it out. I showed it to no-one but my girlfriend/fiancée/wife (remember we're talking about a 20+ years span here), and maybe my parents. I had no beta readers, no critique group, no literary support network, no writer pals, no creative writing classes.

What that meant was that for all the help and encouragement I got from my family, I wasn't getting any kind of constructive response from someone who saw me simply as a writer. My family's thoughts were inevitably complicated by their feelings for me, so the first people who read my book who were NOT already invested in it being good, were the agents and editors to whom I sent it.

This is not a recipe for success. As we all know, rejection letters tend to be light on specifics, so learning about what's wrong with your work this way is like hunting for the proverbial needle in a haystack. Most of the rejections ("Liked it, didn't love it") told me nothing, so I kept on puttering away at the same thing, baffled and feeling like I was shooting in the dark, never really knowing if my next project was any better than the last one.

The fact that you are reading this essay at all suggests you already have me beat. Back in the eighties there were books on writing, but there wasn't anything like this interactive medium (unless it was actual people sitting down together), a place like Magical Words where you can feel part of a community of shared interests. Not only did I not know how to create such a community (or find one), I didn't even know what the value of such a thing was. But it's worse than that. Because if someone had invited me to join a critique group, I almost certainly would have said no.

Some of that was a young writer's arrogance: the surety that I basically knew what I was doing even if the powers-that-be in the publishing world had not recognized that yet. But more of it was the opposite: shyness and fear.

Many writers are private people. We take refuge in our heads and in the stories we build, stories invented largely for our own amusement. The prospect of sending them out into the world, of losing control of them and putting them in the harsh glare of Other People's Opinion is, frankly, terrifying. To this day, I get a rush of panic and anxiety when I offer a new piece for someone to look at (including sympathetic readers like my family, friends, or agent). So it's not surprising that I kept my work to myself, didn't talk about it, didn't ask other people things that might have helped me out, operating as if I might get published by stealth: telling no one until my face was plastered across the *New York Review of Books*.

I can't imagine how much this slowed me down, but I know it did, and probably quite a lot. Even without formal instruction from which I might have learned basic principles, I missed out on the chance to get honest feedback, tips, bits of advice, and criticism coming simply from someone who was interested in whether the book worked as a book, not whether they thought they could sell it. This is a crucial distinction, because for years I was able to hide behind the old lie that my work was *good* but not *marketable*.

We know this one. We use it all the time. I still do when I produce something I can't sell, and I know that sometimes—SOMETIMES—it *is* true.

But usually, it's not.

Unless you are writing something truly experimental or generically very odd, there's a market for it somewhere if it's good. The trick is assessing that last bit: Is it good? We all know readers whose advice is shaky or can't be trusted, that it's marked by jealousy, resentment, or other factors which color their opinion. But we also know that there is no substitute for getting eyes on your work. I learned this the hard way. Writing is private. Publication isn't. If you want your book to be something other than a file on your computer, if you want it out there where people can pick it up from a bookstore shelf, you have to share it with people you trust before sending it out. There's no way round it. You have to swallow your pride, brace for impact, and learn. It's the only way, and it may just help to get you in print a good deal faster than I did.

Carrie Ryan

Great advice! I also think that joining a critique group lets you see other people making similar mistakes that might be easier to spot because it's not your own work so you're not as close to it. I know that it was in judging writer contests that I realized what it meant to have a slow opening or be generic—these were all very well written entries but they helped me understand and recognize that gap between being able to write well and writing a publishable story.

But it did take me a while to feel comfortable sharing my own work. Now I go by the adage: I'd rather hear that it stinks from my critique partner than from my editor, and from my editor than from a reviewer or a reader.

Megan Haskell

Thank you for sharing A.J.! This is something that I've struggled with recently. I've been taking a writing course this summer, and I've loved hearing the feedback from the other students and the professor, even when it's negative (masochistic? me? nah...). However, all that I've shared have been flash fiction pieces that we've written in class or other assignments. When it comes to my novel, I'm holding on to it like a life-preserver in the ocean. Part of this is because it isn't finished and I know that I have a lot of revision work that needs to happen.

So my question is this: How early do you start to get feedback from family/friends, critique groups, and beta readers? And do you share the whole novel all at once, or a chapter at a time?

A.J. Hartley

Megan, this is tough and I'm sure you'll get as many different pieces of advice as there are writers. I generally don't share anything with anyone until the first draft is done and pretty clean (few beta readers are really good at treating a draft as a draft and not a finished product). BUT, there are good reasons to share much earlier than this, and lately my contracts have forced me to block out the entire manuscript in outline. I don't really like doing this, but it forces me to clear up the basic shape of the story and that's invaluable for seeing large issues of arc, rhythm and genre. I'd be wary of working a first novel to a high shine before showing it to anyone in case you start getting notes suggesting you need extensive revision. In outline or draft form it's less of a problem if you start to hear a repeated observation that the book doesn't get going till page 70 and you should probably cut everything before that point.

Many of my beta readers don't want to see the thing in process: they want a true reader's experience as if they've just picked it up in a store. I'm confident enough now that I can do that and know that what I give them is at least in the ball park. Twenty years ago I should have been saying "I have an idea of a book about X: what do you think?" If this is your first book, I'd say start showing it (not sending it to agents or publishers) and see what people say. It might really help you in your revision/editing. That's just my two-cents, of course. But if you DON'T share it with other people yet, have a reason other than fear.

Self-Determination

Faith Hunter

I've been looking into my own psyche lately. I've been looking inside, where the future of my writing life skulks, where my expectations prowl. Or slumber, maybe. What do I expect—what do I really believe will happen with my own writing future?

Do I really believe that I can write? (There lie dragons . . .) Do I really believe that I can build a growing audience? Do I really believe that I will earn a seven-figure advance someday? Do I really believe that I will be a bestseller someday? Do I really believe that I have a book inside me that will be like a tsunami on the reading world? Or do I believe that I will muddle about in the shallow waters of near-obscurity, make a few small splashing waves, and then sink below the surface of the publishing business, to be forgotten? What do I really *believe* about myself . . . ? And how does that belief shape my own writing future?

I've been asking my writing pals what they believed about their futures when they started out. And I've gotten some interesting answers, answers that point into the soul of us all.

One said, "I want to get another book published. That's all. It's always just one more book."

One said, "I'm hoping to be a bestseller in a couple more years."

One writer pal said, "I'm a firm mid-lister."

One said, "I'm in the middle of remaking myself from a mid-lister into who I really am. I'm going to be on Oprah soon. You watch."

I asked a bestseller writer buddy what she expected when she started out. And she said, "I knew I'd be at the top." It wasn't arrogance or conceit. It was the most firm self-confidence I've ever seen. Wow. Just wow.

And suddenly I realized. This is what makes a long-time, successful writer. Unshakeable self-belief. And that understanding rocked me. Because I don't have it. I am still trying to deal with what I learned that day. Still trying to see what I might do with that understanding that will/might/could change me inside and let me grow.

When I started this business, I had two images of myself and my future:

1. I'd write a book a year, making about $25,000 per book to satisfy my inner muse (who was a lot prettier in those days) and to supplement my income.

2. I'd write five books, build an audience, impress a high-placed editor, and then have a breakout book that would put me in the six-figure

income area for twenty books or so, and then I'd retire.

Nowhere in there, in those expectations, was there a vision of myself as a bestseller with four feet of backlist shelf space in every bookstore in the nation. Nowhere in there was the possibility of fabulous success. Was I being sensible? Or have I . . . (deep breath) have I shackled myself?

I do not know. I do not know if I am master of my own vessel (USS Firm Mid-Lister) or if the market made me what I am and I flounder in the wake of others through no fault of my own. And I do not know if I can take the wheel of my own future in my hands and steer myself into new waters, into something fresh and exciting, bigger and better.

But I do know that in some arcane way, our beliefs shape and steer and guide and power us. And so, knowing that, I have to change my self-beliefs. I have to rework my own brain if I want to make it in this fast-changing business. My neurons have to be rewired for success. So, I peer into the depths of my own psyche and say, "Hey, you! What do you believe? Can you do it? Can you be a real writer? Can you envision a future of great things for yourself? Can you be a success?"

So far? A soft, hesitant . . . "Um . . . yeah? Um . . . Maybe?"

David B. Coe

This is a great essay, Faith. It touches on all the emotions with which I grapple these days as I sort through my professional expectations and the realities of my career path thus far. Wonderful stuff.

And yet, I'm troubled by your last paragraph. "Can you be a real writer?" "Can you be a success?" How do we define what either of those things is? In order to be a "real writer" do you have to be a bestseller with six figure advances? I reject that notion entirely. Do we define "being a success" solely in terms of money earned? I'm not sure I accept that, either. I've yet to have a bestseller or a six-figure advance. I know few writers who have had either. But I think that publishing a novel is success. I think that selling a short story is, too. The market is fickle. It values some books that I think are crap and dismisses others that I believe are brilliant. Is that the yardstick I want to use to gauge my own successes and failures?

I understand ambition; I'm ambitious myself. I understand wanting the big contracts and the huge sales numbers. I'm not saying that we shouldn't strive for those things. But I've read your work. I've seen Gwen *and* Faith Hunter filling shelf space in every corner of America. You are a terrific writer; a critically acclaimed writer; an award-winning writer; the author of how many books? Twenty? More? That's success. That should be a source of pride. Not complacency, of course, but pride nevertheless. There are so many ways to measure success; I'd hate to think that money would be the one that you settle on as most important.

Faith Hunter

David, it is success. I'm not really denying that. (Okay, I am, but it's one of those days where I am questioning myself, you know?) What I am gnawing on is more along the lines of, "Have I ham-stringed my own success by applying mental and spiritual reins?" Heck yes. I have to admit that. I have to face it head on. And, "What could I be writing that is better, stronger, faster than a speeding bullet?"

And, "Do I want more? Am I capable of more?"

Not more books, I'm writing as fast as I can. But more . . . something . . . Can I step it up? And if I step it up and let go of the reins, can I, will I, see a change in my book status? And most importantly: Do I care enough to let all that happen? How much do I want it? Did I ever want it at all?

Thank y'all. I am not depressed about this. I *am* soul searching, however (which usually results in a great book in about six months, BTW (laughing)).

Why Bother?

David B. Coe

When last we saw our intrepid author, she was wading into the Slog, the great morass of storytelling, character development, and worldbuilding that stretched to the imaginative horizon, keeping her from her ambitions. Armed only with a keyboard, a thesaurus, and her wits, she strode forth, prepared to face down the horrors which, according to legend, resided in this creative fen: the Minotaur of Narrative lying in wait at the end of a plotting cul-de-sac; the Hydra of Flat Prose that stalks her, looming over every passage, threatening to poison her tale with its noisome breath; the Charybdis of Datadump into which she might fall at any moment, never to be heard from again; and, of course, the dreaded Chimera of Incoherence, which constantly menaces her work, its fiery breath burning narrative bridges right and left. It is hard, dangerous work, and it's a wonder that she even risks the fen in the first place.

Truly, it is a wonder. This essay is not so much a "How-To" piece as it is a "Why-do-we-do-this?" essay. All kidding aside, this *is* hard work. It's discouraging, frustrating, maddening. Getting published at all is incredibly difficult; making a living at it is, for all but a few, next to impossible; making a fortune at it is nothing short of miraculous. It would be so easy simply to give up. Especially now, in the middle of the slog, as I call it. If ever there was a point in the process that would lead people just to chuck it, this is it. Here at Magical Words, we often fall back on the truism that we write because we love it, and that's great. But at this stage in the process it would be easy to call upon the wisdom of that great American philosopher, Keb Mo', who said "That's not love/Love don't feel that bad . . ."

So, why bother?

Last night, my family and I went to see a University production of *A Midsummer Night's Dream*. It was a fine production—great costumes, sparse but effective sets and lighting, good acting; even the original music composed for the play worked well. But these were secondary. The writing was all. The interwoven narratives, the poetry, the humor; the mere fact that at four hundred fifteen years old, it still makes us laugh, it still speaks to us of love and friendship, rivalry and envy. (For A.J.'s sake, I will make no mention of the universality of the human condition, but I'm thinking about it. . . .)

Now, I'm no Shakespeare. No one knows that better than I do; and, forgive me for saying so, but you're probably not Shakespeare reincarnate either. That's okay. We don't have to be in order for me to make my point. We are writers. This is what we do. Sometimes we do it because we love it. Sometimes we do it because not doing it is simply unthinkable. Sometimes we do it because we've started, and we refuse to quit and so the only thing to do is keep moving forward. Maybe, like A.J., we simply love the written word. Maybe, we're driven by a story or a character or a world that we can't get out of our heads. Every one of these is a valid response to "Why bother?"

But there's a larger reason, too. We might not be Shakespeare, but we're not completely divorced from him either. Like him, we are storytellers. We are part of a tradition that is as old as humanity itself. I've been reading Shakespeare for years. I've been reading Poe, Hawthorne, and Dickens; Faulkner, Fitzgerald and Steinbeck; Stegner, Proulx, and Winton. I've also been reading Tolkien and Card and Kay. All of them have shaped my work, my style, my process. I don't think that anyone will be reading my books four hundred and fifteen years from now (although it would be cool if they were). I'm not even sure anyone will be reading them a century from now. But people are reading them now, and will be for years to come.

And maybe some of them will wind up writing, too. Just as I have had stories handed to me over the years that I have then folded into my creative process, maybe they will add my stories to their imaginative mix. And so that narrative tradition will flow on, in part through my work, and through yours, too. We are part of something much larger than the one book with which we happen to be struggling right now. Without thinking ourselves the equal of Shakespeare, or of Hawthorne or Faulkner or Proulx, we can still feel a connection to them.

That's what I felt last night as I listened to the last lines of *Midsummer Night's Dream*. I'd struggled much of the day with rewrites and proofs. When I went to the play I was angry and frustrated and exhausted. I left exhilarated, even proud.

I'm a writer. And that's why I bother.

And as imagination bodies forth
The forms of things unknown, the poet's pen
Turns them to shapes, and gives to airy nothing
A local habitation and a name.
— Act V, scene i

A.J. Hartley

I wondered if some part of that quotation was coming ☺ I thought you would go with the slightly more back-handed "The lunatic, the lover and the poet/Are of imagination all compact." Great post, David. You're absolutely right. It's not just about the need to make up stories: it's about the need to share them. However solitary, writing is finally a communal act. In the context of your theme we might add the closing couplet from sonnet 18: "So long as men can breathe or eyes can see,/So long lives this ⌈my writing⌉ and this gives life to thee."

And thanks for (almost) not mentioning the human condition . . .

John Rea-Hedrick

David, I always appreciate your posts and have been particularly encouraged by this recent series on writers and their writing. I work a full-time day job, but writing has always been my first love—crafting stories in my head during the day then scavenging for time to write them down in the late evenings. I'm not a part of any writing community so your posts (and this blog) have helped me understand I'm not alone in the way I feel about writing or in the frustrations that come with it.

Thanks for helping to keep me inspired!

David B. Coe

John, thanks so much for the kind comment. Writing is a strange endeavor—like painting or sculpture—in that we do it in isolation so that the product of our labor can be enjoyed by (we hope) tens or hundreds of thousands. I'm not part of a writing community where I live, either. But I've come to feel that Magical Words is my writing community, and I'm glad to hear that it serves a similar function for you. I admire you for keeping at the writing even while dealing with the demands of your full-time work. I wish you every success with your book and we're all glad to have you as part of the Magical Words community.

Balancing the Tribal

Faith Hunter

This essay is about . . .

Gardening.

Not really. But it is an essay about balance—the balance of living a life that is comfortable, fulfilling, healthy, full of creativity, full of wonderful words, activities away from the job—or in my case, jobs—and deadlines.

I wrote not too long ago about cutting harmful things and toxic people out of our lives. Yeah, I know, some of those toxic people are family, and may not be cut-able, but most of us can limit the amount of time we spend with toxic people, even family, to improve our lives' balance.

And most of us make time for the good-for-us (non-toxic) family and friends, and make time to go out into the world in social situations like parties, lunch out, tea or coffee with special people. We remember to exercise (sometimes), pray or meditate, and learn new things (which can be read as research, too). But sometimes we forget to do the things that feed our souls, things that are spiritually renewing. Which is where, for me, gardening comes in.

Many people, myself included, go to mosque, synagogue, or church for spiritual renewal, but there are other ways, places, events and experiences that call out to deeper, and far more human, parts of our spiritual natures. And that human, tribal, part of our spiritually often gets left in the dust. All people were once tribal, whether our ancestors were African, AmIn, Celts, people of the steppes, Mongol, South Pacific, whatever, we were tribal long before we settled into cities. And tribal people had rituals to celebrate, recognize, and denote all the different landmarks of human life. As writers, I think we are closer to the ritualistic parts of our human natures than lots of others, and I think we depend on the deeper, mystical, parts of our psyches more than most—which is where those amazing story endings come from that we've spoken of here several times. But we also often forget to nurture those parts of our natures that we depend upon so much. And I am not talking about other creative endeavors, though that may be part of our personal rituals.

For me, those mystical moments come when my hands are in the soil, or my hardboat is moving with the current down a river or rocky creek. I deeply *need* to get my hands in the soil of mother earth. To paddle down her lifeblood is essential. When I don't do both I feel the ache deep inside, and there is a fractured anger that splinters through me, making *me* the toxic person in my own life. For five years I gave up gardening in favor of two books a year, and my soul—though nurtured by kayaking plenty of rivers—missed it deeply.

So, I've begun to terrace the hill in front of my house, and will bring in soil for the garden I've missed so much. It's backbreaking work, hauling stone for retaining walls, shoveling, making level foundations. And yeah, I'm doing it myself, with the help of the hubby. (He got drafted, but he's agreeable.) Gardening is one thing I desperately need—as both writer and human—that I've neglected. I've starved my own creative, human, tribal soul and getting my hands back into the body of the earth is already so fulfilling that I've been able to craft a book proposal in about half the time it usually takes me.

Amy Sanderson

For me, it's always been hiking. I've realized this a lot more fully now that I'm living in a city. Every couple of weeks, I just have to get out into open countryside, away from traffic, noise, crowds, and technology. When I don't do this, I start to go a little bit crazy very quickly! And, of course, as soon as I get away from the keyboard/pen and paper, my head fills up with dozens of story ideas that I can't write down . . .

Misty Massey

Mine is dance. Not just belly dance, but all sorts of musical movement. It reaches me on a deeper, ancient level, the place where my body doesn't hear lyrics or instruments, but recognizes the beat and responds without any prior thought. Doesn't matter if I'm any good to look at. When I'm sweaty and my heart is slamming and my breath is rushing because I've just thrown myself around the room for a while, I feel clean inside.

Stuart Jaffe

I love hiking for a "back to nature" moment. But nothing rejuvenates me more than the Blues. I sit down with my guitar and can just get lost in playing. And if I'm nowhere near my guitar, I'll listen to the Blues greats on my mp3 player.

Changes in the Light
David B. Coe

This morning, instead of my usual workout, I hiked out to one of my favorite viewpoints here in my home town (we sit atop the Cumberland Plateau) and I spent an hour taking pictures. The viewpoint overlooks a narrow valley which opens out into some farmland. The opposite slope is completely undeveloped and covered with white and red oaks, red and sugar maples, tulip poplars, shagbark hickories, and a host of other species of trees that I can't name. In the spring I come here and take pictures of the forest as the trees leaf out in myriad shades of green. Today I was after fall colors, and they were wonderfully intense.

Visual artists do this quite often—return again and again to a spot they've painted or photographed, looking for different patterns, different tones of color, different qualities of light. My brother is a professional artist and he has countless paintings of the same farm or the same streambed which he's painted at different times of day and different times of year. Paul Cezanne painted the Sainte-Victoire in Provence hundreds of times. My favorite works by Claude Monet are his paintings of the Cathedral at Rouen, which he painted under every conceivable lighting condition.

At first blush it would seem that this aspect of visual art has nothing at all to do with writing. But as I embark on a new fiction project I realize that with every new plot line, with every new character, I explore familiar ground from a slightly different perspective. When we try to put names to the spectrum of human emotion—joy, sorrow, anger, contentment, jealousy, indignation, fear— we eventually run out of words. When we think of the conflicts and life events that make for good stories—romance, intrigue, rivalry, betrayal—we soon find ourselves turning back to story points that we've used in past works.

It would be very easy to throw up one's hands in frustration. This has all been done before. *I've* done all of this before! Except that of course I haven't. Just as the facade of Rouen's marvelous cathedral looks one way at dusk on an autumn day and utterly different at dawn in the spring, anger and love and fear change greatly when experienced by different characters. Romance and rivalry are nothing more than the inadequate words we have at our disposal to describe interactions that are as varied as the people they involve.

In fantasy, we have the added bonus of being able to move our stories to different worlds. A story of romance and intrigue set in the Forelands would look nothing like a story with the same elements set in Islevale, the world I've created for my new series. I could take a character I've created for the LonTobyn books and move her to a city in the Southlands, and her life would be unrecognizable.

But for me, the great variable is character. No two people will ever see the world in exactly the same way. And as I step into the mind of a new lead character, I feel my world view shifting to match what I know about him and his past life. Romance has a different meaning for this man, because choices he made decades ago have denied him the one person he ever truly loved. Hardship has a different meaning for him because the sixteen years he spent in prison have left him both calloused and appreciative of small pleasures. I could go on, but I think you probably understand my point.

Part of what makes writing so much fun is that it enables us to find something fresh and exciting in emotions and experiences that might otherwise seem terribly commonplace. When we see the world through the eyes of a new character, the mundane comes alive, the familiar becomes exotic. The light shifts, the colors become more vibrant, patterns emerge that we hadn't seen before. Characters, setting, plot—the variations are endless; there is no such thing as "ordinary."

Misty Massey

David said, "No two people will ever see the world in exactly the same way . . . When we see the world through the eyes of a new character, the mundane comes alive, the familiar becomes exotic."

My dance teacher pointed out once that ten dancers could choreograph their performances to the same piece of recorded music and you'd still be watching ten completely different dances. It's all about the individual interpretation. Writing is the same—the plot may have been done by another writer, but the uniqueness comes from the living, breathing characters the writer creates. Good post, David!

Five Things You Ought To Know About Writers

Misty Massey

The other day, a student came in to my library and looked at me quizzically.

"You wrote a book?" she asked.

"Yes," I said, smiling.

"You don't look like a writer," she said.

"What does a writer look like?" I asked.

"They wear glasses, and they pull their hair back in a knot, and they stare at everyone. Creepy."

I don't know how many writers this child has seen before, but her description made me wonder about how nonwriting people see us. I know most of our readers here are writers themselves, but I thought it might be fun to explain some of the traits nonwriters should know about us.

1. We're watching.

Characters in the most successful stories move and talk and behave in a believable way. So yes, we're watching you. We're looking at the way you walk, and the clothes you chose this morning, and what's in your cup. We're interested in what kind of car you drive, your favorite color, and whether you wanted to be a cowboy or an astronaut when you were a kid. We're not stalking you, really. Don't run away. We're just trying to get the details right.

2. We're listening.

Not long ago I was sitting in a Starbucks waiting on a friend to arrive, and I couldn't help overhearing a conversation between a young woman who was writing a novel, and the young man who was coaching her. She was starry-eyed; he was pretentious, and together they were practically a comedy team. Not that they knew it. I kept my face deadpan and my head down, but I heard almost every word. It's a great way to learn how to write dialogue, after all. Hearing the give and take, the breaths and pauses that happen in between, is vital. And sometimes I hear a sentence that's so individual, so perfect, I rush to scribble it in my notebook, in case one of my characters might say something like that. If you're ever reading along and you run across a familiar turn of phrase, don't be surprised to find that a writer was listening to you.

3. We're not talking about you.

With all that listening and watching, you might worry that our characters are based on real people . . . maybe even you. Most likely not. With all the listening and watching we do, we still prefer to create our own characters. Just because the protag in the novel has brown hair and drives a Santa Fe doesn't make her me. So relax . . . your soul isn't stolen, nor is your secret identity revealed.

4. We occasionally wander in another world.

Sometimes in the middle of a conversation, the writer will seem to drift away. We don't mean to be rude. We can't help it—something pinged a thought and sent us wandering into the world of our imagination. Writers become skillful at pretending to know what they missed in a real-life conversation, because we do this so often. It's easier face to face than on the phone though . . . as my best friend and my sister could tell you. I've done it to them more than once, and felt terrible about it.

5. We're not vampires.

Most of us have day jobs to pay the bills, and have to do our writing at night or on weekends. Time is at a premium. I have to plan my time carefully, to make sure I'm not throwing it away. Sometimes friends will call on the spur of the moment and invite me to some great event, and I have to turn them down because I'd already planned to spend the day with the keyboard. I'd love to go out to the mall or have tea, but if it's between that and getting the writing done, the writing takes precedence. That's just how it has to work. Do you want the next book or not?

> **David B. Coe**
> "We're not vampires."
> 　　Speak for yourself . . .
> 　　I think #4 is key, and I'd add that we're constantly writing in our heads. At least I am. Everything I see, hear, taste, or experience in any other way is grist for the creative mill. And I always find myself searching for the right words to describe whatever it is I'm living at that moment.
>
> **C.E. Murphy**
> "She was starry-eyed; he was pretentious and together they were practically a comedy team." *laughs out loud*
> 　　Ted (my husband) always knows when, during a brainstorming session, he's hit on a particularly good idea, because I do that drift thing. I stop talking and go slack jawed and stare into the distance, and then he's invariably pleased with himself. ☺

Writing On Instinct

A.J. Hartley

I was always a bit of a music head. My tastes have shifted over the years, but I still have the same passion for listening, the same appreciation for clever or emotive songs well-executed. I love virtuoso instrumental work almost as much as I love lyrical complexity and wit, and I always wanted to be able to reproduce those sounds with the kind of casual abandon my idols seemed to manage. So I took lessons in piano and guitar as a kid, formed a band as a teenager, and to this day love to noodle around on my Les Paul. But I learned long ago that I was never going to be a musician.

Sometimes I read about someone like Paul McCartney whose musical gift seems innate, the kind of talent who can get comfortable with almost any instrument in no time and for whom melodies just materialize. But I also know that even for the most gifted musician, technical mastery takes time and work.

Some of it is about labor. For years I misrecognized all those improvised guitar solos as raw, unhoned talent. I figured I could just wander around the fret board and produce the same soaring radiance without actually studying, without endless hours of practice to the detriment of everything else. But the Renaissance had a wonderful word for what we see rock stars do. It's called *sprezzatura*: the feigned naturalness and ease which conceals what is actually carefully studied and prepared. The individual notes of this particular solo might be improvised, but that improvisation has grown out of years of work, and more often than not, even its details have been carefully rehearsed, however spontaneous they might look. We value the spontaneous. We respect it. It feels real, like it comes fully fledged from the soul. Spontaneous is cool.

I never got there, because I never did the work. I never achieved the level of technical mastery that would allow me to simply make stuff up. Even if I could hear the sound in my head, my fingers couldn't execute without hours of rehearsal, and I just didn't try hard enough to make that happen.

My medium is language.

The blessing and curse of writing is that anyone can do it, or rather anyone who speaks the language *seems* to be able to do it. But writing is like singing or acting, an art form where the craft (unlike guitar playing, say) disappears in the performance so that people forget that it took work to get there. It's more *sprezzatura*, but in this case it reinforces the fiction that anyone who has the raw materials (in this case, language) can pull it off effortlessly.

They can't, of course. We know that or else we wouldn't be on a site like this. But we all want shortcuts. We want to pound out the book in a few weeks, dazzle our friends and nail down a mega-contract with a major publisher (preferably with screen rights) when we ought to be practicing the literary equivalent of chord progressions and blues scales. We're so enamored with the seemingly spontaneous out-pouring of talent that we allow ourselves to forget that work has to be done, dues have to be paid.

No news there. But here's the thing. As with any kind of technical mastery, you get to a point where it really does become natural: second nature, almost, even instinctive. Not everyone will like what I write (that's a different issue), but I can now crank out a couple of thousand words in a sitting, and be confident that—with a little polishing—the quality will be far superior to what I used to write, superior even (and here's a confession) to the stuff I used to send out to agents and publishers, certain I was about to be "discovered." I can do it now. The Nobel committee isn't calling me day and night, but I feel good about what I write and can focus on the big idea stuff, confident that I can work the sentence-level execution satisfactorily. That's not a boast any more than it would be for a man who apprenticed as a carpenter for ten years to say he could make a chest of drawers. These are skills that can be mastered. As with most things, talent might make you shine, but success comes largely from work, much of it tedious, time consuming, unglamorous, and marked by small failures.

I'm not sure when it started to come together for me or why, but I suspect it was mainly just time: time spent reading and writing. At bottom, that's what it's all about and it's what I offer as the best and simplest advice to any writer, self-evident though it surely is: Read and write. A lot.

I have never taken a writing class of any kind, though I have taught some and know their potential value. But for years (actually decades) I've worked with language, sometimes through conscious study, sometimes through trial and error, by speaking and writing, and by voracious reading of everything I could get hold of, consuming whole, dwelling on single phrases, mining them for implication and resonance: paying my dues. Now it's what I do and who I am. Language is my instrument. I have learned painfully slowly, but, while I still have a lot to learn, the sounds in my head come out of my fingers as they never did on the guitar.

Writing Organically
David B. Coe

In the course of speaking about my books, I often tell people that I write "organically." And I'm not the only one; I have friends who use the same term when speaking of their own work. But what does this really mean?

Look up "organic" in the dictionary, and among the several definitions listed there you get the following: "Forming an integral element of a whole; fundamental" and "having systematic coordination of parts" and "having the characteristics of an organism; developing in the manner of a living plant or animal." When speaking of my writing, I actually use the word to describe a process that combines all three of these definitions. At this point I realize that I'm muddying the waters more than clarifying them, but bear with me.

I outline when I write, thus providing some framework for my narrative and the evolution of my characters as I proceed through a book. But I don't outline so much that I actually know exactly what's going to happen at every point in the novel. Far from it. I'll write down maybe a paragraph for each chapter. Three or four sentences. "Character 1 goes to this place. S/he finds such and such. This other character shows up. They get a bite to eat." That sort of thing (although hopefully more interesting. . . .) The rest of the plotting, character development, etc. happens as I write. And yes, it happens organically.

I know, I know. I still haven't said what this means. This is where it all gets a bit mystical. When I'm writing, my storylines and the rest just sort of happen. I can explain this any number of ways: my characters assert themselves and carry the plot in directions of their choosing; the narrative presents itself to me and I basically transcribe it into book form; subliminally I know what's going to happen at every point in the book, but I don't realize that I know this until I actually write it. As it happens though, none of these explanations is exactly right; and at the same time every one of them is true to some degree.

I know where my books are going from the very beginning—the day I write page one I already know how the book is going to end. But I have little idea of how I'm going to get from point A to point Z. Every day that I write, I discover just a little bit more about the story I'm telling and the people I'm writing about. For example, this past week I needed to write a scene in which a group of Mettai sorcerers use their magic in a battle, and though this magic helps win the conflict, it also has terrible unforeseen consequences. I knew all of that going in. But I didn't know what magic they would use, how this would work against the enemy, or what the unintended consequences would be. I actually tried to think it through before I wrote the scene and couldn't. So I just started writing. Soon my characters told me which magic they'd use and why. From there I realized what would happen at the end of the scene. And this ending fit in perfectly with something I'd set up in the narrative literally two books ago.

Remember those definitions? "Forming an integral element of a whole; fundamental;" "having systematic coordination of parts;" and "having the characteristics of an organism; developing in the manner of a living plant or animal." They're all there. The solution to the battle scene problem came to me not because I tried to impose an answer on the narrative, but rather because I let it flow out of what had come before. Had I tried to force something, chances are it wouldn't have worked. Instead, I listened to my characters, or, if you prefer, I allowed the narrative to unfold as it was supposed to, or, I knew what had to happen and just had to be patient with myself until I "remembered." Whatever. To my mind, the best way to explain it is to say that it grew out of what I'd already done and laid the foundation for what needs to come next. That's why it worked so well and connected seamlessly with elements of the story that had been established long before.

That's organic writing. I begin with the fundamental elements of storytelling: a setting for my story, characters, and a basic narrative of the events that take us from point A to point Z. Then, rather than deciding from the outset how each of these elements is going to develop during the course of the story, I mix them together, in this case by beginning to write without a crystal clear sense of where it's all going. My characters interact with each other, with the world I've created, with the conflicts and dramas that I've thrown in their path. In other words, the various parts of my story develop symbiotically, feeding off one another, enhancing each other. The story becomes something more than the sum of its parts. It awakens, grows, and even appears to take on a mind of its own. As an author, I can never entirely cede control of my story to this creature I've created, but neither can I make it do everything I want it to.

Pick your metaphor here: if I'm building a house, I have to follow the blueprint and stay within the external walls. But if the flow works better with a room moved here, or a wall eliminated there, so be it. Or . . .

If I'm gardening, I don't want to let the cantaloupes overflow their plot and take over where the beans or tomatoes have been planted. But I can let them roam a bit, give them room to climb up a fence here or wind around a pole there. Or . . .

If I'm raising a child, I can't allow her to live her life without any limits, without any guidance. But I have to give her the freedom to explore who she is, how she wishes to express her individuality, what she wants to make of her life.

So it is with writing a book. Develop the fundamental elements, bring them together and allow them to interact, and give them the freedom to grow and evolve on their own. When I speak of writing organically, that's what I mean.

Misty Massey

It used to make my mother crazy knowing that I write without anything but the most basic of outlines. I would write my term papers first and then make my outline. That alone is probably responsible for a third of my poor mother's silver hairs.

Sometimes I envy the people who can create an unshiftable outline and follow it—it sounds like such an easy way to do things. But after all these years, I know it's not my way. I know how I'm starting, and where I want to end up, but all the gooey bits in the middle happen when they happen. I'm writing in a fashion that's honest to who I am.

Write What You Love
A.J. Hartley

Thus far in my career I've followed the three pieces of advice I always offer to other writers, and all three are really just individual parts of one obvious point. One of them is "Don't Second Guess the Market." That doesn't mean be oblivious to what people are reading—particularly in your genre—but don't set out to write the next [insert current blockbuster title here]. If the vampire-infested bandwagon hasn't been over-run by werewolves by the time your book is ready you'll find yourself competing for the jaded attention of agents and editors with a hundred other manuscripts about the same kind of thing. Originality, the distinctiveness of your voice, sense of story and so forth is unlikely to survive the factory process of imitating something which is already successful.

My second rule of thumb: Don't Write Solely to Impress. I see a lot of younger writers bending over backwards to make the Pulitzer or Booker Prize short list, slaving over a Serious Fiction project which secretly bores them to tears. People often tell you to write what you know—a useful bit of advice, properly handled—but they might better tell you to write what you read. If you like nothing better than to curl up with the new Zadie Smith or Jhumpa Lahiri, then—by all means—try to write that kind of book. But if you read supernatural romance by the crateful, maybe you should be writing that. That way you already know the genre, what other writers are doing within it and—more to the point—you are following your passion. If that passion is literary fiction, great, but don't go down that route just because you think it has more cultural value. (For the record, I think cultural value is in the eye of the beholder and I absolutely reject the idea that genre fiction is less serious than literary fiction. But I digress . . .)

All of which sets up my third rule (which is really the other two rolled into one): Write what you love. Because though I can't speak for every writer, I'm confident that that's what gets most of us into this lark. There are, after all, far surer and—frankly—easier ways to earn a few bucks. We write because we have to. It's a part of who we are.

Now I'm acutely aware that most of us don't have the luxury of lots of spare time, especially those of us who have "day jobs," so I'm going to drop kick the old lie that writers have to write every day. Nonsense. You write when you can and—more importantly—when you have something to say. Sure, a lot of times I don't know that I have something to say till I start to write, but setting yourself unrealistic writing goals is like deciding that you're going to go to the gym every day and lose twenty pounds a month. Shoot for things you can't sustain and you're more likely to fall off the wagon entirely (this being the writing wagon, not the afore mentioned vampire-infested bandwagon). Look at your schedule and set yourself small goals you think you can actually do: maybe a couple of thousand words per week at first, till—as with exercise—you build the habit and skills to do more. In this I think you'll find that writing the book you want to write (rather than something to please your teacher or pump up your bank balance) makes the process a lot easier.

Writing Is A Solitary Business

Faith Hunter

Most people think that writing is what we do at the PC or laptop or with pad and pen. That we live inside our heads and are only working when actively pounding away at the keyboard or scritching madly on the pad. The writers among us know that simply is not true. Our minds get caught up in the lives of our characters and suddenly we find ourselves writing at odd times—driving, eating supper, walking the dogs, paddling a particularly good river (okay that one is mostly just me), and worst of all, while having a conversation that is important to our mates though not so much to us. Or maybe that one is just me, too?

I try not to get *too* personal on MagicalWords.net, but I need to confess something. It's supposed to be good for the soul, yes? When I'm writing I ignore the hubby. A lot. It's not so hard for him when I'm pounding away on the PC, because it's obvious that I am engrossed in someone else. He doesn't even mind that the someone else is often younger, prettier, and more buff then he. And he gave up trying to figure out who I pattern my character's love interests on when he realized that most of them were based on no one at all or a childhood crush or someone I passed on the street or saw on TV, and then totally changed so they are unrecognizable to most folk.

He doesn't mind that I am writing when I'm physically writing. But he does get ticked off—sometimes really ticked off—when we are talking about golf (which I don't play) or a new river he wants to run (which I haven't seen, haven't researched, and have no opinion about yet) and I drift off. I totally lose track of what we are talking about, where we were in the conversation, and he gives me this . . . *look*. Do you know the one I mean? Not quite mad, not quite hurt, not quite disappointed, but sort of . . . painfully exasperated, maybe. I always rush to apologize and turn my total attention to him, but the damage has been done. I was writing and got lost within my own world. The world I was building with him disappeared and I . . . I forgot him. It is a crisis of relationship that many writers face with the their loved ones.

There was a time, for a while after the hubby first fell in love with golf, when we had two totally different conversations every evening on our walks. He was talking about golf, this wonderful shot or this amazing putt, and I was talking about writing, a conversation with an agent, a really great scene, or a difficult plot point I'd worked out. The conversations had no give-and-take, but we both accepted it because it was our lives we were sharing, not really info. But it's different when I drift off and leave him alone in the room. If I am not careful, that can hurt.

My relationships all suffer when I am actively creating—that internal creativity that we do that takes place under the surface of the skin in the deeps of our minds, but sometimes swims to the surface and catches us in its jaws and pulls us down with it. My mom sees it too. Other writers laugh when it happens, when we're having tea or lunch and one of us drifts away. We understand that that no one—no celebrity or politician or *anyone*—is more interesting than the people in our brains. We understand. But we do have to be very careful not to hurt the people we love when we are writing.

Just saying . . .

Misty Massey

Last Saturday when I was out at the faire, Paradiis and Farashah were discussing a particularly challenging dance, and they asked me a question. One I never heard, since at the time I was staring off into the sky. Farashah touched me to get my attention. "Misty, where were you?"

"I was writing," I said.

C.E. Murphy

I'm going to have to ask Ted if I do this. I *know* I do it if I've come to him for help with a plot point or something, because when he hits on The Idea I need, I apparently get this very specific distant expression and often drift into silence while I contemplate the revelation. In those circumstances he's always very pleased with himself, because if I do that it means he's given me the piece I need to make the story work, or he's given me enough that I can see it from there.

But I honestly don't think I drift off into my writing worlds when I'm not working. Granted, "working" is a nebulous term for writers, and plenty of train rides are spent "working" in terms of staring out the window and thinking vague thoughts about the book. But I don't think I drift during conversations and the like. I'll have to ask Ted. ☺

David B. Coe

I certainly do it when I'm driving, hiking, lying in bed waiting to fall asleep, doing mundane stuff like grocery shopping or cutting the lawn. I don't do it when I'm out taking photos—I'm pretty absorbed when I have my camera in hand. I try not to do it in conversations, partic-ularly with my wife and kids, but I know that it happens occasionally. Nancy laughs at me . . . most of the time. The girls get mad at me. To be honest, I get mad at myself, because I know how much it can hurt.

But it's hard to stop, and even if it wasn't hard, I'm not sure I'd want to stop. Inspiration is unpredictable. It can come and go, and when it's there, right in front of me, I have to follow it, because I've set it aside in the past, attempting to be polite, and I've lost whatever idea it was that had come to me. As much as I hate to hurt those I love in this small way, I hate losing ideas even more.

About the Editor

Edmund R. Schubert has served as editor of the online sf/f magazine *Orson Scott Card's Intergalactic Medicine Show* (*IGMS*) since 2006, edited an anthology by the same name (*IGMS*, Tor), and served as executive and managing editor of several business magazines. He is also the author of some 35 short stories, one novel (*Dreaming Creek*, Lachesis Books), and an assortment of articles and interviews. However, he considers his greatest accomplishment to be the time a college professor taught a class about his work—in abnormal psychology. True story.

About the Contributors

David B. Coe is the award-winning author of eleven fantasy novels and the occasional short story. His first trilogy, The LonTobyn Chronicle, received the Crawford Fantasy Award as the best work by a new author in fantasy. His latest fantasy novel, *The Dark-Eyes' War*, is the final volume of his Blood of the Southlands trilogy, which began with *The Sorcerers' Plague* and *The Horsemen's Gambit*. The series is a follow-up to his critically acclaimed Winds of the Forelands quintet. He has written the novelization of director Ridley Scott's recent movie, *Robin Hood*, starring Russell Crowe. David's novels have been translated into a dozen languages.

David received his undergraduate degree from Brown University and then attended Stanford University, where he received both a Master's and a Ph.D in U.S. history. He is currently at work on several projects including a contemporary urban fantasy, a fantasy series for young readers, and the Thieftaker books, historical fantasies set in pre-Revolutionary Boston. The Thieftaker series will be published under the name D.B. Jackson. The first volume will be released in early 2012.

British born writer **A.J. Hartley** joined Magical Words in 2009. He is the *USA Today* and *New York Times* bestselling author of the mystery/thrillers *The Mask of Atreus, On the Fifth Day*, and *What Time Devours*, published by Penguin/Berkley and available world wide in twenty-five languages. His fantasy fiction follows the exploits of Will Hawthorne, a roguish actor with a talent for getting into trouble, in *Act of Will* and *Will Power*, published by Tor/Macmillan. His first young adult novel, *Darwen Arkwright and the Peregrine Pact* will come out from Penguin/Razorbill in Fall 2011, followed by a second in that series a year later.

A.J. has an M.A. and Ph.D. in English literature from Boston University and is currently the Robinson Professor of Shakespeare in the Department of Theatre at the University of North Carolina at Charlotte. He is the director of the Shakespeare in Action Centre, the editor of the performance journal *Shakespeare Bulletin* published by Johns Hopkins UP, and the author of *The Shakespearean Dramaturg* as well as numerous articles in the field. He is currently writing a performance history of *Julius Caesar* for Manchester UP.

As well as being a novelist and academic, he is a screenwriter, theatre director and dramaturg. He makes beer and furniture and has more hobbies than is good for anyone. He is married with a son, and lives in Charlotte.

Faith Hunter, fantasy writer, was born in Louisiana and raised all over the south. Her Rogue Mage novels, a dark, urban fantasy series—*Bloodring, Seraphs,* and *Host*—feature Thorn St. Croix, a stone mage in a post-apocalyptic, alternate reality, urban fantasy world. These novels are the basis for the role playing game, *Rogue Mage.* The Skinwalker series, featuring Jane Yellowrock is taking off like a rocket with *Skinwalker, Blood Cross,* and *Mercy Blade.*

Under pen name **Gwen Hunter**, she writes action-adventure, mysteries, and thrillers. Between Faith and Gwen, she has twenty-one books in print in twenty-six countries.

Hunter fell in love with reading in fifth grade, and best loved SiFi, fantasy, and gothic. She decided to become a writer in high school, when a teacher told her she had talent. Now, she writes full-time and works full-time in a hospital lab, (for the benefits) tries to keep house, and is a workaholic with a passion for travel, jewelry making, white-water kayaking, and writing. She and her husband love to RV, traveling with their dogs to whitewater rivers all over the Southeast.

For more information, including a book list, see www.faithhunter.net and www.gwenhunter.com

Stuart Jaffe is the author of dozens of short stories and articles. Most recently, he has appeared in the anthologies *Rum and Runestones, Under the Rose,* and *New Writings in the Fantastic.* With his wife, he co-hosts The Eclectic Review, a weekly podcast in which they discuss science, art, writing, books, movies, and just about anything else that falls in their laps. For those keeping count—as of this bio writing, we have five cats, one albino corn snake, one rabbit, three aquatic turtles, one box turtle, one tarantula, seven chickens, and a horse. As always, the horse, thankfully, lives at a stable.

Misty Massey is the author of *Mad Kestrel* (Tor), a rollicking adventure of magic on the high seas which was nominated for the 2010 SCASL Book Award. When she's not writing, she studies Middle Eastern dance and is a member of the Beledi Beat dance troupe, which performs at the Carolina Renaissance Faire and many other venues all over the upstate South Carolina area. Misty's short fiction has recently appeared in the *Rum and Runestones* anthology (Dragon Moon Press) and the *Dragon's Lure* anthology (Dark Quest Books). A sequel to *Mad Kestrel, Kestrel's Dance*, is in the works.

C.E. Murphy is an Alaskan-born writer of fantasy novels, short stories, and comic books, who currently lives in Ireland. Her numerous novel series include The Walker Papers, The Old Races Universe, The Inheritor's Cycle, The Strongbox Chronicles, and the forthcoming Worldwalker Duology. She has also written a romance novel trilogy under the pseudonym Cate Dermody.